Better Homes and Gardens®

1991 BEST-RECIPES YEARBOOK

Our seal assures you that every recipe in the
1991 Best-Recipes Yearbook has been tested in the
Better Homes and Gardens® Test Kitchen.
This means that each recipe is practical and reliable,
and meets our high standards of taste appeal.

Editor DAVID JORDAN
Managing Editor LAMONT OLSON
Art Director BRADFORD W.S. HONG

Food and Nutrition
Editor NANCY BYAL
Department Head—Cook Books SHARYL HEIKEN
Senior Food Editor—Magazine JOY TAYLOR
Senior Food Editor—Meredith Publishing Services
MOLLY CULBERTSON
Senior Food Editor—Special Interest Publications
JANET FIGG
Associate Department Heads SANDRA GRANSETH
ROSEMARY HUTCHINSON ELIZABETH WOOLEVER
Senior Food Editors LINDA HENRY
LISA HOLDERNESS JULIA MALLOY
MARY JO PLUTT JOYCE TROLLOPE LOIS WHITE
Associate Food Editors JENNIFER DARLING
KRISTI FULLER HEATHER HEPHNER
SHELLI McCONNELL HEIDI McNUTT
MARY MAJOR WILLIAMS

Test Kitchen
Director SHARON STILWELL
Food Stylist JANET HERWIG

Graphic Design
Associate Art Directors
TIM ALEXANDER PAUL ZIMMERMAN
Cover Designer NANCY KLUENDER
Graphic Designers
KELLY BARTON DAN BISHOP KEVIN S. LUDGATE
SUSAN L. UEDELHOFEN

Copy and Production
Copy Cheif ELIZABETH HAHN BROOKS
Makeup Editor LINDA R. THOMAS
Associate Makeup Editor CINDY L. ALBERTS
Electronic Text Facilitator NANCY HALL
Electronic Design Facilitator MICKIE VORHES

Editorial Marketing Services
Director MARGARET McMAHON
Mail Order Shopping Editor ARLENE AVILES

Editorial Services
Manager of Editorial Services and Planning DAVID S. JOHNSON
Supervisor of Editorial Administrative Services ROSE ANDERSON
Art Business Office Manager DIANE BOYLE *Photo Studio Manager* DON WIPPERMAN
Director, Editorial Research C. RAY DEATON *Research Associate* SCOTT R. TOLAN

Special Interest Publications
Editor WILLIAM J. YATES *Managing Editor* MIKE MAINE *Art Director* DON NICKELL
Food Editor JANET FIGG *Furnishing Editor* HEATHER J. PAPER *Traditional Home Editor* KAROL DeWULF NICKELL
Building and Remodeling Editor GREGORY D. COOK *Crafts Editor* LAURA HOLTORF COLLINS

Meredith Publishing Services
Editor DOUGLAS A. HOLTHAUS *Managing Editor* PATRICIA POLLOCK *Design Director* DEETRA LEECH

BOOKS
Editor GERALD KNOX *Managing Editor* DAVID A. KIRCHNER *Art Director* ERNEST SHELTON
Associate Art Directors NEOMA THOMAS LINDA FORD VERMIE RANDALL YONTZ
Project Editors JAMES D. BLUME MARSHA JAHNS
Project Managers LIZ ANDERSON JENNIFER SPEER RAMUNDT ANGELA K. RENKOSKI
Assistant Art Directors LYNDA HAUPERT HARIJS PRIEKULIS TOM WEGNER
Graphic Designers MARY SCHLUETER BENDGEN MICHAEL BURNS MICK SCHNEPF

Magazine Group Vice President *Editorial Director* **DORIS M. EBY**
Creative Director, Product Development DAVID R. HAUPERT

Senior Vice President-Publishing Director, Better Homes and Gardens
ADOLPH AUERBACHER
Publisher JERRY KAPLAN
Publishing Services Director TERRY UNSWORTH
Advertising Sales Director ROBERT M. BAXTER

MAGAZINE GROUP PRESIDENT **JAMES A. AUTRY**
Magazine Group Vice Presidents
Publishing Directors **ADOLPH AUERBACHER, BURTON H. BOERSMA,**
CHRISTOPHER M. LEHMAN, MYRNA BLYTH
DEAN PIETERS, Operations **MAX RUNCIMAN,** Finance

MEREDITH CORPORATION
Chairman of Executive Committee E. T. MEREDITH III

CORPORATE OFFICERS: **Chairman of the Board ROBERT A. BURNETT**
President and Chief Executive Officer JACK D. REHM
Group Presidents: JAMES A. AUTRY, Magazines
JERAMY LANDAUER, Books
PHILIP A. JONES, Broadcasting **ALLEN L. SABBAG,** Real Estate
Vice Presidents: LEO R. ARMATIS, Corporate Relations
THOMAS G. FISHER, General Counsel and Secretary
JAMES F. STACK, Finance **Treasurer MICHAEL A. SELL**
Corporate Controller and Assistant Secretary LARRY D HARTSOOK

Throughout each year, *Better Homes and Gardens*® publishes a luscious sampler of recipes, including tips and ideas ranging from easy to elegant and healthy to decadent. Here, we invite you to look back on the best from 1990, another outstanding year, in our ninth annual recipe yearbook.

CONTENTS

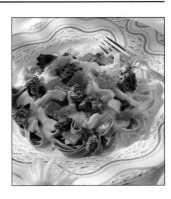

BY LISA HOLDERNESS

20 MIGHTY MEALS

FRESH START *TO A FITTER YOU*

▶ **ALL RECIPES LESS THAN 300 CALORIES**

▶ **LOW IN FAT**

▶ **READY IN 20 MINUTES**

▶ **YOUR FAMILY WILL LOVE THEM!**

Mighty meals are here to save the day, and your family's health.

If you're like most families, coming up with great-tasting, healthful meals that fit a busy schedule is a challenge. Too many cook-quick recipes rate poorly when it comes to good nutrition. To meet that challenge, we created 20 super recipes for hectic weekdays. Each makes eating right more delicious, and a lot easier.

▶ **1 SUPER-EASY SAUCE**
GLAZED CHICKEN AND GRAPES
239 cal. (12% from fat), 3 g fat
This glistening wine and grape sauce uses apple jelly as an instant thickener.

GOOD AND PLENTY SALADS

▲2 BEANS GALORE
HOT GERMAN BEAN SALAD
234 cal. (14% from fat), 4 g fat
Loaded with fiber and that German sweet-and-tangy flavor!

▲3 SIMPLE SEAFOOD
PAELLA SALAD
237 cal. (7% from fat), 2 g fat
Toss shrimp with quick-cooked rice for this Spanish-style salad.

▲4 FRESH TASTE
MINTED HAM SALAD
234 cal. (27% from fat), 7 g fat
Choose low-fat cheese and extra-lean ham for this slimming salad.

SAVE-THE-DAY SUPPERS

5 ▾ JUST 4 INGREDIENTS
MEXICAN TURKEY ROLLS
222 cal. (14% from fat), 4 g fat
Turkey breast stuffed with peppers and slathered with salsa and cheese. Low calorie? You bet!

6 ▾ LESS THAN 200 CALORIES
ZESTY "FRIED" CHICKEN
158 cal. (18% from fat), 3 g fat
One bite of this spiced-up chicken and you'll forget about the Colonel's.

7 ▾ SAY YES TO BURGERS!
JOHNNY APPLESEED BURGERS
239 cal. (25% from fat), 7 g fat
These tasty burgers take less time to cook and serve than running out for fast food.

8 ▾ EXTRA-ENERGY PASTA
EASY ITALIAN VERMICELLI
265 cal. (18% from fat), 5 g fat
Load up on authentic Italian flavor and energizing carbohydrates, all in the same delicious dish.

9

10

JUST–FOR–TWO ENTRÉES

9 SUPER-LOW SODIUM

PLUM CHICKEN KABOBS

260 cal. (12% from fat), 3 g fat

Stir together plum sauce and vinegar for a quick glaze that tastes so great you won't miss the salt.

10 CHOLESTEROL BUSTER

SWORDFISH MARGARITA

180 cal. (23% from fat), 5 g fat

Stock up on omega-3. Swordfish is a good source for this fatty acid, known to reduce blood cholesterol.

SOMETHING-SPECIAL DINNERS

11 GO MEATLESS
MANDARIN TOFU STIR-FRY
297 cal. (23% from fat), 8 g fat
This sweet-and-sour garden dish
gets most of its protein from tofu.

12 NEXT TO NO FAT
MOROCCAN-STYLE FISH
202 cal. (1% from fat), 1 g fat
Trim fat to the bone with fish in
a spiced dried-fruit sauce.

13 LIGHT AND LEAN
MUSHROOM-SAUCED PORK
147 cal. (20% from fat), 3 g fat
Using lean pork tenderloin, you
can feel good about eating meat.

SUPER SOUPS AND SANDWICHES

Shedding unwanted fat can be as simple as changing your cooking habits. These tips can make a difference!

● **Trim all excess fat** from meat and remove the skin from poultry before cooking.

● **Broil, poach, grill, bake, or microwave** meats and vegetables to keep fat to a minimum.

● **To roast meat, place** it on a rack so that the fat drips away from the meat.

● **Use a nonstick skillet or nonstick spray coating** for frying. Or, simmer vegetables in water or broth rather than sautéing.

● **If you do use fat for frying, use** it sparingly and choose cooking oils high in polyunsaturated and monounsaturated fats and low in saturated fat. Examples: canola, safflower, and corn oils.

14 BROWN BAGGIN' IT
HOT-LUNCH STEAK STEW
258 cal. (19% from fat), 5 g fat
Just fix and freeze. Pack this stew in an insulated bag or on ice. At lunchtime, micro-thaw and heat.

15 A TERRIFIC TOTABLE
SALMON-STUFFED PITA BREAD
205 cal. (29% from fat), 7 g fat
Lighten up your lunch box with this salmon-fresh vegetable pita, seasoned with low-calorie dressing.

16 LOW-CALORIE PIZZA
SUPER PIZZA TOSTADAS
236 cal. (22% from fat), 6 g fat
Eating healthfully means enjoying pizza, too. Try our simple tostada-style version.

17 ONLY 5 INGREDIENTS
JAPANESE TORTELLINI SOUP
269 cal. (19% from fat), 6 g fat
When your tummy yearns for rich chicken soup, this easy stuffed-pasta rendition will win you over.

18 MICROWAVE-QUICK
MANHATTAN FISH CHOWDER
177 cal. (8% from fat), 2 g fat
This glorious tomato chowder, cooked in the microwave, takes only 15 minutes from start to finish.

19 6 SATISFYING LAYERS!
SUPER SUBMARINES
270 cal. (20% from fat), 6 g fat
Squelch your craving for a hearty sandwich; layer low-fat cheeses, vegetables, and meat on crusty bread.

ANY-TIME BREAKFAST

20 EGG LOVER'S DREAM
SAUSAGE AND CHEESE SCRAMBLE
254 cal. (27% from fat), 8 g fat

Enjoy this dish guilt free. It uses more egg whites than yolks and turkey sausage to cut fat.

LOW-FAT CHOICES FOR HIGH-FAT FOODS

You can still choose favorite high-fat foods in moderation. Use these tips to make leaner decisions.
● **Substitute egg whites for whole eggs—**
Baked goods and other recipes that use eggs for leavening:
2 whites = 1 whole egg
Scrambled eggs: 2 whites + 1 egg = 2 eggs
● **Choose from these extra-lean cuts of meat—**
Beef: Round, sirloin, chuck, and loin.
Pork: Loin and leg cuts
Lamb: Leg cuts, arm, and loin
● **Lighten up with low-fat dairy products—**
Cheese: Look for part-skim or low-fat cheeses with less than 6 grams fat per ounce. Also, try low-fat cottage cheese, sour cream, and cream cheese.
Milk: Choose skim or 1 percent milk
Yogurt: Nonfat or low-fat, regular and frozen

SAUSAGE AND CHEESE SCRAMBLE

Nonstick spray coating
  8 ounces fully cooked smoked turkey sausage, thinly sliced and quartered
  5 eggs
  4 egg whites
  ¼ cup skim milk
  1 teaspoon dried minced onion
  ¼ teaspoon salt
  ¼ teaspoon dried oregano, crushed
  ¼ teaspoon pepper
  ⅓ cup shredded low-fat cheddar cheese (1½ ounces)
  2 cups fresh *or* frozen broccoli flowerets
  1 15-ounce can sliced potatoes, drained
  2 teaspoons imitation butter granules
Dash dried oregano, crushed
  3 English muffins, split and toasted

● **Spray a cold large skillet** with nonstick coating. Preheat skillet over medium heat. Cook turkey sausage in hot skillet for 2 minutes. Remove skillet from heat.
● **In a mixing bowl beat** eggs, egg whites, milk, onion, salt, ¼ teaspoon dried oregano, and pepper. Stir in *half* of the cheese.
● **Add egg mixture** to the skillet. Cook, without stirring, till mixture begins to set on the bottom and around edges. Using a large spoon or spatula, lift and fold partially cooked eggs so uncooked portion flows underneath. Continue cooking over medium heat about 4 minutes or till eggs are cooked through but are still glossy and moist.
● **Meanwhile,** in a medium saucepan cook broccoli flowerets, covered, in a small amount of boiling water for 8 to 10 minutes (3 to 4 minutes for frozen broccoli), adding potatoes the last 2 minutes of cooking. Drain. Sprinkle butter granules and dash of oregano over cooked vegetables.
● **Spoon** egg mixture atop the English muffin halves. Sprinkle with the remaining cheese. Serve with the cooked vegetables. Makes 6 servings.
Nutrition information per serving:
254 cal., 22 g pro., 25 g carbo., 8 g fat, 250 mg chol., 718 mg sodium, 397 mg potassium, and 2 g dietary fiber. U.S. RDA: 24% vit. A, 34% vit. C, 15% thiamine, 23% riboflavin, 21% niacin, 16% calcium, 15% iron.

January

GLAZED CHICKEN AND GRAPES

Skinned, boneless chicken breast halves make healthy timesavers. They come ready-to-use with only 3 grams of fat—

4 skinned, boneless large chicken breast halves (about 1 pound total)
Nonstick spray coating
¾ cup seedless red grapes
3 parsley sprigs
⅓ cup apple jelly
2 teaspoons lemon juice
2 tablespoons dry sherry
¼ teaspoon salt

● **Wash chicken;** pat dry. Spray a cold large skillet with nonstick coating. Heat the skillet over medium heat. Add chicken to skillet. Cook for 8 to 10 minutes or till no longer pink, turning once during cooking. Transfer chicken to serving plates. Cover to keep warm.
● **Meanwhile, cut the grapes** in half lengthwise and snip the parsley.
● **Add jelly,** lemon juice, sherry, and salt to skillet. Cook and stir till jelly is melted. Add grapes and parsley. Heat through. Spoon over chicken. Serves 4.
Nutrition information per serving: 239 cal., 27 g pro., 24 g carbo., 3 g fat (1 g sat. fat), 72 mg chol., 202 mg sodium, 307 mg potassium. U.S. RDA: 59% niacin.

HOT GERMAN BEAN SALAD

This off-the-shelf dinner nutritiously revamps German potato salad. Fiber-rich beans and lean chicken take the place of potatoes and bacon—

Nonstick spray coating
1 medium carrot, chopped
½ of a small red onion, chopped
1 stalk celery, sliced
¼ cup vinegar
1 tablespoon sugar
1 tablespoon cornstarch
1 teaspoon instant beef bouillon granules
¼ teaspoon celery seed
1 15-ounce can black beans, rinsed and drained
1 8-ounce can red kidney beans, drained
1 5-ounce can chunk-style chicken
4 large lettuce leaves, washed

● **Spray a cold large skillet** with nonstick coating. Heat skillet over medium heat. In the hot skillet stir-fry carrot, onion, and celery for 2 minutes. Remove from heat.
● **In a small bowl stir together** vinegar, sugar, cornstarch, beef bouillon granules, celery seed, and ½ cup *water.* Add to skillet. Cook and stir over medium-high heat for 1 to 2 minutes or till mixture is thickened and bubbly.
● **Stir in** black beans, kidney beans, and chicken. Cook for 2 to 3 minutes or till heated through, stirring occasionally.
● **Meanwhile, arrange** lettuce leaves on individual serving plates. Serve the bean mixture atop. If desired, garnish with halved red onion slices. Serves 4.
Nutrition information per serving: 234 cal., 17 g pro., 34 g carbo., 4 g fat (1 g sat. fat), 22 mg chol., 484 mg sodium, 634 mg potassium, and 11 g dietary fiber. U.S. RDA: 106% vit. A, 18% thiamine, 16% niacin, 18% iron.

PAELLA SALAD

Quick-chill the shrimp mixture in your freezer while you rinse the lettuce and cut the tomato—

1 cup water
1 cup quick-cooking rice
1 teaspoon instant chicken bouillon granules
¼ teaspoon ground turmeric
2 6-ounce packages frozen, peeled, cooked shrimp
1 10-ounce package frozen peas with pearl onions
⅓ cup reduced-calorie Italian salad dressing
⅛ teaspoon ground red pepper
Bibb lettuce leaves
Tomato wedges

● **In a small saucepan heat** water to boiling. Stir in rice, bouillon granules, and turmeric. Remove from heat. Cover and let stand for 5 minutes.

● **Meanwhile,** in a 2-quart microwave-safe casserole or bowl micro-cook the shrimp and peas with onions, covered, on 100% power (high) for 3 minutes, stirring once. Drain, if necessary.
● **Add hot rice,** salad dressing, and red pepper to shrimp mixture; toss to coat well. Place in freezer for 5 minutes or till chilled, stirring occasionally. Serve on lettuce-lined plates and garnish with tomato. Makes 4 servings.
Nutrition information per serving: 237 cal., 23 g pro., 31 g carbo., 2 g fat (0.4 g sat. fat), 166 mg chol., 611 mg sodium, 364 mg potassium, and 3 g dietary fiber. U.S. RDA: 16% vit. A, 17% vit. C, 24% thiamine, 22% niacin, 26% iron.

MINTED HAM SALAD

Save yourself a step and pick up chopped fresh vegetables at your supermarket salad bar—

1 8-ounce carton plain low-fat *or* nonfat yogurt
1 tablespoon skim milk
2 teaspoons horseradish mustard
1 teaspoon dried mint *or* basil, crushed
⅛ teaspoon onion powder
3 cups assorted cut-up fresh vegetables
1 pound extra-lean, fully cooked boneless ham
½ cup shredded low-fat cheddar cheese (2 ounces)
Fresh mint leaves (optional)

● **In a large bowl combine** yogurt, milk, mustard, mint or basil, and onion powder. Add assorted vegetables and toss to coat. Cover vegetable mixture and place in freezer while preparing the remaining ingredients.
● **Cut ham** into ½-inch cubes. Add ham and cheese to vegetable mixture; toss to mix. Serve immediately or chill overnight. If desired, garnish with fresh mint leaves. Makes 4 servings.
Nutrition information per serving: 234 cal., 29 g pro., 14 g carbo., 7 g fat (3.5 g sat. fat), 58 mg chol., 1,524 mg sodium, 691 mg potassium, and 3 g dietary fiber. U.S. RDA: 96% vit. A, 83% vit. C, 14% riboflavin, 26% calcium, 10% iron.

MEXICAN TURKEY ROLLS

Microwave cooking saves time and keeps the turkey steaks moist without adding fat—

- 4 turkey breast tenderloin steaks (1 pound total)
- 1 4-ounce can diced green chili peppers, drained
- ½ cup shredded low-fat cheddar cheese (2 ounces)
- 1 8-ounce jar red salsa
Fresh chili peppers (optional)

● **To assemble turkey rolls, lay** turkey steaks flat. At one end of *each* turkey steak place *one-fourth* of the diced chilies and *1 tablespoon* of the cheese. Carefully fold each turkey steak in half over the chilies and cheese; fasten to the other end with a wooden toothpick.

● **Arrange the turkey steaks** in an 8x8x2-inch microwave-safe baking dish so that the fold of each turkey portion is facing toward the outside of the dish. Cover with vented microwave-safe plastic wrap. Micro-cook on 100% power (high) for 5½ to 7 minutes (low-wattage ovens: 10 to 12 minutes) or till turkey is no longer pink, giving the dish a half-turn once. Drain the liquid from dish and discard.

● **Spoon salsa** on top of the turkey steaks; sprinkle with the remaining cheese. Micro-cook, uncovered, on high about 2 minutes more (low-wattage ovens: 3 minutes) or till cheese is melted. If desired, garnish with fresh chili peppers. Makes 4 servings.

Nutrition information per serving: 222 cal., 39 g pro., 6 g carbo., 4 g fat (2 g sat. fat), 103 mg chol., 877 mg sodium, 518 mg potassium, and 2 g dietary fiber. U.S. RDA: 74% vit. A, 25% vit. C, 15% riboflavin, 44% niacin, 15% calcium, 13% iron.

ZESTY "FRIED" CHICKEN

The cumin-spiked coating turns crunchy and golden on this mock-fried chicken—

- 2 tablespoons yellow cornmeal
- 1 teaspoon paprika
- ½ teaspoon salt
- ½ teaspoon garlic powder
- ½ teaspoon pepper
- ¼ teaspoon ground cumin
- 4 skinned, boneless large chicken breast halves (about 1 pound total)
Nonstick spray coating
Green onions (optional)
Sweet pepper strips (optional)

● **In a medium mixing bowl combine** cornmeal, paprika, salt, garlic powder, pepper, and cumin; mix well.

● **Rinse chicken** (don't dry); coat chicken on all sides with cornmeal mixture.

● **Spray a cold large skillet** with nonstick coating. Heat the skillet over medium heat. Cook chicken for 8 to 10 minutes or till no longer pink, turning occasionally to brown evenly on all sides. If desired, serve with green onions and sweet pepper strips. Serves 4.

Nutrition information per serving: 158 cal., 27 g pro., 4 g carbo., 3 g fat (1 g sat. fat), 72 mg chol., 335 mg sodium, 249 mg potassium. U.S. RDA: 59% niacin.

Buying Ground Turkey

Because there are no official standards for the amount of fat in ground turkey, it may not be as lean as you think. Compare ground turkey to ground beef:

Skinned, boneless turkey breasts, ground (3 ounces): *114 cal., 0.6 g fat, 0.2 g sat. fat; 5% of cal. from fat.*

Purchased ground turkey (3 ounces): *197 cal., 12 g fat, 3 g sat. fat; 56% of the cal. from fat. Values may vary from brand to brand.*

Extra-lean ground beef (3 ounces): *232 cal., 14 g fat, 5 g sat. fat; 54% of the cal. from fat.*

To test the ground turkey recipes in this story, we bought skinned, boneless turkey breast and asked the butcher to grind it (you also can grind it yourself). This way may be a little more expensive than buying preground turkey. These recipes also work well with preground turkey. The choice is yours.

JOHNNY APPLESEED BURGERS

You can have your burgers and eat 'em, too. We've cut out extra fat by combining lean ground beef and ground turkey—

- 1 egg white
- ¾ cup chunk-style applesauce
- ⅓ cup fine dry bread crumbs
- 1 tablespoon dried minced onion
- ¼ teaspoon salt
- ½ pound skinned, boneless turkey breast, ground
- ½ pound lean ground beef
Nonstick spray coating
- 1 small head leaf lettuce
- 2 small apples

● **Preheat the broiler.** Meanwhile, in a medium mixing bowl slightly beat egg white. Stir in ¼ cup of the applesauce, the bread crumbs, onion, and salt. Add turkey and beef; mix well. Shape into five ½-inch-thick patties.

● **Spray a cold rack** of an unheated broiler pan with nonstick coating. Place patties on the rack. Broil 3 to 4 inches from the heat for 5 minutes. Turn over. Broil for 5 to 7 minutes more or till meat is no longer pink.

● **Meanwhile, in a small saucepan** heat the remaining applesauce. Chop the leaf lettuce into thin strips. Slice the apples into wedges. Serve each patty on a bed of chopped lettuce with the warm applesauce and apple wedges. Makes 5 servings.

Nutrition information per serving: 239 cal., 23 g pro., 22 g carbo., 7 g fat (2 g sat. fat), 65 mg chol., 214 mg sodium, 448 mg potassium, and 3 g dietary fiber. U.S. RDA: 12% vit. C, 20% riboflavin, 38% niacin, 14% iron.

EASY ITALIAN VERMICELLI

    4 ounces vermicelli or fine
       noodles
    ½ pound boneless beef top
       round steak
Nonstick spray coating
    ½ of a medium onion, chopped
    1 14½-ounce can tomato wedges
    1 9-ounce package frozen Italian-
       style green beans
    1 4-ounce can sliced mushrooms,
       drained
    ½ of a 6-ounce can Italian-style
       tomato paste
    ½ teaspoon fennel seed
    ¼ teaspoon pepper
    1 tablespoon grated Parmesan
       cheese

● **Cook pasta** according to package instructions. Meanwhile, trim fat from
meat. Thinly slice meat across the
grain into bite-size strips.
● **Spray a cold large skillet** with nonstick coating. Heat the skillet over medium heat. Add the meat strips and
onion; stir-fry for 2 to 3 minutes or till
the meat is brown.
● **Stir in** *undrained* tomatoes, green
beans, mushrooms, tomato paste, fennel seed, and pepper. Bring to boiling.
Reduce heat and simmer, uncovered,
for 7 to 8 minutes or till slightly thickened, stirring frequently. Stir in Parmesan cheese. To serve, ladle meat
mixture over pasta. Makes 4 servings.
Nutrition information per serving:
265 cal., 21 g pro., 35 g carbo., 5 g fat (2 g
sat. fat), 63 mg chol., 506 mg sodium,
773 mg potassium, and 5 g dietary fiber.
U.S. RDA: 31% vit. A, 35% vit. C, 29%
thiamine, 21% riboflavin, 32% niacin,
10% calcium, 23% iron.

PLUM CHICKEN KABOBS

    2 skinned, boneless large chicken
       breast halves (about ½ pound
       total)
    ½ of an 8¼-ounce can pineapple
       slices, drained
    ½ cup plum sauce
    1 tablespoon vinegar
    2 cups loose-pack frozen broccoli,
       baby carrots, and water
       chestnuts
Pineapple slices, cut in half (optional)

● **Cut each chicken breast half** into 4
lengthwise strips. Cut pineapple rings
into quarters. Combine plum sauce and
vinegar. Set aside.
● **Place vegetables** in a 1-quart microwave-safe casserole. Micro-cook, covered, on 100% power (high) for 4 to 5
minutes or till crisp-tender, stirring
once. Toss *2 tablespoons* of the plum
sauce mixture with vegetables. Cover
and set aside.
● **Meanwhile,** on two wooden 10- to 12-
inch skewers thread the chicken strips
accordion-style around the quartered
pineapple slices. Place the kabobs in a
12x7½x2-inch microwave-safe baking
dish. Brush the kabobs with *some* of the
plum sauce mixture.
● **Micro-cook the kabobs,** covered, on
high for 1 minute. Give dish a half-turn
and brush kabobs with sauce. Micro-
cook, covered, on high for 2 to 3 minutes more or till chicken is no longer
pink. Transfer vegetables and kabobs
to a serving platter. If desired, garnish
with additional halved pineapple slices.
Pass any remaining plum sauce mixture. Makes 2 servings.
    Note: This recipe is not recom-
mended for low-wattage ovens.
Nutrition information per serving:
260 cal., 29 g pro., 29 g carbo., 3 g fat (1 g
sat. fat), 72 mg chol., 109 mg sodium,
654 mg potassium, and 5 g dietary fiber.
U.S. RDA: 220% vit. A, 47% vit. C, 13%
thiamine, 14% riboflavin, 63% niacin,
12% iron.

SWORDFISH MARGARITA

Cheers! This tangy fish dish uses the key
ingredients, lime and tequila, that make
the margarita so popular—

    ¾ cup water
    1 teaspoon instant chicken
       bouillon granules
    ¼ teaspoon ground coriander
    2 swordfish *or* tuna steaks (6 to 8
       ounces total), ½ to 1 inch thick
    1 medium lime
    1½ teaspoon cornstarch
    1 teaspoon sugar
Dash pepper
    1 tablespoon tequila
Fresh cilantro (optional)

● **For poaching liquid,** in a medium
skillet combine water, bouillon granules, and coriander. Bring to boiling
over high heat. Measure thickness of
fish. Add fish to skillet. Spoon poaching
liquid over fish. Reduce heat; simmer,
covered, till fish just flakes with a fork
(allow 4 to 6 minutes for each ½-inch
thickness of fish). Using a slotted spatula, transfer fish from skillet to serving
plates; cover and keep warm.
● **Meanwhile, cut the lime** *in half.* Using one half, finely shred *1 teaspoon*
lime peel; set aside. From the same
half, squeeze enough juice to make *1*
tablespoon; set aside. Slice remaining
half of the lime; set aside.
● **For sauce,** measure poaching liquid;
reserve ½ cup. Discard remaining liquid. Combine lime juice, cornstarch,
sugar, and pepper. Add to liquid in skillet along with the lime peel. Cook and
stir till thickened and bubbly. Cook and
stir for 2 minutes more. Stir in tequila.
Drizzle sauce over fish. Serve with lime
slices and, if desired, cilantro. Serves 2.
Nutrition information per serving:
180 cal., 23 g pro., 6 g carbo., 5 g fat (1.3 g
sat. fat), 44 mg chol., 289 mg sodium,
and 359 mg potassium. U.S. RDA: 10%
vit. C, 55% niacin.

MANDARIN TOFU STIR-FRY

Tofu takes on the flavors of what you mix with it. Plus, it's high in protein, low in fat and calories, and cholesterol free—

- 1 cup quick-cooking rice
- 1 pound firm tofu (bean curd)
- ½ cup sweet-and-sour sauce
- ⅛ teaspoon ground red pepper
- Nonstick spray coating
- 6 green onions, bias-sliced into 1-inch pieces
- ½ of a sweet red pepper, cut into strips (½ cup)
- 1 6-ounce package frozen pea pods
- 1 10½-ounce can mandarin orange sections, drained
- 2 tablespoons unsalted dry-roasted peanuts

● **Cook rice** according to package directions, omitting butter or margarine.
● **Meanwhile, press** excess moisture from tofu with paper towels. Cut tofu into ¾-inch cubes. Set aside. In a small bowl combine sweet-and-sour sauce and ground red pepper; set aside.
● **Spray a cold wok** or large skillet with nonstick coating. Heat wok or skillet over high heat. Stir-fry green onions and red pepper strips for 2 minutes. Push vegetables from center of wok.
● **Add sauce mixture and pea pods.** Cook and stir till sauce is bubbly. Carefully fold in tofu, orange sections, and peanuts. Cover and cook for 1 to 2 minutes more or till just heated through. Serve over rice. Makes 4 servings.

Nutrition information per serving: 297 cal., 14 g pro., 47 g carbo., 8 g fat, 0 mg chol., 125 mg sodium, 317 mg potassium, 4 g dietary fiber. U.S. RDA: 49% vit. A, 75% vit. C, 24% thiamine, 11% niacin, 19% calcium, 23% iron.

MOROCCAN-STYLE FISH

If using frozen fish, transfer fillets to the refrigerator the night before to thaw—

- ¾ cup low-sodium chicken broth
- 2 tablespoons sodium-reduced soy sauce
- 2 teaspoons cornstarch
- ½ teaspoon five-spice powder
- ¼ cup mixed dried fruit bits *or* raisins
- 2 tablespoons thinly sliced celery
- 1⅓ cups boiling water
- ⅔ cup couscous
- 1 tablespoon snipped parsley
- ⅛ teaspoon salt
- Nonstick spray coating
- 4 fresh skinless whitefish *or* other fish fillets (12 ounces total), ½ to ¾ inch thick

● **Preheat oven** to 450°. For sauce, in a small saucepan combine chicken broth, *1 tablespoon* of the soy sauce, cornstarch, and five-spice powder. Stir in dried fruit bits or raisins and celery. Cook and stir till thickened and bubbly. Cook and stir for 2 minutes more. Cover sauce to keep warm.
● **In a medium mixing bowl combine** boiling water, couscous, parsley, and salt. Cover; let stand 5 minutes.
● **Meanwhile, spray** a 12x7½x2-inch baking dish with nonstick coating. Measure thickness of fish fillets. Place fillets in baking dish. Brush fish with remaining soy sauce. Bake in a 450° oven till fish just flakes with a fork (allow 4 to 6 minutes per ½-inch thickness of fish). Serve fish over couscous mixture. Ladle sauce atop. Serves 4.

Nutrition information per serving: 202 cal., 20 g pro., 27 g carbo., 1 g fat (0.5 g sat. fat), 37 mg chol., 370 mg sodium, 460 mg potassium, and 3 g dietary fiber. U.S. RDA: 14% niacin

MUSHROOM-SAUCED PORK

Dovetail your work: Microwave a vegetable side dish while you cook these yogurt-sauced pork medaillons on the range top—

- ¾ pound pork tenderloin
- ½ teaspoon lemon pepper
- Nonstick spray coating
- ⅓ cup plain nonfat yogurt
- ¼ cup dry white wine
- ¼ cup water
- 1 tablespoon cornstarch
- 1 teaspoon instant low-sodium beef bouillon granules
- 1 4-ounce can sliced mushrooms, drained
- 2 tablespoons chopped green onion

● **Cut pork** crosswise into 8 slices. Place each slice between 2 sheets of plastic wrap. Using the flat side of a meat mallet, pound slices to ¼-inch thickness; sprinkle with lemon pepper.
● **Spray a cold large skillet** with nonstick coating. Heat skillet over medium heat. Add pork to skillet and cook for 4 minutes. Turn pork over and cook for 2 to 4 minutes more or till no pink remains. Transfer pork to a serving platter; cover and keep warm.
● **For sauce, combine** yogurt, wine, water, cornstarch, and bouillon granules; add to skillet along with mushrooms and onion. Cook and stir till thickened and bubbly. Cook and stir for 2 minutes more. Serve sauce over pork. Makes 4 servings.

Nutrition information per serving: 147 cal., 20 g pro., 6 g carbo., 3 g fat, 60 mg chol., 243 mg sodium, 450 mg potassium. U.S. RDA: 42% thiamine, 19% riboflavin, 17% niacin.

HOT-LUNCH STEAK STEW

½ pound boneless beef top round steak
Nonstick spray coating
½ of a 16-ounce package (2 cups) loose-pack frozen zucchini, carrot, cauliflower, lima beans, and Italian beans
1 14½-ounce can beef broth *or* one 13¾-ounce can reduced-sodium beef broth
1 teaspoon Italian seasoning
1 15-ounce can tomato sauce with onion, celery, and green pepper
1 tablespoon cornstarch
2 teaspoons Worcestershire sauce
½ teaspoon sugar
½ of a 15-ounce can garbanzo beans, drained

●**Trim fat** from meat. Thinly slice meat across the grain into bite-size strips. Sprinkle with pepper.
●**Spray a cold large skillet** with nonstick coating. Heat the skillet over medium heat. Stir-fry meat for 1 to 2 minutes or till evenly browned.
●**Add vegetables,** broth, and Italian seasoning to meat; bring to boiling. Reduce heat. Cover and simmer 5 to 8 minutes or till vegetables are tender.
●**Meanwhile, combine** tomato sauce, cornstarch, Worcestershire sauce, and sugar; stir into the meat mixture. Cook and stir till mixture is thickened and bubbly. Cook and stir for 2 minutes more. Stir in garbanzo beans; heat through. Serve immediately or freeze.* Makes 4 servings.

*__*Note:__* To tote for lunch, pour cooled stew into 4 microwave-safe, airtight containers; cool. Freeze for at least 6 to 8 hours or overnight till solid. Pack frozen stew in an insulated lunchbox or with an ice pack. To thaw and heat, micro-cook, covered, on 100% power (high) for 5 to 7 minutes or till heated through, stirring once.

Nutrition information per serving: *258 cal., 22 g pro., 32 g carbo., 5 g fat (1.5 g sat.), 36 mg chol., 973 mg sodium, 954 mg potassium, and 3 g dietary fiber. U.S. RDA: 67% vit. A, 38% vit. C, 15% thiamine, 19% riboflavin, 26% niacin, 25% iron.*

SALMON-STUFFED PITA BREAD

1 6¾-ounce can skinless, boneless salmon, drained and flaked, *or* one 6½-ounce can tuna (water pack), drained and broken into chunks
½ cup loose-pack frozen peas, thawed
⅓ cup reduced-calorie clear Italian salad dressing
1 medium tomato
½ of a medium cucumber
2 large pita bread rounds, split crosswise
¼ cup soft-style cream cheese with chives and onion
½ cup alfalfa sprouts

●**In mixing bowl** toss salmon or tuna and peas with salad dressing. Thinly slice tomato and cucumber.
●**Spread inside of pita halves** with cream cheese. Divide salmon mixture, tomato, cucumber, and alfalfa sprouts between each of the 4 pita halves. Serve immediately.* Makes 4 servings.

*__*Note:__* For brown bagger's lunch, prepare as directed except divide the salmon mixture, tomato, cucumber, and sprouts between 4 airtight containers. Chill overnight or up to 2 days. Spread each pita with cream cheese just before packing lunch. Wrap each pita in a small plastic bag. Carry 1 pita and 1 container of salmon mixture and vegetables in an insulated lunch box with an ice pack. At lunchtime, add salmon mixture and vegetables to pita.

Nutrition information per serving: *205 cal., 13 g pro., 23 g carbo., 7 g fat, 17 mg chol., 531 mg sodium, 285 mg potassium, 2 g dietary fiber. U.S. RDA: 12% vit. A, 15% vit. C, 12% thiamine, 10% riboflavin, 16% niacin, 10% iron.*

SUPER PIZZA TOSTADAS

6 6-inch flour tortillas
1 small green pepper
1 pound skinned, boneless turkey breast, ground
½ teaspoon dried Italian seasoning
¼ teaspoon crushed red pepper (optional)
½ of a small head lettuce
1 medium tomato
1 8-ounce can pizza sauce
1 4-ounce can chopped mushrooms, drained
¾ cup shredded low-fat mozzarella cheese (3 ounces)

●**Turn oven** to 400°. Immediately arrange tortillas on a baking sheet, overlapping only as necessary. Bake about 10 minutes or till crisp and golden.
●**Meanwhile, cut** green pepper into bite-size pieces. In a 1½-quart microwave-safe dish crumble turkey. Add green pepper, Italian seasoning, and, if desired, crushed red pepper. Microcook, covered, on 100% power (high) for 5 to 7 minutes or till turkey is no longer pink and green pepper is tender, stirring once. Drain.
●**Meanwhile, shred** lettuce and chop tomato; set aside. Stir pizza sauce and mushrooms into turkey mixture. Cook, uncovered, on high about 1 minute more or till mixture is heated.
●**For tostadas, divide** lettuce between tortillas. Spoon *one-sixth* of the turkey mixture (½ cup) onto each tortilla; sprinkle each with *one-sixth* of the cheese and tomato. Makes 6 servings.

Nutrition information per serving: *236 cal., 24 g pro., 22 g carbo., 6 g fat (2 g sat. fat), 56 mg chol., 451 mg sodium, 345 mg potassium, 2 g dietary fiber. U.S. RDA: 12% vit. A, 38% vit. C, 25% riboflavin, 49% niacin, 16% calcium, 14% iron.*

MANHATTAN FISH CHOWDER

½ cup sliced green onion
¼ cup dry white wine *or* chicken broth
¾ pound fresh fish fillets
1 24-ounce can vegetable juice cocktail
1 12-ounce can whole kernel corn with sweet peppers, drained
1 teaspoon Worcestershire sauce
Several dashes bottled hot pepper sauce

● **In a 2-quart microwave-safe dish** combine green onion and wine or broth. Micro-cook, covered, on 100% power (high) 2 minutes or till onion is tender. Meanwhile, cut fish into ¾-inch pieces.
● **Add fish,** vegetable juice cocktail, corn, Worcestershire sauce, and bottled hot pepper sauce to onion mixture. Cook, covered, on high for 8 to 10 minutes or till fish just flakes with a fork and mixture is heated through, stirring twice. To serve, ladle into 4 soup bowls. Makes 4 servings.

Nutrition information per serving: 177 cal., 17 g pro., 24 g carbo., 2 g fat (.1 g sat. fat), 35 mg chol., 957 mg sodium, and 689 mg potassium and 1 g dietary fiber. U.S. RDA: 38% vit. A, 93% vit. C, 16% thiamine, 14% riboflavin, 29% niacin.

JAPANESE TORTELLINI SOUP

2 14½-ounce cans reduced-sodium chicken broth *or* regular chicken broth
1 10-ounce package frozen Japanese-style stir-fry vegetables with seasonings
1 cup refrigerated *or* frozen cheese-stuffed tortellini
Several dashes bottled hot pepper sauce
1 9-ounce package (2 cups) frozen diced, cooked chicken

● **In a large kettle or Dutch oven mix** chicken broth, seasoning packet from vegetables, tortellini, and hot pepper sauce. Bring to boiling. Add vegetables. Return to boiling; reduce heat. Simmer, covered, for 5 minutes.
● **Add chicken** and cook for 5 to 7 minutes more or till tortellini is al dente (tender but still slightly firm) and vegetables are tender. Makes 4 servings.

Nutrition information per serving: 269 cal., 31 g pro., 23 g carbo., 6 g fat (1 g sat. fat), 77 mg chol., 1,247 mg sodium, and 398 mg potassium. U.S. RDA: 21% vit. A, 30% vit. C, 30% thiamine, 30% riboflavin, 99% niacin, 12% calcium, 15% iron.

SUPER SUBMARINES

⅓ cup low-fat ricotta cheese
1 tablespoon grated Parmesan cheese
2 tablespoons skim milk
½ teaspoon Italian seasoning, crushed
⅛ teaspoon garlic powder
½ of a small zucchini
1 medium tomato
½ of a small onion
1 6-ounce package sliced Canadian-style bacon
1 pound loaf French bread (about 15 inches long)

● **Preheat broiler.** In a small mixing bowl stir together ricotta cheese, Parmesan cheese, milk, Italian seasoning, and garlic powder. Set aside.
● **Thinly slice** zucchini, tomato, and onion. Cut bacon slices in half, crosswise. Slice bread in half horizontally. Reserve half of the bread for another use.
● **Spread** remaining half with a *little* of the cheese mixture. Top with bacon slices. Spoon remaining cheese mixture on top of bacon. Top with zucchini, onion, and tomato. Place on a broiler pan.
● **Broil** 4 to 5 inches from heat for 8 to 9 minutes or till heated through. Cut into 8 pieces. Makes 4 servings.

Nutrition information per serving: 270 cal., 18 g pro., 36 g carbo., 6 g fat (2.2 g sat. fat), 27 mg chol., 978 mg sodium, 310 mg potassium, and 2 g dietary fiber. U.S. RDA: 18% vit. C, 39% thiamine, 19% riboflavin, 24% niacin, 10% calcium, 12% iron.

FEBRUARY

FROTHY MIDNIGHT MOCHA

HEARTTHROB CAKES

BERRY TRUE-LOVE CUPS

RASPBERRY ICE WITH
CHOCOLATE LACE

CHOCOLATE!

THE ULTIMATE VALENTINE

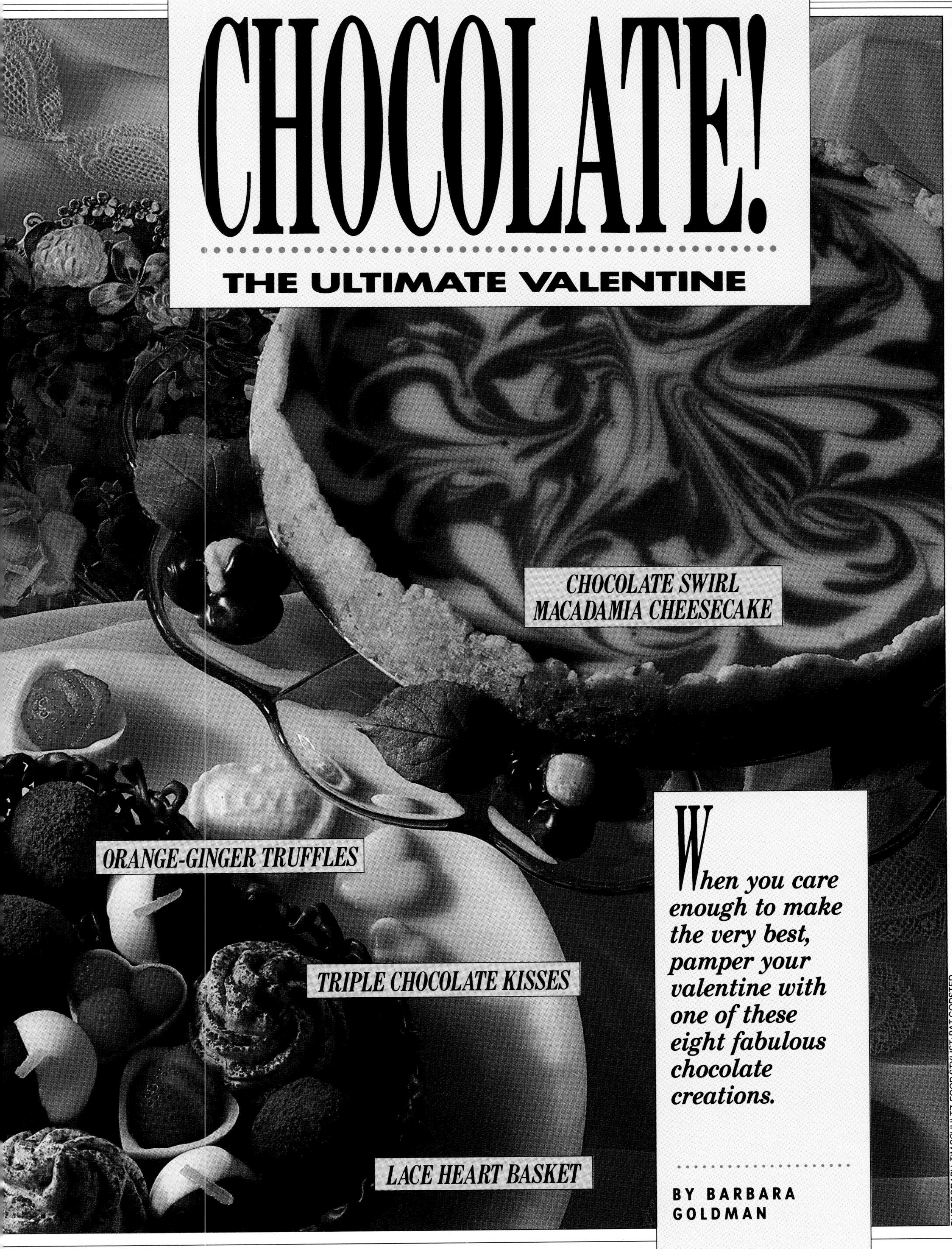
CHOCOLATE SWIRL MACADAMIA CHEESECAKE
ORANGE-GINGER TRUFFLES
TRIPLE CHOCOLATE KISSES
LACE HEART BASKET

PHOTOGRAPH: TIM SCHULTZ; FOOD STYLIST: PAT GODSTED

When you care enough to make the very best, pamper your valentine with one of these eight fabulous chocolate creations.

BY BARBARA GOLDMAN

MELTING CHOCOLATE
The Sweet-and-Simple Way

Follow these steps to melt semisweet chocolate for the Orange-Ginger Truffles, Lace Heart Basket, and Chocolate Lace recipes, as well as for other dipped candy recipes—

● **In a 4-cup glass measure** or 1½-quart glass mixing bowl combine the amount of semisweet chocolate pieces and shortening called for in your recipe. *Or,* use the chocolate-shortening proportions suggested below. Set chocolate mixture aside.

● **In a large glass mixing bowl** pour very warm tap water (100° to 110°) to a depth of 1 inch. Place measure or mixing bowl containing chocolate inside larger bowl. Water should cover bottom half of measure or bowl containing chocolate.

● **Stir the chocolate mixture** *constantly* with a rubber spatula until the chocolate mixture is completely melted and smooth. This takes about 15 to 20 minutes; don't rush the process.

● **If water begins to cool,** remove measure or bowl containing chocolate. Discard cool water; add warm water. Return measure or bowl containing chocolate to bowl containing water. (Avoid getting *any* water in chocolate. Just one drop can cause chocolate to become dull and gummy. *If water gets into chocolate:* stir in additional *shortening,* 1 teaspoon at a time, until mixture becomes shiny and smooth.)

● **If chocolate becomes too thick** while dipping candies, remove measure or bowl containing chocolate and replace water in larger bowl as directed above. Return measure or bowl containing chocolate to bowl containing water. Stir chocolate constantly till it again reaches dipping consistency.

● **Use the melted chocolate** as directed in your specific recipe.

Semisweet chocolate-shortening proportions for melting: Use 1 tablespoon shortening to 6 ounces chocolate, 2 tablespoons shortening to 12 ounces, and 3 tablespoons to 18 ounces.

Note: For 6 ounces of chocolate, use a 2-cup measure or a 3-cup bowl instead of a 4-cup measure or a 1½-quart bowl.

Place the measure containing the stirred semisweet chocolate pieces and shortening into a bowl of very warm inch-deep tap water.

Constantly and thoroughly stir the chocolate mixture with a rubber spatula while it melts. Don't rush the process.

After about 20 minutes the chocolate will be completely melted. The chocolate mixture should look shiny and smooth.

A QUICKER SUBSTITUTION: CONFECTIONERS' COATING

When you don't have time to melt chocolate by the method at left, substitute chocolate-flavored confectioners' coating. The taste can't match chocolate's, but confectioners' coating doesn't require a special melting process: just chop and melt it on the rangetop or in the microwave. Don't add shortening.

IMPORTANT CHOCOLATE TIPS

● **Avoid** humidity, steam, and wet utensils. Moisture can cause melting chocolate to thicken or crumble. Be sure candy-making utensils are dry, and watch carefully to make certain that not even one drop of water enters the melting chocolate. Don't try to melt chocolate on a hot or humid day. Chocolate can be temperamental under these conditions.

● **Constantly scrape and stir** chocolate to ensure even melting. Don't hurry the process; it's important that chocolate be melted slowly and evenly.

● **Use solid vegetable shortening** such as Crisco when melting chocolate the Sweet-and-Simple Way. Do not use butter or margarine. These fats contain moisture that could cause the chocolate to thicken and become grainy.

● **Add only the amount** of shortening called for in your recipe or suggested by our chocolate-shortening proportions. Extending chocolate with extra shortening (or water) will ruin it.

● **To store chocolate pieces** intended for melting, keep them in a cool, dry place between 65° and 70°, with less than 50 percent relative humidity. Higher temperatures or humidity may cause a gray appearance called "bloom" to appear in the chocolate before or after melting. Bloom won't affect the chocolate's flavor or quality.

February

FROTHY MIDNIGHT MOCHA

Wrap containers of the spicy mocha mix for your favorite valentines—but save enough for yourself for late-night sipping, a dessert, or a coffee spree—

- 2½ cups nonfat dry milk powder
- 1 cup sifted powdered sugar
- ½ cup unsweetened cocoa powder
- ¼ cup instant coffee crystals
- ½ teaspoon apple pie spice

● **To make mocha mix,** in a 1-quart airtight storage container combine milk powder, powdered sugar, cocoa powder, coffee crystals, and apple pie spice. Cover and shake well to mix.

● **To make a cup of mocha,** first stir the mix. Place *⅓ cup* of the mix in a blender container or food processor. Cover. With blender or processor running, add *⅔ cup boiling water* through opening in lid or center feed tube. Blend or process till mixed and frothy. Makes 10 (6-ounce) servings.

Nutrition information per serving: 164 cal., 12 g pro., 29 g carbo., 1 g fat, 6 mg chol., 195 mg sodium, 708 mg potassium, 1 g dietary fiber. U.S. RDA: 29% riboflavin, 39% calcium.

CHOCOLATE SWIRL MACADAMIA CHEESECAKE

Treat yourself and those you love to a Valentine's Day splurge—but enjoy this luxurious cheesecake at other times of the year as well—

- ¾ cup all-purpose flour
- 3 tablespoons sugar
- ¼ cup margarine *or* butter
- ¼ cup finely chopped toasted macadamia nuts *or* almonds
- 1 egg white
- ¾ cup milk chocolate pieces
- 3 8-ounce packages Neufchâtel cheese, softened
- 1 cup sugar
- 2 tablespoons all-purpose flour
- 2 eggs
- 1 egg yolk
- ¼ cup white crème de cacao
- Chocolate-covered macadamia nut clusters (optional)
- Chocolate leaves (optional)

● **For crust,** in a medium bowl stir together the ¾ cup flour and the 3 tablespoons sugar. Cut in the margarine or butter till mixture is crumbly. Stir in chopped nuts and egg white.

● **Pat *half* of the dough** onto bottom of an 8- or 9-inch springform pan (with sides removed). Bake in a 375° oven for 8 to 10 minutes or till very light golden brown; cool.

● **Butter sides of pan;** attach sides to bottom. Pat remaining dough 1¾ inches up sides of 8-inch pan or 1½ inches up sides of 9-inch pan; set the prepared pan aside.

● **In a heavy small saucepan melt** chocolate over very low heat, stirring constantly. Remove from heat.

● **For batter,** in a large mixing bowl beat Neufchâtel cheese till fluffy. Stir together the 1 cup sugar and the 2 tablespoons flour; beat into cheese mixture. Add the 2 eggs and the egg yolk all at once, beating on low speed just till blended. Do not overbeat. Stir in the crème de cacao.

● **To ⅔ of the batter (about 3 cups),** stir in melted chocolate. Spoon *half* the chocolate batter into crust-lined pan. Carefully spoon *half* of the remaining plain batter over the chocolate layer. Repeat layers. Carefully run a knife through the layers to swirl.

● **Place on a shallow baking pan** in oven. Bake in a 375° oven for 45 to 50 minutes for the 8-inch pan (35 to 45 minutes for the 9-inch pan) or till center appears *nearly* set. (To test for doneness, gently shake side of pan. When cheesecake is done, frequently a 1-inch portion in the center will jiggle slightly. This portion will set upon cooling.)

● **Cool cheesecake on a wire rack** for 5 minutes. Using a metal spatula, loosen crust from sides of pan, leaving pan sides attached. Cool 30 minutes more; remove sides of pan. Cool 2 hours. Cover and chill thoroughly.

● **To serve,** transfer cheesecake (bottom of springform pan in place) to a serving plate. If desired, garnish plate with chocolate-covered macadamia nut clusters and chocolate leaves before serving. Makes 12 servings.

To make the chocolate-covered macadamia nut clusters: In a heavy saucepan heat 2 ounces of *semisweet chocolate pieces* or *milk chocolate pieces* over very low heat, stirring constantly till the chocolate begins to melt. Immediately remove the chocolate from the heat and stir till smooth. Dip whole *macadamia nuts* into chocolate. Place nuts on a baking sheet lined with waxed paper with sides of 3 nuts touching each other to form a cluster. Top each of the clusters with an undipped macadamia nut; chill till set.

To make chocolate leaves: In a heavy saucepan heat 2 ounces of *semisweet chocolate pieces* or *milk chocolate pieces* over very low heat, stirring constantly till the chocolate begins to melt. Immediately remove the chocolate from the heat and stir till smooth. With a small paintbrush, brush melted chocolate on the underside of nontoxic, pesticide-free, fresh leaves (such as rose, lemon, mint, or ivy), building up layers of chocolate so garnish will be sturdy. Wipe off chocolate that may have run onto the front of the leaves. Place on a baking sheet lined with waxed paper; chill or freeze till set. Just before using, carefully peel the fresh leaves away from the chocolate leaves.

Nutrition information per serving: 399 cal., 9 g pro., 38 g carbo., 24 g fat, 115 mg chol., 301 mg sodium, 141 mg potassium, 1 g dietary fiber. U.S. RDA: 19% vit. A, 13% riboflavin.

A Word About White Chocolate

Many of the recipes in this story call for white baking bar (or pieces) with cocoa butter. You'll often hear this product referred to as white chocolate. Although these recipes were tested using this product, you may substitute products such as candy coating, confectioners' coating, and almond bark.

25

HEARTTHROB CAKES

You can bake these minicakes in small heart-shape pans or mini muffin pans. Look for the 3½x1-inch heart-shape pans in a kitchen specialty shop—

- 1 cup all-purpose flour
- 1 cup sugar
- ½ teaspoon baking powder
- ¼ teaspoon baking soda
- ¼ teaspoon salt
- ¾ cup milk
- ¼ cup peanut butter
- 2 envelopes (2 ounces) premelted unsweetened chocolate product
- ½ teaspoon vanilla
- 1 egg
- Peanut Butter Icing
- ¼ cup chopped peanuts

● **In a large mixing bowl** stir together the flour, sugar, baking powder, baking soda, and salt. Add milk, peanut butter, chocolate product, and vanilla. Beat with an electric mixer on low speed till combined. Beat on medium speed for 2 minutes. Add egg and beat for 2 minutes more.

● **Spoon a scant ¼ *cup*** of the batter into each of 12 greased and floured 3½x1-inch heart-shape minicake pans. If necessary, bake *half* of the batter at a time; let remaining batter stand at room temperature. (*Or,* spoon a scant tablespoon of the batter into 48 greased and floured 1¾-inch muffin pans. If necessary, bake *one-fourth or half* of the batter at a time; let the remaining batter stand at room temperature.)

● **Bake** the 3½x1-inch hearts in a 350° oven for 15 minutes or till a toothpick inserted near the center comes out clean. (Bake the 1¾-inch cakes for 8 to 9 minutes.) Cool for 10 minutes on a wire rack. Remove from pans.

● Cool cakes completely. Pour Peanut Butter Icing over heart cakes, completely covering top and sides (drizzle icing over the smaller cakes). If desired, sprinkle with peanuts. Makes 12 (3½x1-inch) heart-shape cakes or 48 (1¾-inch) miniature cakes.

Peanut Butter Icing: In a small mixing bowl beat 3 tablespoons *peanut butter* till light and fluffy. Gradually add ¾ cup sifted *powdered sugar*, beating well. Beat in ¼ cup *milk* and ½ teaspoon *vanilla*. Gradually beat in an additional 1 cup sifted *powdered sugar*. Beat in additional milk (1 to 2 tablespoons), if necessary, to make an icing of pouring consistency. (Icing should be thin enough to flow over the cakes so heart shape is distinct.) Makes enough to ice 12 3½x1-inch cakes or drizzle over 48 1¾-inch cakes.

Nutrition information per 3½x1-inch cake: *263 cal., 6 g pro., 45 g carbo., 8 g fat, 24 mg chol., 160 mg sodium, 147 mg potassium, 1 g dietary fiber. U.S. RDA: 12% niacin.*

BERRY TRUE-LOVE CUPS

Tuck fresh raspberries and strawberries inside candy hearts—

- 12 ounces white baking bar *or* pieces with cocoa butter, finely chopped
- 2 tablespoons shortening
- Several 1¼-inch *and/or* 1½-inch heart-shape candy molds
- 1 to 2 cups fresh raspberries, *and/or* sliced strawberries, rinsed, well dried, and at room temperature

● **In a heavy saucepan** melt white baking bar or pieces and shortening over very low heat, stirring constantly. Remove from heat; stir till smooth.

Paint the inside of the candy molds.

● **Using a small paintbrush** or small spoon, spread some of the mixture inside heart-shape candy molds. (The molds need to be about 1½ inches in diameter and about 1 inch deep in order to hold fruit. If your sheets of molds also have smaller hearts, fill them with chocolate to accent a candy tray.)

● **Place molds in freezer** for 2 to 3 minutes. Remove. Repeat spreading mixture inside molds, coating evenly. Freeze about 5 minutes or till firm. Immediately turn molds upside down and gently tap against a hard surface or press molds to remove candy hearts. Chill. Continue to mold hearts with remaining mixture. If mixture thickens, reheat over very low heat till melted.

● **Fill hearts with berries.** (You'll need the larger amount of fruit to fill *all* hearts. Or, fill half the hearts, and place remaining unfilled hearts atop as covers, slightly ajar.)

● **Chill** 2 to 3 minutes in freezer or 15 to 20 minutes in refrigerator. Store filled hearts in refrigerator up to 24 hours. Before serving, let stand at room temperature 10 to 15 minutes. Makes 40.

Nutrition information per heart, with fruit: *55 cal., 1 g pro., 6 g carbo., 3 g fat, 2 mg chol., 8 mg sodium, 35 mg potassium, 1 g dietary fiber.*

RASPBERRY ICE WITH CHOCOLATE LACE

- 1 **10-ounce package frozen red raspberries, thawed**
- ¼ **cup sugar**
- 3 **tablespoons crème de cassis**
- ½ **teaspoon finely shredded orange peel**
- 1 **6-ounce package (1 cup) semisweet chocolate pieces**
- 1 **tablespoon shortening**
- 3 **ounces white baking bar *or* pieces with cocoa butter, finely chopped**
- 1 **tablespoon shortening**

● **In a covered blender container** or food processor bowl puree the thawed raspberries. Sieve puree to remove seeds. Discard seeds. (You should have about *1¼ cups* of puree.) Add the sugar, crème de cassis, and orange peel. Cover and blend till sugar dissolves. Pour raspberry mixture into a 9x5x3-inch loaf pan. Cover; freeze for 3 to 4 hours or till almost firm.

● **Break frozen mixture** into chunks. Transfer to a chilled large mixing bowl. Beat with an electric mixer on medium speed till smooth but not melted. Return to cold pan. Cover and freeze for 6 to 8 hours more or till firm.

● **For chocolate lace,** in a 2-cup glass measure or 3-cup mixing bowl stir together the semisweet chocolate pieces and 1 tablespoon shortening. Follow directions for melting chocolate, *page 24.* This melting process takes about 15 minutes for 6 ounces of chocolate.

● **Line a baking sheet** with waxed paper or foil. Using a pastry bag fitted with a writing tip or a heavy-duty plastic bag with a small hole cut in one corner, quickly drizzle the melted chocolate mixture over the waxed paper. For each piece of lace, drizzle a 2x1½-inch zigzag shape, forming an open, lacy design or pattern. Repeat with the remaining melted chocolate to make about 40 pieces of lace. Chill in the freezer about 5 minutes or till set.

● **Meanwhile, in a small saucepan** melt the finely chopped white baking bar or pieces and 1 tablespoon shortening over very low heat, stirring constantly. Using a pastry bag fitted with a writing tip or a heavy-duty plastic bag with a small hole in one corner, randomly drizzle the white mixture atop each chocolate design, forming a variegated white and chocolate pattern. Chill in the freezer about 5 minutes or till set. Store lace pieces, covered, in a cool, dry place between 65° and 75° till ready to serve.

Drizzle white designs over chocolate.

● **To serve,** let raspberry ice stand about 5 minutes at room temperature. Meanwhile, carefully remove chocolate lace from waxed paper.

● **For each serving,** arrange 3 small scoops of raspberry ice on a serving dish. Garnish each serving with 1 or 2 pieces of the chocolate lace. Store the remaining chocolate lace in the freezer in layers with foil or plastic wrap between layers. Store up to 4 weeks. Makes 4 servings.

Nutrition information per serving (with 2 pieces chocolate lace): 234 cal., 1 g pro., 47 g carbo., 6 g fat, 1 mg chol., 5 mg sodium, 122 mg potassium, 4 g dietary fiber. U.S. RDA: 20% vit. C.

TRIPLE CHOCOLATE KISSES

You'll love eating your way through to the soft and chewy centers—

- 2 **egg whites**
- ¼ **teaspoon cream of tartar**
- ¼ **teaspoon almond extract**
- ½ **cup sugar**
- 1 **square (1 ounce) semisweet chocolate, grated**
- 24 **milk chocolate kisses**

Unsweetened cocoa powder

● **For meringue,** in a small mixing bowl beat egg whites, cream of tartar, and almond extract on medium speed till soft peaks form (tips curl). Gradually add sugar, beating on high speed till stiff peaks form (tips stand straight). Fold in grated semisweet chocolate. Spoon meringue into a decorating bag fitted with a large star tip.

● **On a lightly greased cookie sheet** pipe *some* of the meringue into 24 rounds, *each* about 1¼ inches in diameter. Lightly press a chocolate kiss into each meringue round. Pipe meringue around each kiss in a concentric circle, starting at the base and working toward the top, till kiss is completely covered. Dust with cocoa powder.

Pipe the meringue around candies.

● **Bake in a 325° oven** for 20 to 25 minutes or till light brown on the edges. Immediately remove from cookie sheet; cool on a wire rack. Makes 24 kisses.

Nutrition information per kiss: 44 cal., 1 g pro., 7 g carbo., 2 g fat, 1 mg chol., 10 mg sodium, 23 mg potassium.

ORANGE-GINGER TRUFFLES

You can dip these creamy confections in chocolate or roll them in cocoa powder. Either way, they're terrific. For instructions on melting chocolate for dipping these luscious centers, turn to page 24—

  6 **squares (6 ounces) semisweet chocolate, coarsely chopped**
⅓ **cup whipping cream**
¼ **cup margarine *or* butter**
  1 **beaten egg yolk**
  2 **tablespoons finely chopped crystallized ginger**
½ **teaspoon finely shredded orange peel**
  1 **12-ounce package (2 cups) semisweet chocolate pieces**
  2 **tablespoons shortening**
  4 **ounces white baking pieces with cocoa butter (about 1 cup) *or* white baking bar with cocoa butter, cut up**
  2 **tablespoons shortening**
Crystallized ginger (optional)
Unsweetened cocoa powder (optional)

● **For centers,** in a heavy medium saucepan combine the 6 squares semisweet chocolate, whipping cream, and margarine or butter.
● **Cook and stir** over low heat till chocolate is melted, stirring constantly. Gradually stir about *half* of the hot mixture into the egg yolk. Return all of the mixture to the saucepan. Cook and stir over medium-low heat for 3 minutes. Remove from heat.
● **Transfer chocolate mixture** to a small mixing bowl; chill about 1½ hours or till mixture is completely cool and is smooth, stirring occasionally. Beat the cooled chocolate mixture with an electric mixer on medium speed till slightly fluffy. Fold in finely chopped ginger and orange peel. If necessary, chill about 15 minutes more or till mixture holds its shape. If you plan to dip balls in chocolate, roll chilled mixture into 1-inch balls. If you plan to coat balls with cocoa powder, roll mixture into 1½-inch balls. Chill about 30 minutes more or till firm.

● **If dipping balls in chocolate,** in a 4-cup glass measure or 1½-quart glass mixing bowl, stir together the chocolate pieces and 2 tablespoons shortening. Follow directions for melting chocolate, *page 24.* This process takes about 20 minutes for 12 ounces of chocolate.
● **To coat balls,** with a fork dip 1-inch balls, one at a time, into the melted chocolate mixture; place on waxed-paper-lined baking sheet. If the chocolate becomes too thick while dipping, follow the instructions for rewarming chocolate, *page 24.* Continue dipping. Chill candies in the freezer for 5 minutes or till chocolate is set.
● **Meanwhile,** in a heavy small saucepan melt the white baking pieces or bar and 2 tablespoons shortening over very low heat, stirring constantly. Holding balls with a fork, decorate by dipping balls in the white chocolate mixture so that the white chocolate coats half of the ball. If desired, top each ball with a small piece of crystallized ginger.
● ***Or,* if desired,** roll larger chilled balls in unsweetened cocoa powder rather than dipping them in chocolate.
● **Store candies,** covered, in a cool, dry place between 65° and 70°. Makes 36 (1-inch) chocolate-dipped candies or 24 (1½-inch) cocoa-coated candies.

    Nutrition information per dipped candy: *125 cal., 1 g pro., 11 g carbo., 10 g fat, 11 mg chol., 20 mg sodium, 80 mg potassium, 1 g dietary fiber.*

LACE HEART BASKET

Who can resist a chocolate lace heart filled with Berry True-Love Cups, Triple Chocolate Kisses, and Orange-Ginger Truffles? Here's how to make this standout centerpiece—

  1 **6-ounce package (1 cup) semisweet chocolate pieces**
  1 **tablespoon shortening**

● **Press** a large piece of foil over inside bottom and up sides of a 7½-inch heart-shape baking pan. Chill in freezer.
● **Meanwhile,** in a 2-cup glass measure or 3-cup glass mixing bowl, stir together chocolate pieces and shortening. Follow directions for melting chocolate, *page 24.* This process takes about 15 minutes for 6 ounces of chocolate.

● **Using a pastry bag** fitted with a writing tip (a No. 4 works well) or a heavy-duty plastic bag with a small hole cut in one corner, drizzle the chocolate mixture randomly over the bottom and sides of chilled foil on the inside of the cake pan. Chill in the freezer about 5 minutes or till set.

Randomly pipe melted chocolate over foil.

● **To unmold,** lift chocolate-coated foil from pan. Carefully peel foil from chocolate. Place chocolate heart on a serving tray. To store, cover and place in a cool dark place. Fill with Triple Chocolate Kisses, Orange-Ginger Truffles, and Berry True-Love Cups. Makes 1 7½-inch basket (six 1-ounce servings).

    Nutrition information per serving: *162 cal., 1 g pro., 16 g carbo., 12 g fat, 1 mg sodium, 92 mg potassium, 2 g dietary fiber.*

    To make a 9-inch basket: Follow recipe as directed, *except* substitute a 9-inch heart-shape cake pan, and use *12 ounces* semisweet chocolate pieces and *2 tablespoons* shortening. The melting process will take about 20 minutes for 12 ounces of chocolate. You will have a little more chocolate than you need for the basket. Use just *two-thirds* of the chocolate mixture to make the heart basket. Reserve the remaining chocolate to use for "repairs" if the chocolate lace heart breaks while being removed from foil. (Spread remaining chocolate over waxed-paper-lined baking sheet. Chill till set. Chop and use in other recipes.)

TWICE AS NICE

BY
BARBARA GOLDMAN

Cook Once for Two Meals

Isn't it great when you cook one meal and end up with the makings for another? For these doubleheader recipes, serve half the first night and refrigerate or freeze the rest. The second night, a few more ingredients create a delicious new dinner.

PHOTOGRAPHS: TIM SCHULTZ; FOOD STYLIST: PAT GODSTED

1st NIGHT

Beef and Vegetable Stew

A homey, warming meal that'll brighten a winter day, with plenty of healthful vegetables, and bulgur on the side. Though you'll be tempted to eat more, remember to save half the stew for another night.

2nd NIGHT

Quick Beef Potpie

Stir up a simple sauce, add the stew, mushrooms, and peas, and cook until bubbly. Pour into a casserole, top with refrigerated biscuits, and bake 10 minutes.

BEEF ON THE DOUBLE

29

FROM STIR-FRY TO SOUP

Pork works a sleight of hand as it debuts in a sizzling stir-fry, then vanishes into a steaming bowl of oriental soup.

1st NIGHT Pork, Pepper, and Carrot Stir-Fry

Carrots and sweet red peppers pack plenty of vitamin A—and plenty of taste—into this perky stir-fry. Freeze or chill part of the stir-fry for a second meal that's just as wonderful.

2nd NIGHT

Oriental Hot and Sour Soup

Mix up this tangy soup in just 15 minutes. It's no trick at all, thanks to preshredded cabbage with carrots, canned chicken broth, and the remaining stir-fry. Add tofu for extra nutrition, mushrooms and seasonings for extra flavor.

1st NIGHT

Chicken Breasts Dijon
with Fresh Vegetables

Snow peas and baby red-skinned potatoes combine nicely with this healthful offering of tasty, tender chicken breasts. Prepare the chicken with a little mustard and a little wine, but with no added fat.

QUICK-CHANGE CHICKEN

Transform a simple but elegant chicken entrée into another terrific meal of pasta and chicken.

2nd NIGHT

Pasta with Chicken
and Artichokes

Be ready for dinner in 20 minutes or less. Your second chicken dish goes together with tricolor pasta, artichokes, pimiento, and garbanzo beans.

TWO-WAY TURKEY

A speedy broiler entrée with a delectable chutney sauce evolves into a down-home skillet of Turkey Country Captain.

1st NIGHT — Chutney-Sauced Turkey Tenderloins

The perfect answer to a hurry-up call for a company dinner. A turn under the broiler and a slathering of chutney sauce produces a succulent turkey entrée that's a dinner winner.

2nd NIGHT — Turkey Country Captain

New seasonings recycle a turkey dinner. Onions, garlic, a hint of curry powder, and ground red pepper combine with the turkey, canned tomatoes, and strips of sweet pepper to fashion a robust, family-style dish. It's ready in 30 minutes.

1st NIGHT

South-of-the-Border Spuds

Bring this saucy meal to the table in just half an hour. While the meat sauce simmers, slip the potatoes into the microwave. Serve the cooked, sliced potatoes topped with meat sauce and the fixin's—cheese, tomato, and green onion.

SOUTHWESTERN SWITCH

Two zesty meat sauce partnerships prove the simpler, the better. First, pair the sauce with a potato, next with a bun.

2nd NIGHT

Southwestern Heroes

Your search for a bold and brave hero ends here. Though humble in every way, this one has what it takes—a snappy manner with plenty of crust.

BEEF AND VEGETABLE STEW

Simply stir a jar of gravy, wine, and seasonings into the pot of browned meat, add the vegetables, and simmer an hour for terrific flavor—

    2 pounds beef round steak,
       cut into 1-inch cubes
    2 tablespoons cooking oil
    1 12-ounce jar brown gravy
    ¼ cup dry red wine
    ½ teaspoon dried thyme, crushed
    ¼ teaspoon pepper
    8 medium carrots, cut into 1½-inch
       pieces
    3 medium turnips, peeled and cut
       into 1½-inch pieces
    3 medium onions, quartered
    1 cup bulgur
    1 medium zucchini, cut into thin
       strips

● **In a Dutch oven brown** steak cubes, *half* at a time, in hot oil. Drain off excess fat. Return all meat to Dutch oven. Stir in gravy, wine, thyme, and pepper. Add the carrots, turnips, and onions to the meat in Dutch oven. Bring to boiling; reduce heat. Cover and simmer about 1 hour or till meat is tender.

● **About 15 minutes before dinner,** cook bulgur according to package directions. Place zucchini strips atop bulgur for the last 5 minutes of cooking time. Transfer zucchini to a small plate or bowl. Cover to keep warm.

● **To serve, spoon bulgur mixture** into one side of *each* of 4 soup bowls or plates. Reserve half of the stew (about 4 cups) and chill up to 48 hours or freeze for Quick Beef Potpie; see recipe, *at right*. Spoon the remaining half of the stew into the other side of the 4 bowls or plates. Place cooked zucchini strips atop bulgur in each bowl or plate. Makes 4 servings.

Nutrition information per serving: 399 cal., 28 g pro., 46 g carbo., 12 g fat, 62 mg chol., 112 mg sodium, 804 mg potassium, 11 g dietary fiber. U.S. RDA: 407% vit. A, 25% vit. C, 20% thiamine, 17% riboflavin, 28% niacin, 29% iron.

QUICK BEEF POTPIE

Refrigerated biscuits and leftover Beef and Vegetable Stew make this homey potpie a breeze to prepare—

    ½ recipe (about 4 cups) Beef and
       Vegetable Stew (thawed, if
       frozen)
    3 tablespoons margarine *or* butter
    ¼ cup all-purpose flour
    ⅛ teaspoon dried rosemary,
       crushed
   1½ cups milk
    ¾ cup loose-pack frozen peas
    1 4-ounce can whole mushrooms,
       drained
    1 package (6) refrigerated biscuits
Dried rosemary, crushed (optional)

● **If frozen,** thaw the Beef and Vegetable Stew overnight in the refrigerator. *Or,* place the frozen stew in a 2-quart microwave-safe casserole and microcook, covered, on 30% power (medium-low) for 30 to 35 minutes, stirring occasionally.

● **In a large saucepan melt** margarine or butter over medium heat. Stir in flour and the ⅛ teaspoon rosemary. Add the milk all at once; cook and stir till thickened and bubbly. Stir in the stew, peas, and mushrooms. Cook and stir till bubbly. Pour into a 2-quart casserole. Halve biscuits crosswise. Arrange biscuits in two rings on top of the casserole. If desired, sprinkle with dried rosemary.

● **Bake in 450° oven** for 8 to 10 minutes or till biscuits are golden brown. Serve immediately. Serves 4 or 5.

Nutrition information per serving: 424 cal., 25 g pro., 35 g carbo., 20 g fat, 55 mg chol., 578 mg sodium, 683 mg potassium, 4 g dietary fiber. U.S. RDA: 335% vit. A, 22% vit. C, 23% thiamine, 25% riboflavin, 25% niacin, 22% iron.

PORK, PEPPER, AND CARROT STIR-FRY

Rice wine vinegar lends a sweet-sour flavor to the saucy stir-fry—

   1½ pounds lean boneless pork
    ½ cup sodium-reduced soy sauce
    ¼ cup rice wine vinegar *or* red wine
       vinegar
    2 teaspoons cornstarch
    1 teaspoon ground ginger
    ½ teaspoon crushed red pepper
    1 tablespoon cooking oil
    6 medium carrots, thinly bias-
       sliced (3 cups)
    2 sweet red peppers, cut into thin
       bite-size strips (2 cups)
    2 small onions, cut into wedges
    2 cloves garlic, minced
Hot cooked rice
Fresh cilantro *or* parsley sprigs
   (optional)
Garlic chives (optional)

● **Cut pork on bias** into matchstick-size strips (about 2x¼x¼ inches).

● **For sauce,** stir together soy sauce, vinegar, cornstarch, ginger, and crushed red pepper. Set aside.

● **Preheat a wok** or a 12-inch skillet over high heat. Add oil. (Add more oil as necessary during cooking.) Add carrots, sweet red peppers, onions, and garlic. Stir-fry for 4 to 5 minutes or till vegetables are crisp-tender. Remove vegetables from wok.

● **Add** *one-third* **of pork** to hot wok or skillet. Stir-fry about 3 minutes or till no longer pink. Remove pork. Repeat twice with remaining pork. Return all the pork to wok or skillet. Push pork from center to outer edges.

● **Stir the soy sauce mixture;** add to center of wok. Cook and stir till thickened and bubbly. Return vegetables to wok. Stir ingredients together. Cover and cook for 1 to 2 minutes or till heated through. (Reserve 3 cups of the pork mixture and chill up to 48 hours or freeze for Oriental Hot and Sour Soup; see recipe, *page 35*.) Serve remaining portion over hot cooked rice. If desired, garnish with cilantro or parsley and garlic chives. Makes 4 servings.

Nutrition information per serving (including ½ cup cooked rice): 411 cal., 31 g pro., 38 g carbo., 14 g fat, 81 mg chol., 940 mg sodium, 716 mg potassium, 3 g dietary fiber. U.S. RDA: 389% vit. A, 96% vit. C, 69% thiamine, 18% riboflavin, 34% niacin, 16% iron.

ORIENTAL HOT AND SOUR SOUP

Crushed red pepper adds the hotness, and rice wine vinegar makes it sour. Look for rice wine vinegar in the Oriental section of your grocery store or in an Oriental specialty store—

      3 cups Pork, Pepper, and Carrot
         Stir-Fry (thawed, if frozen)
      1 49½-ounce can chicken broth
      1 cup sliced fresh mushrooms
      1 tablespoon soy sauce
    ¼ teaspoon crushed red pepper
      1 8-ounce package tofu, drained
         and cut into ½-inch cubes
         (about 1¾ cups)
  1½ cups shredded cabbage with
         carrot
      2 tablespoons rice wine vinegar *or*
         red wine vinegar

● **If frozen,** thaw Pork, Pepper, and Carrot Stir-Fry overnight in refrigerator. *Or,* place the stir-fry mixture in a 1½-quart microwave-safe casserole and micro-cook, covered, on 30% power (medium-low) for 11 to 13 minutes, turning the dish once.
● **In a Dutch oven combine** the chicken broth, mushrooms, soy sauce, and crushed red pepper. Bring to boiling. Add the thawed stir-fry, tofu, shredded cabbage with carrot, and vinegar. Return to boiling. Spoon into 4 soup bowls. Makes 4 servings.

Nutrition information per serving: 265 cal., 27 g pro., 13 g carbo., 12 g fat, 41 mg chol., 1,855 mg sodium, 847 mg potassium, 3 g dietary fiber. U.S. RDA: 273% vit. A, 60% vit. C, 37% thiamine, 21% riboflavin, 44% niacin, 12% calcium, 19% iron.

CHICKEN BREASTS DIJON WITH FRESH VEGETABLES

Here's a lightly sauced chicken main dish that tastes as delicious as it is good for you—

    ¾ pound whole tiny new potatoes
      8 ounces fresh pea pods
    ¾ cup hot water
      1 teaspoon instant chicken
         bouillon granules
    ¼ cup dry white wine
      3 to 4 teaspoons Dijon-style
         mustard

    ½ teaspoon dried basil, crushed
    ¼ teaspoon dried tarragon,
         crushed
    ⅛ teaspoon pepper
      8 boned skinless chicken breast
         halves (about 1½ pounds total)
Nonstick spray coating
Halved orange slices (optional)
Cucumber curls (optional)
Fresh basil *and/or* tarragon sprigs
  (optional)

● **In a large saucepan** cook the potatoes, covered, in a small amount of boiling salted water for 20 minutes. Add the pea pods and cook for 2 to 4 minutes more or till potatoes are tender and pea pods are crisp-tender. (*Or,* in a 3-quart casserole, micro-cook potatoes and 2 tablespoons *water*, covered, on 100% power (high) for 5 minutes. Add the pea pods. Cook, covered, on high for 3 to 5 minutes more or till potatoes are tender and the pea pods are crisp-tender.)
● **Meanwhile, in a small bowl** combine the ¾ cup hot water and chicken bouillon granules. Add the wine, mustard, basil, tarragon, and pepper. Set aside.
● **Rinse chicken** and pat dry. Halve each chicken breast half lengthwise. Spray a cold large skillet with nonstick coating. Heat the skillet over medium-high heat. Add the chicken pieces. Cook until the chicken is golden brown on both sides, turning once. (Allow about 2 minutes per side.) Remove skillet from heat. Carefully add the bouillon mixture to the chicken; bring to boiling. Reduce heat. Simmer, covered, about 5 minutes or till the chicken is no longer pink.
● **Remove *two-thirds*** of the chicken; keep warm. (Reserve remaining *third* of the chicken and *half* of the pan juices and chill up to 48 hours or freeze for Pasta with Chicken and Artichokes; see recipe, *at right*.)
● **If necessary,** boil the remaining pan juices, uncovered, till reduced to ¼ cup (about 1 minute). Divide the chicken among 4 serving plates. Pour the pan juices over the chicken. Serve the chicken with the cooked vegetables. If desired, garnish with the halved orange slices, cucumber curls, and basil or tarragon sprigs. Makes 4 servings.

Nutrition information per serving: 286 cal., 39 g pro., 20 g carbo., 5 g fat, 96 mg chol., 195 mg sodium, 838 mg potassium, 3 g dietary fiber. U.S. RDA: 41% vit. C, 16% thiamine, 13% riboflavin, 86% niacin, 14% iron.

PASTA WITH CHICKEN AND ARTICHOKES

The tangy marinade from the artichokes combines with the mustard-wine-flavored pan juices for a tangy pasta and chicken supper—

    ⅓ recipe Chicken Breasts Dijon
         including juices (thawed, if
         frozen)
      4 ounces (about 1½ cups)
         corkscrew macaroni (rotelle)
      1 6-ounce jar marinated artichoke
         hearts
      1 cup canned garbanzo beans
      1 2-ounce jar sliced pimiento,
         drained
    ¼ cup grated Parmesan cheese
      2 tablespoons snipped parsley

● **If frozen,** thaw Chicken Breasts Dijon and pan juices overnight in refrigerator. *Or,* in a 10x6-inch microwave-safe baking dish micro-cook the chicken pieces and juices, covered, on 30% power (medium-low) for 5 to 7 minutes. Cut the chicken into bite-size pieces.
● **In a large saucepan cook** the pasta according to package directions; drain. Return pasta to saucepan.
● **Drain marinated artichoke hearts,** reserving *2 tablespoons* liquid. Cut large artichokes in half. To pasta, add the artichokes and reserved liquid, the chicken and reserved juices, the garbanzo beans, and sliced pimiento.
● **Cook, stirring gently,** over medium heat for 5 minutes or till most of the liquid is absorbed. To serve, sprinkle the Parmesan cheese and parsley over the pasta and chicken mixture. Makes 4 servings.

Nutrition information per serving: 343 cal., 27 g pro., 37 g carbo., 9 g fat, 53 mg chol., 474 mg sodium, 431 mg potassium, 6 g dietary fiber. U.S. RDA: 11% vit. A, 22% vit. C, 14% thiamine, 12% riboflavin, 46% niacin, 15% calcium, 16% iron.

CHUTNEY-SAUCED TURKEY TENDERLOINS

Slip the turkey under the broiler and add a sweet-sour chutney sauce. Then serve the succulent turkey with rice— but not until you've reserved part for another great meal—

- ¾ cup chutney
- 1 tablespoon margarine *or* butter
- 1 tablespoon lemon juice
- 1 tablespoon water
- ⅛ teaspoon pepper
- ⅔ cup long grain rice
- ½ teaspoon ground turmeric
- 8 turkey breast tenderloin steaks (about 2 pounds total)
- 2 tablespoons margarine *or* butter, melted
- ¼ cup sliced almonds
- Green grape clusters (optional)
- Green onion curls (optional)

● **Snip any large pieces** of chutney. In a 1-quart saucepan stir together the chutney, the 1 tablespoon margarine or butter, lemon juice, water, and pepper. Cook mixture over medium heat till margarine melts and mixture bubbles, stirring occasionally. Remove from heat; keep warm.
● **Cook rice** according to package directions, adding the turmeric to the cooking water.
● **Meanwhile, preheat broiler.** Place turkey steaks on the unheated rack of a broiler pan. Brush with the 2 tablespoons melted margarine or butter. Broil 4 to 5 inches from heat for 4 minutes. Turn; broil turkey 6 to 8 minutes more or till no longer pink, brushing with some of the chutney sauce during the last 2 minutes of broiling.
● **Spoon remaining sauce** over the turkey steaks. (Reserve 4 turkey steaks with sauce and chill up to 48 hours or freeze for Turkey Country Captain; see recipe, *at right*.)
● **Spoon rice** onto a serving platter. Top with remaining turkey steaks and sauce. Sprinkle almonds over turkey. If desired, garnish with grapes and green onion curls. Makes 4 servings.

Nutrition information per serving: *355 cal., 25 g pro., 43 g carbo., 9 g fat, 59 mg chol., 144 mg sodium, 369 mg potassium, 1 g dietary fiber. U.S. RDA: 12% thiamine, 33% niacin, 15% iron.*

TURKEY COUNTRY CAPTAIN

- ½ recipe Chutney-Sauced Turkey Tenderloins, with sauce (thawed, if frozen)
- 2 medium sweet yellow *and/or* green peppers, cut into thin strips (2 cups)
- 1 medium onion, chopped (½ cup)
- 1 clove garlic, minced
- 1 tablespoon cooking oil
- 1 14-ounce can whole Italian-style tomatoes, cut up
- 1 teaspoon curry powder
- ½ teaspoon salt
- ⅛ to ¼ teaspoon ground red pepper
- 2 cups hot cooked couscous *or* rice

● **If frozen,** thaw Chutney-Sauced Turkey Tenderloin Steaks overnight in the refrigerator. *Or,* in a 10x6x2-inch microwave-safe baking dish micro-cook frozen turkey with sauce, covered, on 30% power (medium-low) for 7 to 9 minutes, turning the dish once.
● **In a large skillet** cook peppers, onion, and garlic in hot oil over medium-high heat till the vegetables are tender but not brown.
● **Stir in the *undrained* tomatoes,** curry powder, salt, and ground red pepper. Cook, uncovered, about 5 minutes or till some of the liquid evaporates. Add the thawed turkey tenderloin steaks with sauce. Spoon vegetable mixture over turkey; cover.
● **Reduce heat; simmer** for 10 to 12 minutes or till heated through. Serve with hot cooked couscous. Serves 4.

Nutrition information per serving: *388 cal., 27 g pro., 51 g carbo., 9 g fat, 59 mg chol., 662 mg sodium, 679 mg potassium, 8 g dietary fiber. U.S. RDA: 21% vit. A, 108% vit. C, 12% thiamine, 10% riboflavin, 34% niacin, 19% iron.*

Microwave directions: In a 12x7½x2-inch microwave-safe baking dish, micro-cook peppers, onion, garlic, and oil, covered, on 100% power (high) for 5 to 6 minutes or till tender. Stir in the *undrained* tomatoes, curry powder, salt, and ground red pepper. Cook, uncovered, on high for 5 minutes. Add the thawed turkey tenderloin steaks with sauce. Spoon vegetable mixture over turkey. Cook, covered, on high for 5 to 7 minutes or till heated through, giving the dish a half-turn after 3 minutes. Serve as above.

Freezing Homemade Meals

To keep frozen foods in tip-top shape, choose a wrap or a container that is moistureproof, vaporproof, and able to withstand temperatures of zero or below. The following wraps and containers meet these requirements.

● **Aluminum foil:** Heavy-duty foil provides better protection for frozen foods than regular foil. Mold the foil to the shape of the food to keep air out. Be sure the foil doesn't get punctured while you're wrapping the food.

Avoid using foil to wrap foods that contain acid, such as tomato products. Acid reacts with the aluminum, changing the flavor of the food. If you must use foil, wrap the food first in clear plastic wrap, then overwrap with foil.
● **Freezer plastic wrap:** This type is sturdier than everyday plastic wrap. Because not all plastic wraps are alike, read the label to be sure your plastic wrap is freezer safe.
● **Laminated paper:** Sturdy laminated paper, also known as heavy freezer wrap, is white, shiny on one side and dull on the other. Wrap the food with the shiny side of the paper facing toward the inside next to the food.
● **Polyethylene freezer bags:** These bags are made from pliable plastic film and are moisture- and vaporproof. These bags work well for solid foods, but they don't store easily when filled with liquids.
● **Plastic freezer cartons:** These containers come in a variety of sizes and shapes with tight-fitting lids.
● **Baking dishes:** In the freezer, use baking dishes that are recommended for freezer-to-oven and/or freezer-to-microwave oven use.
● **Aluminum containers:** These are available in many sizes and styles with tight-fitting lids. Many are reusable and can go from oven to freezer and back again.
● **Waxed cartons:** Reusable waxed cardboard containers come in a variety of shapes and sizes. If you intend to pack them with foods that stain, line them first with polyethylene bags.

SOUTH-OF-THE-BORDER SPUDS

Pair these chili-topped potatoes with fresh baked corn mufffins—

- 1 pound lean ground beef
- 1 large onion, chopped (1 cup)
- 1 16-ounce can crushed tomatoes
- 1 15½-ounce can red kidney beans, drained
- 1 8-ounce can tomato sauce
- 2 4-ounce cans diced green chili peppers
- 1 tablespoon chili powder
- ½ teaspoon garlic salt
- 4 medium baking potatoes (6 to 8 ounces each)
- 4 cups shredded lettuce
- 1 medium tomato, chopped
- ¼ cup sliced green onion
- 1 cup shredded American cheese (4 ounces)

● **In a large skillet cook** ground beef and onion till beef is brown and onion is tender. Drain off fat.

● **Stir in** the *undrained* crushed tomatoes, kidney beans, tomato sauce, chili peppers, chili powder, and garlic salt. Bring to boiling; reduce heat. Simmer, uncovered, for 15 minutes. (Reserve 2½ cups of the meat mixture and chill up to 48 hours or freeze for Southwestern Heroes; see recipe, *at right*.)

● **Meanwhile, scrub potatoes** and prick them several times with a fork. Arrange the potatoes on a microwave-safe plate. Micro-cook, uncovered, on 100% power (high) for 14 to 17 minutes or till tender, rearranging the potatoes once. Let potatoes stand for 5 minutes.

● **Arrange** *1 cup* of the lettuce on *each* of 4 individual plates. Slice potatoes; arrange slices over lettuce, overlapping the slices. Spoon the hot meat mixture over potato slices. Top with chopped tomato, sliced green onion, and shredded cheese. Makes 4 servings.

Nutrition information per serving: *386 cal., 24 g pro., 44 g carbo., 14 g fat, 60 mg chol., 1,080 mg sodium, 1,531 mg potassium, 7 g dietary fiber. U.S. RDA: 98% vit. A, 80% vit. C, 21% thiamine, 20% riboflavin, 29% niacin, 24% calcium, 26% iron.*

SOUTHWESTERN HEROES

For a cooling salad to accompany these spicy hot sandwiches, toss together orange sections, jicama strips, and sliced celery—

- 2½ cups meat mixture from South-of-the-Border Spuds recipe
- Few drops bottled hot pepper sauce (optional)
- 4 French-style rolls
- 1 cup shredded Monterey Jack *or* Cojack cheese (4 ounces)
- ½ of a 6-ounce container frozen avocado dip, thawed
- ½ of a 2¼-ounce can sliced pitted ripe olives (optional)

● **In a covered** 1½-quart microwave-safe casserole or covered 1½-quart saucepan, reheat frozen or chilled meat mixture till heated through. (See reheating times, *at right*.*) Stir in hot pepper sauce.

● **Meanwhile, cut a thin slice** off the top of each roll. Using a fork, lightly scrape and remove some of the bread from each half, leaving a ½- to ¾-inch shell. (Reserve and use another time for bread crumbs.) Broil bread, cut side up, 5 to 6 inches from heat, for 2 to 3 minutes or till lightly browned.

● **Evenly spoon** *one-fourth* of the hot meat mixture over *each* roll on broiler rack. Top the meat mixture with cheese. Broil about 1 minute more or till cheese just melts. Transfer sandwiches to serving plates. Spoon avocado dip over each roll. If desired, top with olives and the top slice of roll. Makes 4 servings.

*To reheat chilled meat mixture: In a microwave-safe 1½-quart casserole micro-cook meat mixture, covered, on 100% power (high) about 4 minutes or till mixture is heated through, stirring twice. *Or,* in a covered 1½-quart saucepan cook the meat mixture over medium heat about 10 minutes, or till the meat mixture is heated through, stirring frequently.

*To reheat frozen meat mixture: In a 1½-quart microwave-safe casserole micro-cook the meat mixture on 100% power (high) about 10 minutes or till heated through, stirring several times. *Or,* in a covered 1½-quart saucepan cook the meat mixture over medium heat about 20 minutes or till heated through, stirring frequently.

Nutrition information per serving: *534 cal., 31 g pro., 59 g carbo., 19 g fat, 70 mg chol., 1,548 mg sodium, 765 mg potassium, 4 g dietary fiber. U.S. RDA: 103% vit. A, 44% vit. C, 31% thiamine, 28% riboflavin, 32% niacin, 30% calcium, 33% iron.*

Foods to Freeze

Whether you're freezing a make-ahead dish or leftovers, refer to this chart for maximum freezer storage times.

Food	Freezer Shelf Life
Casseroles (fish, poultry, or meat with vegetables or pasta)	2 to 4 weeks
Leftovers (meat with gravy)	1 to 3 months
Sandwiches (avoid salad vegetables, hard-cooked egg, salad dressing, mayonnaise, and jam)	2 months
Soups and Stews	1 to 3 months

BY
NANCY BYAL
AND
LISA HOLDERNESS

LOW FAT

AND LOVING IT

Top food professionals of the ProjectLEAN team gathered at *Better Homes and Gardens*® magazine to cook up their healthful recipes.

14 TOP CHEFS PROVE THAT LEAN IS LUSCIOUS

Join the lean bandwagon, and discover a wealth of new, satisfying dinners—even desserts. To help you lighten up, a team of nationally known chefs and food writers reveal their best low-fat recipes (no more than 30 percent of the calories in each recipe comes from fat). You'll feel at ease fixing any one of these family recipes because each dish relies on familiar ingredients and cooking methods. Best of all, you'll savor every bite along the way.

PROJECTLEAN

Low-fat eating will be the norm in the '90s. A national campaign called ProjectLEAN (*Low-fat Eating for America Now*) is popularizing low-fat shopping, cooking, and dining tactics. Also, food companies and restaurants will provide tastier, leaner food choices.

The Henry J. Kaiser Family Foundation and 30 other leading health and food organizations back ProjectLEAN.

PHOTOGRAPHS: SCOTT LITTLE AND PERRY STRUSE. FOOD STYLIST: JANET HERWIG

EL PASO PILAF

You need just one pan and 30 minutes to fix this fiber-rich, bean-and-rice main dish. See recipe, page 50.

''When I develop recipes, I want them to look as delicious as they taste. Basic foods like corn, beans, and tomatoes paint this pilaf with warm, Tex-Mex colors. Stir in bottled salsa for zesty flavor.''

—TOM NEY, Director of Rodale Food Center, Emmaus, Pa.

CRISPY POTATO CHICKEN

First, smear mustard over the chicken, then smother with shredded potato. The tangy mustard adds snap to this crunchy, golden chicken. See recipe, page 51.

"In New York, fried chicken is in, with one difference. It's not fried. Often the chicken is topped and baked with shredded potato for the crispy taste we love, without all the fat."

—JANE FREIMAN (incognito), Restaurant Critic, *New York Newsday,* New York, N.Y.

PAPAYA-CRAB QUESADILLA

Ever-popular quesadillas can have a healthful as well as tasty image. Serve this lightened-up version in wedges as an appetizer or whole as an entrée. See recipe, page 52.

"When creating recipes for our restaurant, we take advantage of low-fat foods. For this menu favorite, we reworked a south-western classic by relying on crab, papaya, and lean cheese."

—MICHAEL FRANKS with BILL DONNELLY, Chez Melange Restaurant, Redondo Beach, Calif.

MANDARIN CHOW MEIN

This stir-fry makes a budget-wise meal. You can feed a family of three or four with a half pound of meat. See recipe, page 51.

"A little chop chop, a few minutes in the wok, and you have dinner. I use instant noodles to save time; to save on fat, use less meat and more vegetables."
—MARTIN YAN, *Yan Can Cook* television show, Foster City, Calif.

CARAMEL APPLE TART

This lean version of Tart Tatin is made in a skillet, just like the original.

"At our culinary school, we were searching for the perfect low-fat pastry crust. When one of our chefs made his mother's ricotta cheese pastry, we knew it was a winner. Now we use this low-fat crust for our version of the famous Tart Tatin."

—Robert Briggs, The Culinary Institute of America, Hyde Park, N.Y.

2 cups all-purpose flour
2 teaspoons baking powder
Vanilla low-fat yogurt (optional)

●**Place the first ⅓ cup sugar** in a 10-inch ovenproof skillet. Cook the sugar over *medium-high* heat till it begins to melt, shaking the skillet occasionally to heat sugar evenly. Reduce heat to *low* and cook till sugar is melted and golden brown (about 5 minutes more). Stir occasionally after sugar begins to melt. Add margarine or butter and sliced apples. Gently stir till apples are coated with the caramelized sugar. Cook, uncovered, for 8 to 10 minutes or till apples are crisp-tender.

●**Meanwhile, for the pastry,** in a large mixing bowl stir together the ricotta cheese, the remaining ⅓ cup sugar, the milk, egg white, oil, vanilla, and salt. Add the flour and baking powder and stir till just combined. Divide the pastry in half. On a lightly floured surface roll *half* of the pastry into a 10-inch circle. Wrap and freeze the remaining half of the pastry to use another time.

●**Carefully place the rolled pastry** atop the hot apples in the skillet. Press the pastry lightly to the edge of the skillet. Cut slits in the pastry for steam to escape. Bake in a 350° oven for 20 to 25 minutes or till pastry is golden. Cool 10 minutes on a wire rack. Invert onto a serving platter. To serve, cut into wedges and, if desired, dollop with yogurt. Makes 8 to 10 servings.

Nutrition information per serving:
200 cal. (18% from fat), 3 g pro., 39 g carbo., 4 g fat (saturated fat 1 g), 6 mg chol., 75 mg sodium, 142 mg potassium, and 2 g dietary fiber.

CARAMEL APPLE TART

For the caramelized apples, start with white sugar in the skillet and watch it melt and turn golden as it cooks—

⅓ cup sugar
1 tablespoon margarine *or* butter
6 medium tart cooking apples such as Jonathan or Granny Smith, peeled, cored, and sliced (6 cups)
½ cup low-fat ricotta cheese
⅓ cup sugar
3 tablespoons skim milk
1 egg white
2 tablespoons safflower oil *or* cooking oil
1½ teaspoons vanilla
Dash salt

THE NEW BEEF STEW

The flavor of this stew is as appealing as ever—only the extra fat is missing. In fact, this has 14 percent less fat than a traditional stew recipe.

"To keep the stew portions generous and the fat at a minimum, I cut back on meat and stock up on a variety of fresh vegetables. For a new taste, stir in a little bit of shredded orange peel."

—ANNE LINDSAY, cookbook author, Toronto, Canada

2 stalks celery, cut into ½-inch
  pieces
1 cup frozen peas
¼ cup snipped fresh parsley *or*
  1 tablespoon dried parsley flakes
½ cup cold water
2 tablespoons all-purpose flour

● **Cut beef into 1-inch pieces.** Spray a Dutch oven or a large, heavy saucepan with nonstick coating. Heat the pan over medium-high heat; add beef. Cook and stir till meat is brown on all sides. Remove from heat.
● **Carefully add the water to the pan** and return to heat. Bring to boiling, scraping up any brown bits on the bottom of pan. Add the onion, orange peel, beef bouillon granules, bay leaf, thyme, oregano, and pepper. Cover; return to heat and simmer for 1 hour.
● **Cut carrots, parsnips, and turnip** into ¾-inch pieces. Add carrots and turnips to the beef mixture and simmer for 10 minutes. Add parsnips, potatoes, and celery and simmer for 20 minutes or till vegetables are tender. Add peas and parsley. Cover and cook for 5 minutes more. With a slotted spoon, remove the meat and vegetables from broth. Cover and keep warm.
● **Mix the cold water and flour** till smooth; stir into broth. Cook and stir till thickened and bubbly. Return meat and vegetables to broth; heat through. Season with salt to taste. Serves 4.

Nutrition information per serving: *343 cal. (18% from fat), 27 g pro., 44 g carbo., 7 g fat (saturated fat 3 g), 61 mg chol., 418 mg sodium, 1,287 mg potassium, and 8 g dietary fiber. U.S. RDA: 314% vit. A, 95% vit. C, 26% thiamine, 20% riboflavin, 29% niacin, 11% calcium, and 30% iron.*

THE NEW BEEF STEW

¾ pound lean beef stew meat
Nonstick spray coating
4 cups water
3 medium onions, halved
1 tablespoon grated orange peel
1 tablespoon instant beef bouillon
  granules

1 bay leaf
1 teaspoon dried thyme, crushed
½ teaspoon dried oregano,
  crushed
¼ teaspoon pepper
3 medium carrots, peeled
2 parsnips, peeled
½ medium turnip (about ½ pound)
2 medium potatoes, peeled and cut
  into 1-inch pieces

BANANA YOGURT CAKE

Part of making low-fat desserts appealing is making them look good. Decorate this impressive cake with a chocolate icing design and fresh berries.

"I strive to make low-fat cakes that still taste rich and satisfying. For this moist cake, I substitute whipped egg whites for whole eggs and reduce the oil to cut fat. To add flavor I use banana, lemon peel, and a nonfat chocolate icing."

—FLO BRAKER, cookbook author, baking instructor, and food columnist, Palo Alto, Calif.

BANANA YOGURT CAKE

- 2 cups all-purpose flour
- ⅓ cup sugar
- ¾ teaspoon baking powder
- ¾ teaspoon baking soda
- ¼ teaspoon salt
- ⅔ cup plain low-fat yogurt
- ½ cup mashed ripe banana
- ¼ cup cooking oil
- 1 teaspoon finely shredded lemon peel
- 1 teaspoon vanilla
- 3 egg whites
- ¾ cup sugar
- 2 tablespoons light corn syrup
- 2 tablespoons water
- ¼ cup unsweetened cocoa powder
Fresh raspberries (optional)

● **In a large mixing bowl stir together** flour, the ⅓ cup sugar, baking powder, baking soda, and salt; set aside. In a medium bowl stir together the yogurt, banana, cooking oil, lemon peel, and vanilla; set aside.

● **In a small mixing bowl beat** egg whites till soft peaks form (tips curl). Gradually add remaining ¾ cup sugar, beating on high speed till stiff peaks form (tips stand straight). Stir yogurt-banana mixture into flour mixture till moistened. Fold in about a *fourth* of the egg-white mixture to soften; then fold in remaining egg whites.

● **Pour the batter evenly** into a greased (or sprayed with nonstick spray coating) and floured 9x9x2-inch baking pan. Bake in a 350° oven for 40 to 45 minutes or till a wooden toothpick inserted near the center comes out clean. Cool cake in pan on a wire rack for 10 minutes. Remove cake from pan and cool completely on the wire rack. Place cake in a storage container or wrap with plastic wrap and store; this cake slices better when held overnight.

● **For icing, stir together** the corn syrup and water; add cocoa powder, stirring till smooth. Drizzle chocolate over cake in a lacy design. Let stand till set (about 30 minutes). You also can drizzle icing in a lacy design on each serving plate and top with a piece of cake (as pictured *above*). Serve with raspberries, if desired. Makes 12 servings.

Nutrition information per serving: *223 cal. (24% from fat), 4 g pro., 41 g carbo., 6 g fat (saturated fat 1 g), 1 mg chol., 168 mg sodium, 113 mg potassium, and 1 g dietary fiber. U.S. RDA: 10% thiamine.*

celery in skillet for 2 minutes. Add water (use 1½ cups for basmati rice; 2 cups for long grain rice), rice, lemon juice, bay leaf, and salt. Simmer, covered, 20 minutes or till rice is tender.

● **Meanwhile, cut salmon into 4 portions;** brush with oil. Spray cool grill rack with *nonstick spray coating.* Grill salmon directly on grill rack over *medium-hot* coals for 5 minutes. Turn salmon. Grill 4 to 7 minutes more or till fish flakes with a fork. If desired, grill lemon slices till heated through, turning once.

● **For sauce,** combine the lemon peel, yogurt, green onions, dill, and capers. Add *half* of the mixture to a blender container; cover and blend till smooth. Stir into remaining mixture.

● **To serve, spoon** about *2 tablespoons* of sauce onto center of each dinner plate. Top with salmon. Serve with basmati rice and, if desired, grilled lemon slices. Store any remaining sauce, covered, in the refrigerator for another use. It may be used as a salad dressing or meat accompaniment. Serves 4.

Nutrition information per serving: 366 cal. (22% from fat), 25 g pro., 46 g carbo., 9 g fat (saturated fat 2 g), 56 mg chol., 232 mg sodium, 646 mg potassium, 1 g dietary fiber. U.S. RDA: 106% vit. A, 10% vit. C, 29% thiamine, 17% riboflavin, 34% niacin, 14% calcium.

SALMON WITH DILL SAUCE AND RICE

Low-calorie, great-tasting salmon is also a good source of omega-3. Studies suggest that this fatty acid may help protect your body from heart disease.

"Learning to cook low fat can be a big challenge. Our advice is to keep things simple. For this recipe from our health spa, grill naturally healthful salmon and serve it with lemon-flavored rice and an easy dill sauce made in the blender." —TRACY PIKHART RITTER with SHERI LEE SHANSBY, The Golden Door health spa, Escondido, Calif.

GRILLED SALMON WITH DILL SAUCE AND BASMATI RICE

¼ cup finely chopped onion
1 carrot, finely chopped
1 stalk celery, finely chopped
1½ to 2 cups water
1 cup basmati rice *or* long grain rice
½ teaspoon finely shredded lemon peel
3 tablespoons lemon juice
1 bay leaf
¼ teaspoon salt

1 12-ounce fresh *or* frozen salmon fillet, skinned and thawed (about 1 inch thick)
1 tablespoon olive oil *or* cooking oil
Lemon slices (optional)
1 8-ounce carton plain low-fat yogurt
¼ cup sliced green onions
¼ cup snipped fresh dill *or* 1 teaspoon dried dillweed
1 teaspoon capers

● **Spray a large skillet** with *nonstick spray coating.* Cook onion, carrot, and

CINNAMON BRAN PANCAKES

For a quick fruit syrup, combine equal parts of fruit spread or preserves and maple syrup. Heat through and drizzle over pancakes.

CINNAMON BRAN PANCAKES

¾ cup oat bran
¾ cup all-purpose flour
1 tablespoon sugar
½ teaspoon baking powder
½ teaspoon ground cinnamon
¼ teaspoon baking soda
2 slightly beaten egg whites
1¼ cups buttermilk
1 tablespoon cooking oil

● **Combine** oat bran, flour, sugar, baking powder, cinnamon, soda, and ⅛ teaspoon *salt.* In another bowl combine *continued on page 48* egg whites, buttermilk, and oil; beat with fork just till combined. Add to dry ingredients, stirring just till combined.

● **Spray a cold griddle** or large skillet with *nonstick spray coating;* heat. For each pancake, spoon a *¼-cup* portion of batter onto hot griddle. Cook over medium heat till golden, turning once. Makes 8 to 10 pancakes.

Nutrition information per pancake: 115 cal. (23% from fat), 5 g pro., 17 g carbo., 3 g fat (saturated fat 1 g), 1 mg chol., 140 mg sodium, 129 mg potassium, and 2 g dietary fiber. U.S. RDA: 11% thiamine.

"I like creating low-fat breakfast recipes because many traditional options are far from healthful. These revamped pancakes use egg whites and less oil to cut fat, plus oat bran to add fiber."

—ABBY MANDEL, cookbook author and food columnist, Winnetka, Ill.

THREE-BEAN CHILI

The mixture of beans in this one-dish meal provides ample protein per serving and satisfies more than half of the recommended fiber for one day. See recipe, page 52.

"I like to create recipes using ingredients that most people, myself included, usually have on hand. This chunky, meatless chili uses common pantry foods like canned tomatoes and beans. For extra zest, blend a spoonful of mustard in with the other seasonings."

—SUSIE HELLER, recipe development consultant, Shaker Heights, Ohio

CHICKEN CACCIATORE

For the best flavor, simmer the mixture slowly atop the stove or finish it off in the oven.

''At the restaurant, for our low-fat menu items, I lighten up traditional favorites. To make this well-known dish a healthful hit, I skin the chicken and cut down on cooking oil.''

—KELLY MILLS, Chef, Four Seasons Clift Hotel, San Francisco, Calif.

CHICKEN CACCIATORE

6 boned skinless chicken breast halves (3 ounces each)
2 tablespoons olive oil *or* cooking oil
3 cups (8 ounces) small fresh mushrooms *or* two
  4½-ounce jars whole mushrooms, drained
2 medium sweet red *or* green peppers, cut into strips
1 large onion, thinly sliced and separated into
  rings (1 cup)
2 cloves garlic, minced
½ cup dry white wine
1 small serrano chili pepper, seeded and
  finely chopped *or* ¼ teaspoon crushed red
  pepper (optional)

1 28-ounce can tomatoes, cut up
2 tablespoons tomato paste
2 tablespoons lemon juice
2 teaspoons dried basil, crushed
1 teaspoon sugar
1 teaspoon dried thyme, crushed
Hot cooked mostaccioli *or* rigatoni (optional)

● **In a heavy 12-inch skillet** or Dutch oven brown chicken in hot olive oil or cooking oil on all sides (4 to 5 minutes total). Remove chicken; set aside. Add mushrooms (if using fresh), sweet peppers, onion, and garlic to skillet drippings. Cook till vegetables are tender.

● **Add mushrooms** (if using canned), wine, and serrano or crushed red pepper to vegetable mixture. Bring to boiling; reduce heat. Simmer, uncovered, till almost all liquid evaporates, stirring occasionally. Add *undrained* tomatoes, tomato paste, lemon juice, basil, sugar, thyme, ½ teaspoon *salt*, and ¼ teaspoon *pepper*. Return chicken to pan.

● **Simmer, uncovered,** for 15 minutes or till chicken is tender and no longer pink. *Or,* after returning chicken to pan, bake, uncovered, in a 350° oven for 10 to 15 minutes or till chicken is done (use an ovenproof skillet for this method). If desired, serve over cooked pasta. Serves 6.

Nutrition information per serving: *253 cal. (28% from fat), 29 g pro., 13 g carbo., 8 g fat (saturated fat 2 g), 72 mg chol., 511 mg sodium, 806 mg potassium, and 3 g dietary fiber. U.S. RDA: 22% vit. A, 57% vit. C, 13% thiamine, 20% riboflavin, 73% niacin, 18% iron.*

TURKEY BURGERS
WITH SPRING VEGETABLES

Enjoy these lean burgers either grilled or sautéed. For low-fat sautéing, simply spray a large skillet with nonstick coating before cooking.

TURKEY BURGERS WITH SPRING VEGETABLES

- 2 **egg whites**
- ⅓ **cup soft bread crumbs**
- ⅓ **cup finely chopped onion**
- 2 **tablespoons snipped fresh parsley**
- 2 **cloves garlic, minced**
- 1 **teaspoon dried basil, crushed**
- ¼ **teaspoon dried tarragon, crushed**
- 1½ **pounds boned skinless turkey *or* chicken breast, ground, *or* 1½ pounds purchased ground raw turkey**
- **Nonstick spray coating**
- **Spring Vegetables**

● **Beat egg whites till foamy.** Stir in bread crumbs, onion, parsley, garlic, basil, tarragon, ½ teaspoon *salt*, and ⅛ teaspoon *pepper*. Add turkey; mix well. Shape into eight ½-inch-thick patties.

● **Spray cool grill rack** with nonstick coating. Grill over *medium-hot* coals 12 to 14 minutes or till no longer pink, turning once. Or, to broil, spray cool broiler pan with nonstick coating. Broil 4 to 5 inches from heat 9 to 10 minutes or till no longer pink, turning once. Serve atop sautéed Spring Vegetables. Makes 8 servings.

"In New Orleans, flavor— and lots of it—is everything. To turn mild ground turkey into great-tasting burgers, I add a combination of savory herbs. Surround these burgers with seasoned vegetables to make a colorful meal."

—EMERIL LAGASSE, Executive Chef, Commander's Palace Restaurant, New Orleans, La.

Spring Vegetables: In a 12-inch skillet cook 1 medium *zucchini*, sliced; 1 medium *yellow summer squash*, halved lengthwise and bias-sliced (1½ cups); 1½ cups sliced fresh *mushrooms*; and ⅓ cup chopped *onion* in 1 tablespoon hot *safflower oil* or other *cooking oil* over medium-high heat till crisp-tender. Stir in 1 medium *tomato*, peeled, seeded, and chopped; 1 tablespoon snipped *parsley;* ½ teaspoon dried *basil*, crushed; ¼ teaspoon dried *tarragon*, crushed; and ⅛ teaspoon *pepper*. Heat through. Serves 8.

Nutrition information per serving including vegetables: 161 cal. (28% from fat), 21 g pro., 7 g carbo., 5 g fat (saturated fat 1 g), 49 mg chol., 205 mg sodium, 533 mg potassium, 2 g dietary fiber. U.S. RDA: 12% vit. A, 16% vit. C, 9% thiamine, 15% riboflavin, 23% niacin, 12% iron.

Note: Because there are no official standards, the amount of fat in purchased ground turkey can vary by producer. To assure the leanest ground turkey for this recipe, we bought boned skinless turkey breast and asked the butcher to grind it (or you can grind it yourself). Either fresh ground or purchased ground turkey works well for this recipe; the choice is yours.

EL PASO PILAF

For extra crunch, serve this meat-free main dish with carrot chips made by thinly slicing a carrot with a vegetable peeler. Curl carrot slices by placing them in ice water—

- ½ **cup chopped onion**
- 2 **teaspoons olive oil *or* cooking oil**
- 1 **15-ounce can red kidney beans, drained**
- 1¾ **cups chicken broth *or* water**
- 1 **cup long grain rice**
- 1 **cup frozen corn**
- 1 **cup chunky salsa**
- ¼ **cup dry lentils, rinsed and drained**
- ¼ **cup chopped sweet red pepper *or* one 2-ounce jar diced pimiento**
- ½ **teaspoon chili powder**
- **Dash garlic powder**
- 8 **tomato slices**

● **In a large saucepan cook** the onion in hot olive oil or cooking oil over medium heat about 5 minutes or till the onion is tender but not brown.

● **Add** the beans, broth or water, rice, corn, salsa, lentils, red pepper or pimiento, chili powder, and garlic powder. Bring to boiling; reduce heat. Cover; simmer for 20 minutes or till rice and lentils are tender and most of the liquid is absorbed. Serve over tomato slices. Makes 4 servings.

Nutrition information per serving: 407 cal. (8% from fat), 16 g pro., 77 g carbo., 4 g fat (saturated fat 1 g), 0 mg chol., 729 mg sodium, 822 mg potassium, and 13 g dietary fiber. U.S. RDA: 13% vit. A, 22% vit. C, 35% thiamine, 11% riboflavin, 22% niacin, 31% iron.

CRISPY POTATO CHICKEN

For a crisp, golden potato "skin," make sure you pat the potato shreds as dry as possible—

1 large potato (8 ounces), peeled
3 to 4 tablespoons Dijon-style mustard
1 large clove garlic, minced
2 whole large chicken breasts (1 pound), skinned and split in half
1½ teaspoons olive oil *or* cooking oil
Ground black pepper
Snipped fresh parsley, cilantro, rosemary, *or* chives

● **In a food processor** fitted with a medium shredding disc, coarsely shred potato. (Or, shred with a grater.) Transfer shredded potato to a bowl of ice water; let stand for 5 minutes.
● **Meanwhile, in a small bowl** combine the mustard and garlic; mix well. Rinse chicken and thoroughly pat dry with paper towels. Brush or spread the mustard mixture evenly on the meaty side of the chicken breast halves. Place the chicken, bone side down, on a foil-lined 15x10x1-inch baking pan.
● **Drain potato.** Thoroughly pat dry with paper towels; place in a medium mixing bowl. Add olive oil or cooking oil; toss to mix well. Top each piece of chicken with about ⅓ cup potato mixture in an even layer, forming a "skin." Sprinkle lightly with pepper.
● **Bake in a 425° oven** for 35 to 40 minutes or till chicken is no longer pink and potato shreds are golden. (If potatoes are not browning, transfer pan to broiler. Broil about 5 minutes or till golden, watching closely.) Sprinkle with desired herb. Serve immediately. Makes 4 servings.

Nutrition information per serving: *253 cal. (25% from fat), 36 g pro., 9 g carbo., 7 g fat (saturated fat 1 g), 96 mg chol., 417 mg sodium, 463 mg potassium, and 1 g dietary fiber. U.S. RDA: 80% niacin.*

Choosing and Using Dried Chili Peppers

To add fire to salsas, sauces, and main dishes, Southwesterners rely heavily on chili peppers. Look for the following dried chili peppers in the produce department at your grocery store or at a Mexican food store.
● **Pasilla chili peppers:** These long, slender, medium-size peppers range from mild to medium-hot. Their skins are wrinkled and blackish-brown. Pasillas often are used along with ancho peppers.
● **Ancho chili peppers:** The most common of the dried peppers, anchos are used in red chili sauces and as a major ingredient in chili powder. These mild to medium-hot chilies are dried poblano peppers and have the same large, triangular size and shape as poblanos with wrinkled, reddish-brown skin.
● **New Mexican chili peppers:** Ranging from mild to hot in taste, these dark red peppers are about 4 inches long with shiny, fairly smooth skin. Before using, check the package to find out the degree of hotness.
● **Handling chili peppers:** Because chili peppers contain volatile oils that can burn skin and eyes, wear plastic or rubber gloves or work under cold running water. If your bare hands touch the chili peppers, wash hands and nails well with soap and water.

MANDARIN CHOW MEIN

2 3-ounce packages quick-cooking Oriental noodles (with *or* without flavor packet)
2 tablespoons soy sauce
4 teaspoons catsup
1 tablespoon Worcestershire sauce
1 teaspoon sugar
½ teaspoon sesame oil
Nonstick spray coating
4 cloves garlic, minced
¼ teaspoon crushed red pepper
½ pound lean boneless pork such as pork loin *or* sirloin, cut into thin strips
3 cups thinly sliced cabbage
1 8-ounce can sliced bamboo shoots, drained and rinsed
½ cup coarsely shredded carrot
2 green onions, cut into 2-inch lengths

● **Cook noodles** in 4 cups boiling water for 3 minutes or just till tender, omitting flavor packet, if present. Drain and rinse noodles; set aside.
● **For sauce,** in a small bowl stir together the soy sauce, catsup, Worcestershire sauce, sugar, and sesame oil; set aside.
● **Spray a wok or large skillet** with nonstick coating; preheat over medium-high heat. Add garlic and red pepper to hot wok or skillet; cook over medium-high heat for 10 seconds. Add pork; stir-fry 1 minute. Add cabbage, bamboo shoots, carrot, and onion. Stir-fry for 2 to 3 minutes more or till onions are just crisp-tender and pork is no longer pink. Add noodles and sauce; heat through, about 1 minute, stirring gently to coat. Makes 3 servings.

Nutrition information per serving: *430 cal. (25% from fat), 26 g pro., 54 g carbo., 12 g fat (saturated 4 g), 104 mg chol., 633 mg sodium, 651 mg potassium, and 4 g dietary fiber. U.S. RDA: 121% vit. A, 49% vit. C, 69% thiamine, 29% riboflavin, 38% niacin, 19% iron.*

PAPAYA-CRAB QUESADILLA

When shopping for farmer cheese, look for brands made from skim milk. They have a texture similar to mozzarella cheese—

- 1 cup thinly sliced papaya
- 4 ounces farmer cheese, finely shredded
- 4 ounces Dungeness crab (leg meat) *or* frozen crabmeat, thawed
- 3 tablespoons snipped fresh cilantro
- 3 green onions, sliced
- 4 6-inch flour tortillas
- Roasted Tomato Salsa *or* 3½ cups purchased salsa

● **For quesadillas, layer** papaya, cheese, crab, cilantro, and green onion evenly atop *half* of *each* tortilla. Fold plain half of each tortilla over the filled half. Place on an ungreased baking sheet. Bake in a 350° oven for 8 to 10 minutes or till light brown. For appetizer portions, cut each quesadilla into quarters before serving. Top with Roasted Tomato Salsa or purchased salsa. Makes 4 quesadillas.

Roasted Tomato Salsa: In a small saucepan combine 1 cup *chicken broth;* 2 dried *pasilla chili peppers,* seeded; 1 dried *ancho chili pepper,* seeded; and 1 dried *New Mexican chili pepper,* seeded. Simmer about 5 minutes or till chilies soften. Remove from heat and set aside.

Place 3 small *tomatoes* and 4 *tomatillos,* outer husks removed, on a baking sheet and bake in a 425° oven about 20 minutes or till brown blisters form on the skins. Carefully core tomatoes. Place the unpeeled tomatoes and tomatillos in a blender container or food processor bowl along with the chili mixture, ¼ cup snipped fresh *cilantro,* ¼ cup chopped *onion,* and 3 cloves *garlic.* Cover and blend or process to desired consistency. Add salt and pepper to taste. Makes about 3½ cups. Place any leftover salsa in a storage container and chill for up to 2 weeks.

Nutrition information per quesadilla with ¼ recipe salsa: *213 cal. (30% from fat), 16 g pro., 23 g carbo., 8 g fat (saturated fat 3 g), 34 mg chol., 423 mg sodium, 417 mg potassium, and 3 g dietary fiber. U.S. RDA: 28% vit. A, 79% vit. C, 17% thiamine, 21% riboflavin, 21% niacin, 29% calcium, 7% iron.*

THREE-BEAN CHILI

- 3 cloves garlic, minced
- 1 tablespoon olive oil *or* cooking oil
- 1 28-ounce can Italian-style tomatoes, cut up
- 1 cup water
- 1 6-ounce can tomato paste
- 1 tablespoon chili powder
- 1 tablespoon Dijon-style mustard
- 1 teaspoon dried basil, crushed
- 1 teaspoon dried oregano, crushed
- ½ teaspoon ground cumin
- ½ teaspoon pepper
- 1 15-ounce can red kidney beans, drained
- 1 15-ounce can great northern beans, drained
- 1 15-ounce can garbanzo beans, drained
- 1 cup chopped carrots
- 1 cup fresh *or* frozen whole kernel corn
- 1 cup chopped zucchini
- Several dashes bottled hot pepper sauce
- ¾ cup shredded *or* grated Parmesan cheese
- Whole fresh green chili peppers (optional)

● **In a Dutch oven cook** garlic in hot olive or cooking oil for 30 seconds. Stir in the *undrained* tomatoes, water, tomato paste, chili powder, mustard, basil, oregano, cumin, and pepper. Add the kidney beans, great northern beans, and garbanzo beans; bring mixture to boiling. Reduce heat and simmer, covered, for 10 minutes.

● **Stir in** the chopped carrots, corn, and chopped zucchini. Simmer, covered, for 10 minutes more. Add hot pepper sauce to taste. Spoon into serving bowls. Top *each* serving of chili with *2 tablespoons* Parmesan cheese and, if desired, a green chili pepper. Makes 6 servings.

Nutrition information per serving: *359 cal. (22% from fat), 21 g pro., 54 g carbo., 9 g fat (saturated fat 3 g), 10 mg chol., 776 mg sodium, 1,312 mg potassium, and 18 g dietary fiber. U.S. RDA: 159% vit. A, 47% vit. C, 29% thiamine, 16% riboflavin, 17% niacin, 31% calcium, 36% iron.*

Figuring Percent Fat

A well-rounded, low-fat diet means a more healthful one. ProjectLEAN suggests that no more than 30 percent of your daily calories come from fat.

Choose from any of these family-style recipes, created by top food professionals, to help keep the fat in your diet to a minimum. Each recipe featured has less than 30 percent fat per serving.

To figure your daily fat intake, keep track of the total calories and grams of fat in the foods you eat. Then use this formula to figure the percent of fat in your diet:

Total fat calories = total fat (in grams) × 9 (9 is the number of calories in 1 gram of fat)

Percent of calories from fat = (total fat calories ÷ total calories) × 100

Low-Fat Meals

To order Better Homes and Gardens® *Low-Fat Meals Cook Book,* send check or money order for $11.95 to: Better Homes and Gardens® Reader Service, Department 8BB, Box 374, Des Moines, Iowa 50336. Specify Product Number 16324. All 118 recipes in this 128-page hardcover volume meet Project LEAN guidelines.

HAVE YOUR CAKE AND FIBER, TOO

GREAT TASTE AND A BIT OF FIBER IN EVERY BITE

BY JOY TAYLOR

No-Cholesterol Apple Cake: Less than 150 calories per serving, with 2 grams dietary fiber.

For everyday sweet-tooth satisfaction, opt for these healthful cakes. They're made with less fat than most cakes. Plus, these whole grain desserts are especially good for you because each piece contains some dietary fiber, and every little bit of fiber helps.

Studies have shown that a high-fiber, low-fat diet may reduce colon cancer risk, and it appears that soluble fiber (as in oat bran and apples) lowers blood cholesterol.

Try a slice of moist and tender Cornmeal Spice Cake.

NO-CHOLESTEROL APPLE CAKE

Leave the peel on the apples because that's what gives you lots of fiber—

Nonstick spray coating
- ⅔ cup sugar
- ½ cup packed brown sugar
- ¼ cup vegetable oil
- 3 egg whites
- ⅔ cup all-purpose flour
- ⅔ cup whole wheat flour
- ½ cup oat bran
- 1½ teaspoons baking soda
- 1 teaspoon ground cinnamon
- ¼ teaspoon ground allspice *or* nutmeg
- 3 cups shredded unpeeled apples

Powdered sugar

Spray a 13x9x2-inch baking pan with nonstick coating; set aside. In a large mixing bowl combine sugars, oil, and egg whites. Beat with a wooden spoon till well blended. Add flours, oat bran, baking soda, cinnamon, and allspice or nutmeg; stir just till moistened. Stir in shredded apples. Pour batter into the prepared pan.

Bake in a 350° oven for 25 to 30 minutes. Cool. If desired, sift powdered sugar atop cake. Makes 16 servings.

Nutrition information per serving: 147 cal., 2 g pro., 4 g fat, 0 mg chol., 1,057 mg sodium, 100 mg potassium, and 2 g dietary fiber.

CORNMEAL SPICE CAKE

A slice of this cake makes a delicious snack along with a cup of coffee or tea—

Nonstick spray coating
- 1¼ cups all-purpose flour

- ⅔ cup whole wheat flour
- ½ cup cornmeal
- 2 teaspoons baking powder
- ½ teaspoon baking soda
- ¼ teaspoon ground cardamom *or* ground nutmeg
- ⅔ cup honey
- ½ cup cooking oil
- 1 teaspoon vanilla
- 3 slightly beaten eggs
- 1 8-ounce carton plain yogurt

Honey-Spice Syrup

Spray a 10-inch fluted tube pan with nonstick coating; set aside. Combine flours, cornmeal, baking powder, baking soda, and cardamom; set aside.

In a large mixing bowl combine honey, oil, vanilla, and beaten eggs. Mix well. Add flour mixture and yogurt alternately to egg mixture, stirring well after each addition. Pour batter into prepared pan.

Bake in a 325° oven for 50 to 55 minutes or till done. Cool 15 minutes in pan on a wire rack. Remove from pan; place on the rack over a shallow pan.

With a fork, prick top of cake generously. Gradually drizzle warm Honey-Spice Syrup over cake till all syrup is absorbed. Let cool on wire rack. Makes 10 servings.

Honey-Spice Syrup: In a medium saucepan combine ¾ cup *water*, ½ cup *honey*, and ¼ teaspoon *ground cardamom* or *nutmeg*. Bring to boiling; cook and stir syrup for 1 minute. Remove from heat. Let syrup stand till just slightly warm.

Nutrition information per serving: 362 cal., 6 g pro., 13 g fat, 84 mg chol., 91 mg sodium, 154 mg potassium, 2 g dietary fiber. U.S. RDA: 12% thiamine, 11% riboflavin, 10% calcium.

53

MICROWAVE EASY

Like burgers on the grill, fresh vegetables in your microwave oven promise great eating. Try our collection of light spring dishes.

Spring
VEGETABLES

BY

JOY TAYLOR

Artichokes

Asparagus

Greens

New Potatoes

Peas

Radishes

Photographs: Mike Dieter. Food stylist: Janet Herwig

Be patient when you eat an artichoke, and savor it one fleshy leaf at a time. Your just reward: the tender heart.

ARTICHOKE CHICKEN SALAD

Simple chicken salad becomes sensational when you add artichokes, raisins, and chutney—

- **2 medium artichokes**
- **Lemon juice**
- **2 tablespoons water**
- **2 cups chopped cooked chicken**
- **½ cup sliced celery**
- **¼ cup raisins**
- **¼ cup sliced green onion**
- **8 large romaine leaves**
- **½ cup reduced-calorie mayonnaise**
- **¼ cup plain yogurt**
- **1 tablespoon chutney**
- **Dash garlic salt**
- **Dash paprika**
- **4 cherry tomatoes, halved**

● **Cut the stems** and loose outer leaves from artichokes. Cut off 1 inch from tops; snip off sharp leaf tips. Brush cut edges with lemon juice. Place the artichokes in an 8x4x2-inch microwave-safe loaf dish; add water.

● **Micro-cook,** covered, on 100% power (high) for 7 to 10 minutes (low-wattage oven: 10 to 12 minutes) or till a leaf pulls away easily, turning dish once. Drain. Let stand, uncovered, to cool.

● **When cooled,** remove all outer leaves from artichokes. Wrap leaves in plastic wrap and chill. Discard the center leaves (cone) and choke, reserving hearts. Cut hearts into thin strips (you should have about ⅓ cup). Wrap and chill.

● **For salad,** in a large bowl combine chicken, celery, raisins, and onion. Finely shred *two* romaine leaves (you should have about 1 cup). Stir shredded romaine into chicken mixture.

● **For dressing,** in a small bowl stir together the mayonnaise, yogurt, chutney, garlic salt, and paprika. Add to chicken mixture. Toss to mix well. Cover and chill for 1 to 2 hours.

● **To serve,** line a serving plate with remaining romaine leaves. Spoon the chicken salad into the center. Arrange strips of artichoke heart on top of salad. Arrange artichoke leaves and tomatoes around salad. Makes 4 main-dish servings.

Nutrition information per serving: 342 cal., 26 g pro., 30 g carbo., 15 g fat, 75 mg chol., 392 mg sodium, 811 mg potassium, and 3 g dietary fiber. U.S. RDA: 26% vit. A, 25% vit. C, 16% riboflavin, 38% niacin, 20% iron.

STUFFED FETA ARTICHOKES

Serve this first-course salad (opposite) with a light red wine such as Beaujolais or a light white wine such as chardonnay—

- **2 medium artichokes (about 10 ounces each)**
- **Lemon juice**
- **2 tablespoons water**
- **3 tablespoons lemon juice**
- **2 tablespoons olive oil *or* salad oil**
- **1 tablespoon water**
- **½ teaspoon dried oregano, crushed**
- **½ cup bulgur**
- **¼ teaspoon salt**
- **½ cup crumbled feta cheese (2 ounces)**
- **¼ cup snipped parsley**
- **1 large tomato, peeled, seeded, and chopped**
- **Shredded lettuce**
- **1 tomato, cut into wedges**

● **Cut the stems** and loose outer leaves from the artichokes. Cut off 1 inch from the tops and snip off the sharp leaf tips. Brush the cut edges with lemon juice. Place artichokes in a 1½- or 2-quart microwave-safe casserole; add the 2 tablespoons water.

● **Micro-cook artichokes,** covered, on 100% power (high) for 7 to 10 minutes (low-wattage oven: 10 to 12 minutes) or till a leaf pulls away easily, turning the dish once. Drain. When cool, halve each artichoke lengthwise. Discard center leaves (cone) and choke.

● **For dressing,** combine the 3 tablespoons lemon juice, the oil, the 1 tablespoon water, and oregano. Place the artichoke halves in a plastic bag; place in a bowl. Pour the dressing over artichokes; seal bag. Turn to coat. Chill the artichokes several hours, turning bag occasionally.

● **Meanwhile,** in a bowl combine bulgur, salt, and 1 cup *hot water;* let stand for 1 hour. Drain well, pressing out excess water. Combine the drained bulgur, the feta cheese, the snipped parsley, and the chopped tomato. Cover and chill the mixture thoroughly.

- **To serve,** drain artichokes, reserving dressing. Place, cut side up, on shredded lettuce. Stir dressing into bulgur mixture; spoon into artichoke halves.
- **Place** any additional bulgur mixture in a bowl and serve with artichokes. Arrange the tomato wedges around artichokes. Makes 4 side-dish servings.

Nutrition information per serving: 249 cal., 8 g pro., 35 g carbo., 10 g fat, 13 mg chol., 399 mg sodium, 635 mg potassium, 6 g dietary fiber. U.S. RDA: 23% vit. A, 35% vit. C, 14% thiamine, 15% riboflavin, 15% calcium, 21% iron.

ARTICHOKES WITH TARRAGON CREAM

As an appetizer or salad, these artichokes are perfect for rounding out a meal—

- **4 medium artichokes**
- **Lemon juice**
- **6 green onions, chopped**
- **1 8-ounce package Neufchâtel cheese**
- **2 tablespoons lemon *or* lime juice**
- **¼ teaspoon dried tarragon, crushed**
- **⅛ teaspoon pepper**
- **¼ cup milk**
- **Lemon slices (optional)**
- **Fresh tarragon (optional)**

- **Cut the stems** and the loose outer leaves from artichokes. Cut off 1 inch from tops; snip off sharp leaf tips. Brush cut edges with lemon juice. Place the artichokes in an 8x8x2-inch microwave-safe baking dish. Add 2 tablespoons *water.*
- **Micro-cook,** covered, on 100% power (high) for 14 to 15 minutes or till a leaf pulls out easily, rearranging artichokes once. Drain. Let stand, uncovered, to cool. Cover and chill.
- **For cream mixture,** in a 1-quart microwave-safe bowl combine green onions and 2 tablespoons *water.* Cook, covered, on high for 2 to 3 minutes or till onions are tender. Drain. Add cheese; cook on high for 10 seconds or till softened. Stir in lemon or lime juice, tarragon, and pepper. Stir in milk.
- **Remove center leaves** and chokes from artichokes. Spread leaves slightly. Spoon cream mixture into center of each. If desired, garnish with lemon slices and fresh tarragon. To eat, remove and dip leaves in the cream mixture. Makes 4 side-dish servings.

Nutrition information per serving: 296 cal., 14 g pro., 36 g carbo., 14 g fat, 44 mg chol., 433 mg sodium, 952 mg potassium, and 2 g dietary fiber. U.S. RDA: 45% vit. A, 43% vit. C, 19% riboflavin, 19% calcium, 26% iron.

Note: Recipe is too large for low-wattage ovens.

ARTICHOKE ETIQUETTE

Before cooking a whole artichoke, cut off 1 inch from the top and snip off sharp leaf tips. Brush cut edges with lemon juice. Micro-cook till a leaf pulls out easily; drain and chill.

To eat, pull a leaf off the globe, and draw the leaf through your teeth, scraping off and eating only the tender flesh at the base. Discard the rest of the leaf. Continue till a cone of young leaves appears. Pull away the cone, eating a little bit of the soft flesh. Then scoop out and discard the fuzzy "choke." Eat the remaining heart with a fork, dipping each bite in sauce.

Baby vegetables are in, and the oldest baby of them all is the new potato. These tiny, immature potatoes cook up fast to tender tidbits.

NEW POTATOES CAESAR

- **1 pound whole tiny new potatoes (12 to 16 potatoes)**
- **2 tablespoons water**
- **½ cup reduced-calorie Caesar salad dressing**
- **1 small head Bibb lettuce**
- **2 hard-cooked eggs, sliced**
- **8 large cherry tomatoes, sliced**
- **2 tablespoons shredded Parmesan cheese**
- **Cracked pepper**
- **12 rolled anchovy fillets with capers**

● **Wash new potatoes;** slice into ¼-inch slices. In a 1-quart microwave-safe casserole combine potatoes and water. Micro-cook, covered, on 100% power (high) for 6 to 9 minutes (low-wattage oven: 9 to 11 minutes) or just till tender, stirring once. Drain. Pour salad dressing over potato slices. Cover and chill for 1 to 3 hours.

● **To serve,** arrange lettuce leaves on salad plates. With

a slotted spoon, remove potato slices from dressing, reserving dressing. Arrange potato, egg, and tomato on lettuce. Drizzle with reserved dressing. Sprinkle with cheese and pepper. Top with anchovies and capers. Makes 4 side-dish servings.

Nutrition information per serving: 192 cal., 10 g pro., 25 g carbo., 6 g fat, 146 mg chol., 628 mg sodium, 963 mg potassium, and 3 g dietary fiber. U.S. RDA: 23% vit. A, 37% vit. C, 12% thiamine, 12% riboflavin, 14% niacin, 11 calcium, 12% iron.

NEW POTATOES GRUYERE

Gruyère cheese has a mild, nutty flavor similar to Swiss cheese—

- **2 pounds whole tiny new potatoes (24 to 32)**
- **⅓ cup water**
- **1 small onion, sliced and separated into rings**
- **¼ teaspoon salt**
- **1 tablespoon all-purpose flour**
- **⅛ teaspoon garlic powder**
- **⅛ teaspoon ground white pepper**
- **½ cup milk**
- **¼ cup chicken broth**
- **½ cup shredded process Gruyère cheese (2 ounces)**
- **Snipped parsley (optional)**

● **Wash new potatoes** thoroughly. Halve any large potatoes. With a vegetable peeler, peel a strip around the center of each remaining whole potato. In a 1½- or 2-quart microwave-safe casserole combine the potatoes, the water, the onion, and salt.

● **Micro-cook,** covered, on 100% power (high) for 14 to 18 minutes (low-wattage oven: 17 to 20 minutes) or till the potatoes are tender, stirring mixture twice. Let vegetables stand, covered, while preparing the sauce.

● **For sauce,** in a 2-cup glass measure combine the flour, the garlic powder, and the pepper. Stir in the milk and the chicken broth. Cook, uncovered, on high for 2½ to 3½ minutes (low-wattage oven: 3 to 4 minutes) or till the mixture is thickened and bubbly, stirring every 30 seconds during cooking time. Stir in the cheese. Cook, uncovered, on high for 1 to 1½ minutes or till cheese is melted, stirring every 30 seconds.

● **Drain** the potato mixture. Add the cheese sauce to potatoes. Gently toss till the potatoes are well coated with cheese sauce. If desired, sprinkle the snipped parsley over the potato mixture to garnish. Makes 4 to 6 side-dish servings.

Nutrition information per serving: 266 cal., 11 g pro., 45 g carbo., 6 g fat, 18 mg chol., 259 mg sodium, 1,324 mg potassium, and 4 g dietary fiber. U.S. RDA: 53% vit. C, 16% thiamine, 11% riboflavin, 19% niacin, 20% calcium.

Asparagus

It's a sure sign that spring is here when fresh asparagus spears greet you in the grocery store. Enjoy asparagus at its best— simply prepared in the microwave.

GINGER-CREAM ASPARAGUS

- 1 pound asparagus spears
- ⅓ cup light cream
- ¼ cup chicken broth
- 1½ teaspoons cornstarch
- ¼ teaspoon grated gingerroot
- ¼ teaspoon finely shredded lemon peel

● **Wash asparagus.** Snap off and discard woody ends. Place in an 8x8x2-inch or 10x6x2-inch microwave-safe baking dish. Add 2 tablespoons *water.* Cover dish with clear plastic wrap; vent by leaving a small area unsealed at edge of dish.

● **Micro-cook** on 100% power (high) for 7 to 9 minutes (low-wattage oven: 9 to 11 minutes) or till tender, rearranging asparagus once by switching center spears with those on the edges. Drain; cover to keep warm.

● **For sauce,** in a 2-cup glass measure combine cream, chicken broth, cornstarch, gingerroot, and lemon peel. Cook on high for 2 to 3 minutes or till thickened and bubbly, stirring after 1 minute, then every 30 seconds. Pour sauce over asparagus. Makes 4 side-dish servings.

Nutrition information per serving: 70 cal., 4 g pro., 6 g carbo., 4 g fat, 13 mg chol., 59 mg sodium, 381 mg potassium, and 2 g dietary fiber. U.S. RDA: 23% vit. A, 44% vit. C.

WARM SALAD OF ASPARAGUS AND GREENS

- 2 cups asparagus, cut into 2-inch pieces
- 4 slices bacon, cut into 1-inch pieces
- 1 small onion, sliced into rings
- 2 tablespoons vinegar
- 1 tablespoon sugar
- ½ teaspoon fines herbes, crushed
- ⅛ teaspoon salt
- 1 cup torn Bibb *or* Boston lettuce
- 1 cup torn kale *or* 1½ cups torn sorrel
- 1 tomato, chopped

● **In a 1-quart** microwave-safe casserole cook the asparagus in 2 tablespoons *water,* covered, on 100% power (high) for 5 to 7 minutes (low-wattage oven: 6 to 8 minutes) or till asparagus is just tender. Drain.

● **For dressing,** in a 1½-quart microwave-safe casserole cook bacon, covered, on high for 3 to 5 minutes (low-wattage oven: 8 to 9 minutes) or till crisp, stirring once. Remove bacon; set aside.

● **Cook onion in drippings,** covered, on high for 2 to 3 minutes (low-wattage oven: 3 to 4 minutes). Stir in vinegar, sugar, fines herbes, and salt. Stir asparagus, bacon, greens, and tomato into dressing; toss and serve. Makes 4 side-dish servings.

Nutrition information per serving: 89 cal., 5 g pro., 10 g carbo., 4 g fat, 6 mg chol., 197 mg sodium, 410 mg potassium, and 3 g dietary fiber. U.S. RDA: 45% vit. A.

A + ASPARAGUS

● Select firm, straight spears with compact, closed tips. Choose spears of the same size; they'll cook more evenly.

● Wash and scrape off scales. Break off woody bases at point where spears snap easily.

● Arrange spears in a microwave-safe dish. If spears are short, place tips in center. Add 2 tablespoons *water.* Cover with a microwave-safe lid.

● Micro-cook on 100% power (high) till tender, rearranging asparagus once by switching center spears with those on the edges. Allow 4 to 6 minutes for ½ pound; 7 to 9 minutes for 1 pound. Drain; season.

Ah, sweet pea! Like sweet corn, peas have natural sugars that start converting to starch once they leave the vine. So cook peas soon after buying or picking.

DILLED PEA SOUP

- 1 10-ounce package frozen peas *or* 2 cups shelled peas
- 2 green onions, cut up
- 1 14½-ounce can chicken broth
- ½ teaspoon dried dillweed
- 1 8-ounce carton plain yogurt *or* dairy sour cream
- Plain yogurt *or* dairy sour cream (optional)
- Sliced green onion (optional)

● **In a 1-quart** microwave-safe casserole combine peas, cut-up onions, ¼ *cup* of the chicken broth, and dillweed. Micro-cook, covered, on 100% power (high) for 8 to 10 minutes or till very tender. *Do not drain.* Uncover; cool slightly. Add the remaining chicken broth.

● **In a blender container** or food processor bowl blend or process pea mixture, *half* at a time, till smooth. Transfer to a storage container. Cover and chill.

● **At serving time, use** a

wire whisk to blend in the carton of yogurt or sour cream. If desired, dollop with additional yogurt or sour cream and lightly sprinkle with sliced green onion before serving. Makes 3 or 4 side-dish servings.

Nutrition information per serving: 146 cal., 12 g pro., 20 g carbo., 2 g fat, 5 mg chol., 595 mg sodium, 456 mg potassium, and 5 g dietary fiber. U.S. RDA: 15% vit. A, 21% vit. C, 19% thiamine, 17% riboflavin, 18% niacin, 17% calcium, 11% iron.

VELVETY PEAS AND RADISHES

- 1 cup radishes, sliced
- 1 cup fresh *or* frozen shelled peas
- 2 tablespoons water
- ½ cup milk
- 1 tablespoon all-purpose flour
- ¼ teaspoon dried dillweed
- ⅛ teaspoon salt
- ⅛ teaspoon lemon pepper
- Fresh dill (optional)

● **In a 20-ounce** microwave-safe casserole stir together the sliced radishes and the peas; add the water. Micro-cook, covered, on 100% power (high) for 5 to 7 minutes or till vegetables are tender, stirring once. Drain. Cover and keep warm.

● **In a 2-cup glass** measure combine milk, flour, dillweed, salt, and lemon pepper. Cook, uncovered, on high 1½ to 2½ minutes or till bubbly, stirring every 30 seconds. Stir into hot vegetables. Top with fresh dill. Makes 3 side-dish servings.

Nutrition information per serving: 74 cal., 4 g pro., 12 g carbo., 1 g fat, 3 mg chol., 197 mg sodium, 230 mg potassium, and 3 g dietary fiber.

PERFECT PEAS, PLEASE

To cook 2 cups shelled peas:

● **In a 1-quart** microwave-safe casserole combine peas and 2 tablespoons *water.*

● Micro-cook, covered, on 100% power (high) for 6 to 8 minutes or till tender, stirring once. Drain.

To cook 6 ounces (2 cups) pea pods:

● Remove tips and strings.

● **In a 1-quart** microwave-safe casserole combine pea pods and 2 tablespoons *water.*

● Micro-cook, covered, on 100% power (high) for 3 to 5 minutes (low-wattage oven: 4 to 6 minutes) or till crisp-tender, stirring once. Drain.

More than a salad ingredient, radishes cook up tender and sweet—still with "heat." As a relish, the vegetable goes haute.

RADISH RELISH

- 1 pound radishes, cut up
- 1 medium onion, quartered
- 1 medium carrot, cut into 1-inch pieces
- 2 tablespoons whole allspice
- ¼ teaspoon whole cloves
- 1 cup white vinegar
- ¾ cup sugar

- ¾ cup water
- 1 teaspoon mustard seed
- ½ teaspoon salt

● **In a blender container** or food processor bowl combine *half* the radishes, *half* the onion, and *half* the carrot. Cover; blend or process till finely chopped. Remove from blender. Repeat with remaining vegetables.

● **For spice bag,** tie allspice and cloves in cheesecloth. In a 2-quart (low-wattage oven: 1½-quart) microwave-safe casserole combine vegetable mixture, spice bag, vinegar, sugar, water, mustard seed, and salt.

● **Micro-cook,** covered, on 100% power (high) for 7 to 9 minutes (low-wattage oven: 12 to 14 minutes) or till boiling. Stir. Cook, covered, on 50% power (medium) for 12 to 14 minutes (low-wattage oven: 100% power for 12 to 14 minutes) or till vegetables are tender, stirring twice.

● **Let stand, uncovered,** to cool. Spoon into airtight containers and freeze. *Or,* pack into hot, clean pint jars, leaving ½-inch headspace. Wipe rims; adjust lids. Process in boiling water bath for 15 minutes (start timing when water boils). Serve at room temperature or chilled. Makes 4 cups.

Nutrition information per tablespoon: 12 cal., 3 g carbo., 19 mg sodium, and 26 mg potassium.

Greens

SPRING GREEN FRITTATA

- 4 ounces fresh spinach, sorrel, *or* arugula
- 1 tablespoon margarine *or* butter
- ¼ cup sliced green onion
- 6 beaten eggs
- ⅓ cup light cream
- ¼ teaspoon salt

Dash pepper

- ½ cup shredded Swiss cheese (2 ounces)
- 1 small tomato, seeded and chopped

● **Wash and trim greens.** In a 1½-quart microwave-safe casserole micro-cook greens, covered, on 100% power (high) for 2 to 3 minutes or till wilted. Drain. Chop; set aside.

● **In a 9-inch pie plate** cook margarine uncovered, on high 45 to 60 seconds or till melted; swirl to coat pie plate. Add onion and cook, uncovered, on high for 2 minutes. Spread greens evenly over onions.

● **Combine eggs,** cream, salt, and pepper; pour over greens. Cook, uncovered, on high 4 to 6 minutes or till eggs are set but still shiny, lifting cooked edges and letting uncooked portions flow underneath after every minute. Give the pie plate a half-turn after every minute.

● **Sprinkle with cheese.** Micro-cook, uncovered, on high 1 to 1½ minutes more or till cheese melts. Top with tomato. To serve, cut into wedges. Serves 4.

Nutrition information per main-dish serving: 249 cal., 15 g pro., 4 g carbo., 19 g fat, 438 mg chol., 332 mg sodium, 339 mg potassium. U.S. RDA: 56% vit. A, 13% vit. C, 22% riboflavin, 23% calcium, 14% iron.

"W e're making brunch Sunday and would love to have you join us. We'll start cooking about 10:00 and plan to eat about 11:30. Be sure to bring the kids."

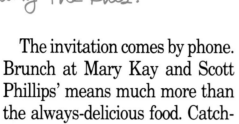

The invitation comes by phone. Brunch at Mary Kay and Scott Phillips' means much more than the always-delicious food. Catching up on family news, chatting with friends, relaxing in the sun, and watching children play—everyone shares in the fun that makes this springtime morning memorable.

Because Mary Kay and Scott both work, they simply don't have time for formal entertaining. For them, a relaxed brunch for family and friends is much easier. To keep things manageable, Mary Kay relies on a menu she feels comfortable with, and that includes some make-ahead dishes, a quick-fix coffee cake, and platters of fresh fruits and vegetables. She also gets everyone involved in the cooking, leaving plenty of time for her and the guests to relax, play, and enjoy

A Morning in May

BY LISA HOLDERNESS

Mary Kay decorates her brunch table with a piled-high bowl of berries and toppings for Fresh Berry Sundaes. The Pecan Streusel Coffee Cake looks just as tempting. This elegant cake starts with a mix and can be made ahead.

A Morning in May

With kisses and hugs, Thomas, 11, and Christine, 8, join Mary Kay in welcoming their grandparents, Carl and Dolores D'Aquila. When the D'Aquilas are in town, they love to come early and help out.

"I learned from my mother to keep entertaining simple. And if you make it fun, everyone will love to come over."

"Successful party decorations needn't be complicated, fussy, or expensive," Mary Kay says. "A casual look helps everyone feel at home so they can kick back and relax."

As an interior designer, Mary Kay has a knack for creating beautiful table settings with items she's collected over the years for her home.

In the morning hours on brunch day, Mary Kay gathers her prized quilts, assorted colorful sheets, and baskets of every shape from around the house. It's not unusual to find a quilt and a striped sheet teamed as a tablecloth. And a pitcher, overflowing with fresh garden flowers, complements the fabrics' soft spring colors and simple designs.

The Party Vegetable Platter, with assorted fresh vegetables and a creamy mustard dressing, is a brunch tradition at the Phillips house.

A Morning in May

When Minnesota weather allows, the Phillipses' backyard serves as center stage for the brunch activities. Spring flowers, budding trees, and singing birds set up an inviting backdrop for the festive brunch table.

The buffet-style meal lets guests help themselves, choosing what and how much they want to eat. After eating, high-spirited yard games, coffee, and conversation follow.

With so many delicious choices, plates fill up fast. Everyone looks forward to Mary Kay's ham- and pineapple-topped chicken and her scrambled-egg casserole.

"Thomas and Christine share a moment with their grandparents, LaVerne and Bill Phillips, while filling their plates with favorite foods."

A Morning in May

The kids cook up the pancakes assembly-line style. As Christine Phillips makes the cakes, Eric Gustafson, a friend, pours syrup atop.

"What an idyllic way to spend the last day of the weekend—outdoors, with loved ones and great food."

The kids take over at dessert time (with a little help from Mary Kay, of course). Lafayette Pancakes, a light yet sweet finale of minicakes topped with fresh berries and syrup, are easy enough for amateur chefs to make. When the young cooks convene, they take dessert-making seriously. Each has a special job as they work together, clanging dishes and talking.

The adults, wary of how the pancakes would turn out, enjoy the freshly made results. And the youngsters, forgetting how much they have already eaten, eagerly dig into their fruit-topped, mini dessert cakes.

Brunch winds down with Lafayette Pancakes drizzled with syrup. These silver-dollar-size dessert cakes can be made ahead if needed and warmed up before serving. Mary Kay sprinkles them with a handful of berries for extra flavor and color.

A Morning in May

A SPRINGTIME BRUNCH

MENU

Serve these recipes together as a menu or pick and choose just a few for a more intimate brunch—

Party Vegetable Platter

Chicken Hawaiian

Cheese and Mushroom
Brunch Eggs

Pecan Streusel
Coffee Cake

Fresh Berry Sundaes

Lafayette Pancakes

Champagne with
Orange juice

Orange juice and milk

Coffee and tea

Mary Kay, her mother, and husband, Scott, make cooking part of the fun.

Making Brunch Manageable

To keep entertaining lighthearted and hassle free, Mary Kay follows a brunch plan that allows her to get the grocery shopping done early and to spread the menu preparation time throughout the week.

For a head start on this spring-fresh brunch menu, follow these easy make-ahead steps.

Several days ahead
● Precook the chicken and the pineapple sauce up to two days in advance for the Chicken Hawaiian. Cover and chill.
● Bake the Pecan Streusel Coffee Cake several days ahead; cover the pan with freezer wrap or foil and freeze.
● For the Cheese and Mushroom Brunch Eggs, make the cheese sauce up to a week before needed. Cool sauce thoroughly, cover, and chill.
● Stir together the mustard dressing for the Party Vegetable Platter up to a week before brunch. Cover and chill.

The day before
● Finish up brunch eggs, using made-ahead sauce. Instead of baking, cover with plastic wrap and chill.

● For the Party Vegetable Platter, clean, cut up, and steam vegetables and arrange on the platter. Cover and chill. Wait to drizzle on the dressing till just before serving time.
● If desired, you can make the Lafayette Pancakes ahead. Wrap them in foil and chill till needed.

On brunch morning
● Thaw and warm coffee cake first. Cover and keep warm.
● Top chicken with ham, reheat in oven, and pour on sauce.

Laverne Phillips gives Mary Kay a hand with her brunch eggs.

● Bake brunch eggs alongside chicken.
● Dish up the toppings for berries.
● If pancakes were made ahead, warm in oven to serve. Heat syrup through immediately before serving.
● Drizzle the Party Vegetable Platter with the mustard dressing.

HAWAIIAN CHICKEN

You can make this chicken and ham dish up to two days in advance. Just follow the make-ahead instructions—

- 12 **boned, skinless chicken breast halves (4 ounces each)**
- ¼ **cup all-purpose flour**
- ½ **teaspoon salt**
- ¼ **cup margarine or butter**
- 1 **20-ounce can pineapple tidbits (juice pack)**
- ½ **cup dry sherry**
- 2 **cups sliced celery**
- 1½ **cups sliced onion**
- 2 **tablespoons all-purpose flour**
- 2 **cups fully cooked ham cut into thin strips**

● **Rinse chicken;** pat dry. Stir together the ¼ cup flour and salt. Roll chicken pieces in flour mixture to coat.

● **In a 12-inch skillet cook** the chicken, *half* at a time, in hot margarine or butter till chicken is brown, turning once. Transfer chicken to a 13x9x2-inch baking dish, reserving drippings in skillet. Bake, uncovered, in a 350° oven for 25 minutes.

● **Meanwhile, for sauce,** drain pineapple, reserving juice. Add sherry to drippings in skillet. Cook and stir over medium heat, stirring to scrape up browned bits. Add pineapple tidbits, celery, and onions. Bring to boiling. Reduce heat; simmer, uncovered, about 5 minutes or till celery starts to soften.

● **Combine** reserved pineapple juice and the 2 tablespoons flour; stir into the sauce mixture in the skillet. Cook and stir till thickened and bubbly. Remove from heat.

● **Spoon off any juices** from chicken in the baking dish. Sprinkle ham over chicken. Pour sauce over all. Bake, uncovered, about 10 minutes more or till chicken is tender and no longer pink. Makes 12 servings.

Make-ahead directions: Prepare chicken as directed, *except* bake, uncovered, (without sauce) for 35 minutes (instead of 25 minutes) or till tender and no longer pink. Cool slightly. Drain. Cover and chill up to 2 days.

Prepare sauce as directed, *except do not* pour over chicken. Cool slightly. Transfer to a storage container; cover and chill up to 2 days.

To reheat, sprinkle ham over the chilled chicken and bake, covered with foil, in a 350° oven about 40 minutes or till heated through. Meanwhile, in a medium saucepan cook and stir the sauce over medium heat about 15 minutes or till heated through. Pour the sauce over the ham and chicken, and serve immediately.

Nutrition information per serving: *196 cal., 18 g pro., 13 g carbo., 7 g fat, 46 mg chol., 462 mg sodium, 317 mg potassium, and 1 g dietary fiber. U.S. RDA: 14% vit. C, 19% thiamine, 34% niacin.*

PARTY VEGETABLE PLATTER

For a springtime brunch Mary Kay chooses fresh asparagus because it's in season and plentiful. Other seasons, she substitutes fresh green beans—

- 1½ **pounds asparagus spears or 1 pound green beans**
- 2 **small heads cauliflower, broken into flowerets**
- ½ **cup white wine vinegar**
- ⅓ **cup Dijon-style mustard**
- 2 **tablespoons sugar**
- ⅔ **cup olive oil or salad oil**
Leaf lettuce
Cherry tomatoes, halved
Pitted ripe olives
Lemon slices, halved (optional)
Fresh thyme sprig (optional)

● **Place a steamer basket** in a saucepan. Add water to just below the bottom of the steamer basket. Bring to boiling. Add asparagus or green beans. Steam, covered, till crisp-tender (5 to 8 minutes for asparagus; 18 to 22 minutes for green beans). Remove asparagus or green beans from steamer basket; chill till serving time.

● **Add water** to just below the bottom of the steamer basket, if necessary. Return to boiling. Add cauliflower. Steam, covered, for 8 to 12 minutes or till crisp-tender. Remove cauliflower from steamer basket; chill till serving time.

● **For dressing,** in a blender container or food processor bowl combine wine vinegar, mustard, and sugar. Cover and blend or process for 5 seconds. With blender running slowly, add oil in a thin, steady stream through the opening in the lid. (When necessary, stop blender or processor and use a rubber scraper to scrape sides.) Season to taste with *salt* and *pepper*. Cover and chill till serving time.

● **To serve, arrange** asparagus or green beans on one side of a large platter. Line remaining half of the platter with lettuce. Arrange cauliflower on top of the lettuce. Add several cherry tomatoes and ripe olives. Drizzle vegetables with the dressing. If desired, garnish with the lemon slices and the thyme sprig. Makes 12 servings.

Make-ahead directions: Make the dressing up to a week before serving. Store in a covered container in the refrigerator. The day before, clean and steam the asparagus or green beans and cauliflower. Arrange on the platter. Cover and chill. Just before serving, add cherry tomatoes and olives. Drizzle with dressing.

Nutrition information per serving: *170 cal., 3 g pro., 9 g carbo., 14 g fat, 0 mg chol., 303 mg sodium, 463 mg potassium, and 3 g dietary fiber. U.S. RDA: 20% vit. A, 75% vit. C.*

FRESH BERRY SUNDAES

As pictured on page 64, Mary Kay serves the berry toppings in an eclectic assortment of china teacups, adding her personalized touch to the table—

Fresh strawberries *and/or*
  blackberries
Vanilla yogurt
Ground nutmeg
Brown sugar
Granola
Toasted coconut
Toasted sliced almonds

● **Plan on** about 1 cup of berries per person. (Mary Kay uses strawberries and blackberries, but any combination of berries will work.) Remove stems from berries. Rinse the berries in cold water and drain well. Transfer the berries to a large serving bowl.
● **For toppings, set out cups** of vanilla yogurt sprinkled with ground nutmeg, brown sugar, granola, coconut, and sliced almonds. This way, guests can build their own berry sundaes.

Nutrition information per 1 cup berries with 1 tablespoon yogurt, 1 teaspoon brown sugar, and 1 teaspoon almonds: 102 cal., 2 g pro., 21 g carbo., 2 g fat, 1 mg chol., 12 mg sodium, 330 mg potassium, and 5 g dietary fiber. U.S. RDA: 67% vit. C.

PECAN-STREUSEL COFFEE CAKE

For a tasty variation, add ½ teaspoon finely shredded orange or lemon peel to the cake mix—

  1 **cup chopped pecans**
  ⅔ **cup packed brown sugar**
  2 **tablespoons margarine** *or* **butter, melted**
1½ **teaspoons ground cinnamon**
  1 **27¼-ounce package cinnamon streusel cake mix**
  ½ **cup dairy sour cream**

● **For topping,** in a mixing bowl stir together pecans, brown sugar, margarine or butter, and cinnamon. Set aside.
● **Prepare the cake mix batter** according to the package directions, *except* stir the sour cream into the prepared batter. Spread *two-thirds* (about 4 cups) of the batter into a greased and floured 13x9x2-inch baking pan. Sprinkle batter with the streusel mix from the package. Carefully spread with the remaining batter. Sprinkle with the nut topping.
● **Bake in a 350° oven** for 35 to 40 minutes or till a toothpick inserted near the center comes out clean. Cool slightly in pan. Meanwhile, prepare glaze from the cake mix according to package directions. Drizzle glaze over warm coffee cake. Makes 14 to 16 servings.

Make-ahead directions: Cool coffee cake completely and do not add glaze. Cover the pan with heavy foil or remove coffee cake from pan and wrap in freezer wrap. Freeze up to 6 months. To serve, if used freezer wrap, remove wrap and cover loosely with foil. Bake, covered, in a 350° oven for 25 to 30 minutes or till heated. Glaze as directed above.

Nutrition information per serving: 375 cal., 3 g pro., 49 g carbo., 19 g fat, 55 mg chol., 223 mg sodium, 113 mg potassium, 1 g dietary fiber.

Jeanne Gustafson, Mary Kay's best friend, helps serve the coffee cake.

Hassle-Free Shopping

For manageable entertaining, start by taking the hassle out of grocery shopping. Use these tips to organize your shopping list and cut valuable time from your trip.
● **Make a list and check it twice.** Try to get everything you need for your brunch in one trip (you may need to make a last-minute run for perishable goods as well). Divide foods into categories such as produce, dairy products, meat, canned foods, frozen foods, breads, bakery items, and beverages. Cross off items on your list as you pick them up so you won't forget anything. Call ahead to make sure specialty items are in stock. This also may save an extra trip.
● **Shop wisely with coupons and store specials.** On your shopping list, mark the items and brands that you have coupons for. Also, check the newspaper for store specials and mark those items and brands.
● **Stick to a store you know.** Because grocery stores are arranged differently, choose one you are familiar with so you can find the items you need quickly.
● **Avoid aisle traffic jams.** (The most congested times are usually from 5 to 6:30 in the evenings and any time on weekends.) Shop on weekdays or after 6:30 on weeknights when the aisles are free of carts and people and when the checkout lines are short.

CHEESE AND MUSHROOM BRUNCH EGGS

By serving scrambled eggs casserole-style, Mary Kay knows the eggs will stay hot till all the guests are served—

```
  3 tablespoons margarine or butter
  ¼ cup all-purpose flour
2½ cups milk
  1 cup shredded process Swiss
    cheese (4 ounces)
  ½ cup grated Parmesan cheese
  ¼ cup dry white wine
Nonstick spray coating
  3 cups sliced fresh mushrooms
  ½ cup thinly sliced green onions
  2 tablespoons margarine or butter
 24 beaten eggs
Tomato slices, cut in half
Sliced green onions
```

● **For sauce, in a saucepan melt** the 3 tablespoons margarine or butter. Stir in flour. Cook for 1 minute. Add milk all at once. Cook and stir over medium heat till thickened and bubbly. Stir in cheeses. Cook and stir over medium heat till cheeses melt. Remove from heat; stir in wine. Cool.

● **For eggs,** spray a *cold* 12-inch skillet with nonstick coating. Heat skillet over medium heat. Add mushrooms and the ½ cup green onions to the hot skillet; cook till tender. Transfer vegetables to a bowl; set aside.

● **In the same skillet** melt *1 tablespoon* of the margarine or butter. Add *half* of the eggs. Cook over medium heat without stirring till eggs begin to set on the bottom and around the edge. Using a large spoon, lift and fold the partially cooked egg mixture so the uncooked portion flows underneath. Continue cooking till eggs are set throughout, but still glossy and moist. Transfer scrambled eggs to a 13x9x2-inch broiler-proof baking pan or au gratin dish. Scramble remaining eggs using remaining margarine or butter; remove from heat.

● **Spread** *half* of the mushroom mixture over the eggs in the baking pan or au gratin dish. Drizzle about *half* the sauce atop. Top with the remaining scrambled eggs, mushroom mixture, and sauce.

● **Bake, uncovered, in a 350° oven** about 25 minutes or till heated through. For a golden brown top, transfer to broiler and broil 4 inches from the heat for 3 to 4 minutes or till surface starts to brown. Top with tomato wedges and remaining sliced green onions. Let stand 10 minutes before serving. Makes 12 servings.

Make-ahead directions: Prepare sauce as directed above; cover and chill up to one week. Scramble the eggs and assemble the casserole using the prepared sauce. Cover and chill up to 24 hours. To serve, bake, uncovered, in a 350° oven about 55 minutes or till heated through. Continue as directed.

Nutrition information per serving: 301 cal., 19 g pro., 8 g carbo., 21 g fat, 566 mg chol., 324 mg sodium, 324 mg potassium, and 1 g dietary fiber. U.S. RDA: 26% vit. A, 10% thiamine, 32% riboflavin, 27% calcium, 15% iron.

LAFAYETTE PANCAKES

Turn pancakes into dessert with Mary Kay's berry-topped petite cakes—

```
  3 egg yolks
  1 cup buttermilk
  2 cups all-purpose flour
  3 tablespoons sugar
  2 teaspoons baking powder
  ¼ teaspoon baking soda
  ½ cup buttermilk
  6 tablespoons margarine or butter,
    melted
  3 egg whites
```

Berry *or* maple syrup
Margarine *or* butter
Fresh raspberries, blueberries,
   or sliced strawberries (optional)

● **In a large mixing bowl** blend together the egg yolks and the 1 cup buttermilk. In another bowl combine the flour, sugar, baking powder, and baking soda; add to the egg yolk mixture. Mix to combine. Stir in the ½ cup buttermilk and the melted margarine or butter.

● **In a mixer bowl beat** egg whites till stiff peaks form (tips stand straight). Gently fold beaten egg whites into flour mixture, leaving a few fluffs of egg white. *Do not overmix.*

● **For each pancake, spoon** about *1 tablespoon* of the batter onto a hot, lightly greased griddle or heavy skillet. If batter is too thick to spread slightly when dropped onto a hot griddle, stir in 2 to 4 tablespoons additional milk. Cook till golden brown, turning to cook second side when pancakes have a bubbly surface and slightly dry edges.

Before serving, in a small saucepan warm syrup over medium-high heat till heated through, stirring occasionally. Serve pancakes with warm syrup and, if desired, fresh berries. Makes about 16 to 24 pancakes.

Make-ahead directions: Bake pancakes as directed above. Cool completely. Arrange *half* of the pancakes in a single layer on a piece of foil (about 20x12 inches). Top with another piece of foil and remaining pancakes. Place a third piece of foil atop; seal edges of foil together with a double fold, making a packet. Chill pancakes up to 24 hours. To reheat, place foil packet in a 350° oven 15 minutes or till heated through. Remove from foil; serve as directed.

Nutrition information per 2 pancakes with 2 teaspoons butter and 2 tablespoons berry syrup: 340 cal., 5 g pro., 46 g carbo., 15 g fat, 69 mg chol., 282 mg sodium, 159 mg potassium, and 1 g dietary fiber. U.S. RDA: 13% vit. A, 14% thiamine, 12% riboflavin, and 12% calcium.

summertime

BY
JOY TAYLOR

AND THE GRILLING IS EASY

Summer sizzles
with the smells
and the tastes of
outdoor cooking.
And our passion
for grilling grows
stronger each year.
This recipe
collection includes
the easiest and best
choices for laid-
back barbecuing.
Catch the sizzle. . . .

The best of summer:
smoking barbecues,
icy drinks, and
family chit-chat
out in the yard.

**Fish Steaks with
Fresh Fruit Salsa**

Spiced and Smoked Ribs

FABULOUS FISH, LEAN AND SIMPLE

- Because fish is so low in fat, it needs a little special attention.
- Brush the cold grill rack with oil before grilling to prevent fish from sticking.
- Baste fish during grilling with olive oil, melted butter, or leftover marinade.
- Figure cooking time according to thickness. Allow 4–6 minutes for each half inch of thickness. If fish is thicker than an inch, turn it once during cooking.

RIB TICKLERS

- For the most tender ribs, first cook them in simmering water about 30 minutes. After boiling, smoke them for 45 minutes.
- To smoke in flavor, use hardwoods from fruit or nut trees. Best bets: hickory, mesquite, apple, or cherry. Soak the chips in water so they smolder rather than flame when added to red-hot coals.
- Smoke-cooked foods take on a pink color even though they're fully cooked.

summertime AND THE GRILLING IS EASY

BARBECUE LOVERS' VEGETABLE PLATTER

● You can cook almost any vegetable over an open fire. For starters, try asparagus, squash, carrots, peppers, and leeks.

● Longer-cooking vegetables (such as new potatoes) need a few minutes of precooking in the microwave oven or on the range top.

● Generously brush vegetables with melted margarine, butter, or olive oil for flavor and to prevent sticking. Cook directly over *medium-hot* coals till fork-tender and slightly charred.

Grilled
Summer
Vegetables

Outdoors, the dining is easy. The food tastes so good. No wonder we love cookouts.

Fresh Garden Chicken

Greek
Kabobs
With
Bulgur
Pilaf

AND THE GRILLING IS EASY

summertime

KABOBS ARE JUST RIGHT

- Kabobs make a great do-ahead meal. Marinate the meat, precook those vegetables that need it, and chill everything overnight till you're ready to grill.
- Have the whole family thread their own sticks—you can use long metal skewers or dampened short bamboo skewers.
- Leave a small space between each piece of food on the skewer to allow even cooking.

CHICKEN AT ITS BEST

- It's hard to resist the aroma of grilling chicken, but don't rush dinner.
- Remove chicken from the grill when meat next to the bone is no longer pink. That takes 35 to 45 minutes for pieces or quarters.
- Get chicken quarters to lie flat on the grill by breaking the wing, hip, and drumstick joints. Twist those little wing tips under the back.

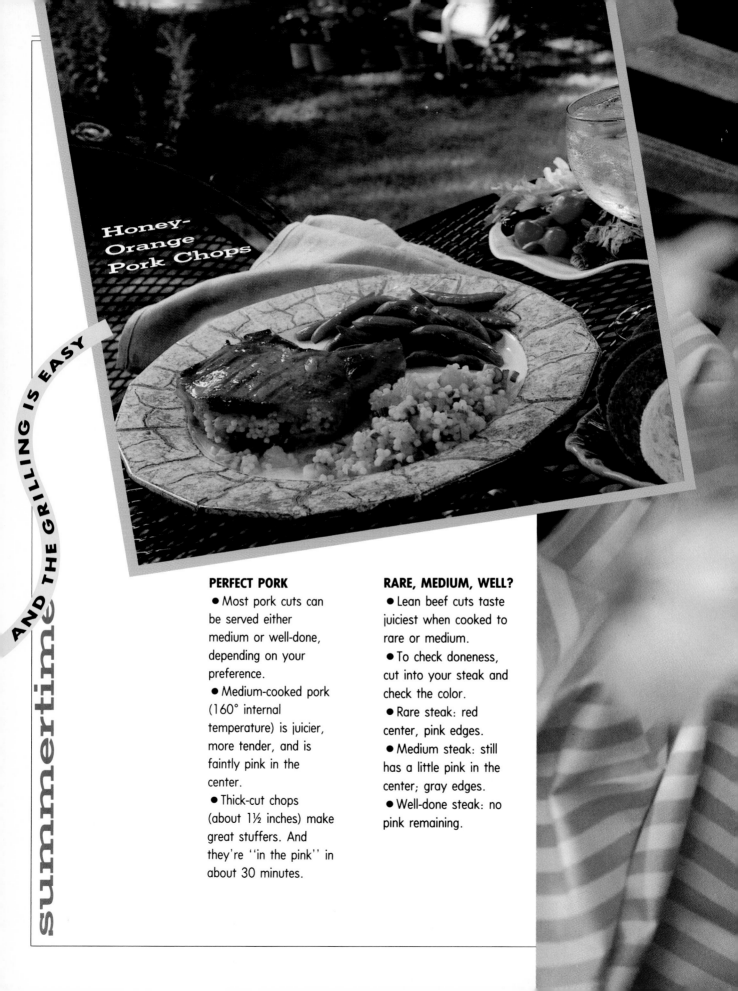

Honey-Orange Pork Chops

PERFECT PORK

- Most pork cuts can be served either medium or well-done, depending on your preference.
- Medium-cooked pork (160° internal temperature) is juicier, more tender, and is faintly pink in the center.
- Thick-cut chops (about 1½ inches) make great stuffers. And they're ''in the pink'' in about 30 minutes.

RARE, MEDIUM, WELL?

- Lean beef cuts taste juiciest when cooked to rare or medium.
- To check doneness, cut into your steak and check the color.
- Rare steak: red center, pink edges.
- Medium steak: still has a little pink in the center; gray edges.
- Well-done steak: no pink remaining.

Why is it that your neighbor's cookout always smells better than your own?

**Stuffed
Sirloin
With Mixed
Mushroom
Sauté**

Salad Burger

A BEVY OF BURGERS

What kind of burger are you hungry for? Create one to your liking—

1 beaten egg
Liquid
Bread crumbs *or* **grain**
Vegetable *or* **condiment**
Seasoning
1 pound lean ground beef, pork, lamb *or* **mixture of**
½ pound ground turkey and
½ pound ground beef
Bread *or* **bun, toasted**
Topping

● **In a mixing bowl** combine egg and liquid. Stir in bread crumbs or grain, vegetable or condiment, and seasoning. Add ground meat; mix well.

● **Shape meat mixture** into four ¾-inch-thick patties. Grill on an uncovered grill directly over *medium* coals (see tip, *page 87*) 15 to 18 minutes or till well done, turning once. Serve on bread or bun with topping. Serves 4.

Nutrition information per All-American Burger: 397 cal., 26 g pro., 19 g fat, 141 mg chol., 827 mg sodium, 2 g dietary fiber.

	LIQUID	BREAD/GRAIN	VEGETABLE/CONDIMENT	SEASONING	BREAD/BUN	TOPPING
ALL-AMERICAN BURGERS	1 tablespoon prepared mustard and 1 tablespoon catsup	¼ cup fine dry bread crumbs	⅓ cup finely chopped pickle	½ teaspoon onion salt; dash pepper	Hamburger buns	Onion slices; tomato slices; lettuce leaves; pickle slices
PIZZA BURGERS	2 tablespoons pizza sauce	¼ cup fine dry seasoned bread crumbs	⅓ cup chopped pitted ripe olives or chopped canned mushrooms	½ teaspoon salt; ½ teaspoon dried Italian seasoning	1-inch-thick French bread slices	Warm ½ cup pizza sauce with ¼ cup sliced pitted ripe olives. Spoon atop burgers. Top with mozzarella cheese slices.
SALAD BURGERS	2 tablespoons creamy cucumber or buttermilk salad dressing	3 tablespoons bulgur wheat	⅓ cup chopped cucumber	½ teaspoon garlic salt; ¼ teaspoon dried marjoram, crushed; dash pepper	Kaiser bun or pita bread halves	¼ cup creamy cucumber or buttermilk salad dressing; alfalfa sprouts; cucumber and avocado slices
GERMAN-STYLE BURGERS	2 tablespoons beer	¼ cup dry rye bread crumbs	¼ cup shredded Muenster cheese	½ teaspoon caraway seed; ½ teaspoon salt; ¼ teaspoon pepper	Rye or pumpernickel bread	Spread bread with mustard. Stir ¼ teaspoon caraway seed into ½ cup drained sauerkraut. Spoon atop burgers; top with Muenster cheese.

summertime AND THE GRILLING IS EASY

FISH STEAKS WITH FRESH FRUIT SALSA

Brighten each dinner plate with a fresh sprig of rosemary, a leaf of purple kale, and steamed baby summer squash, as pictured on pages 76–77—

- 4 fresh *or* frozen halibut, swordfish, shark, *or* salmon steaks, cut 1 inch thick (about 2 pounds)
- ½ small ripe papaya, peeled, seeded, and chopped
- 1 small ripe nectarine, pitted and chopped
- 1 fresh jalapeño chili pepper, seeded and chopped* *or* 1 tablespoon capers, drained
- 1 tablespoon snipped fresh rosemary, basil, *or* thyme
- 1 tablespoon olive oil

Olive oil

● **Thaw fish, if frozen.**
● **Several hours ahead,** for fruit salsa, stir together the papaya, nectarine, jalapeño pepper or capers, rosemary, basil or thyme, and 1 tablespoon olive oil. Cover and chill thoroughly.
● **Lightly brush the cold grill rack** with olive oil. Brush both sides of steaks with olive oil. Grill fish on an uncovered grill directly over *medium-hot* coals (see tip, *page 87*) for 4 minutes. Using a wide spatula, carefully turn fish over. Brush with olive oil. Grill for 4 to 8 minutes more or till fish just flakes with a fork. Serve fish with the fruit salsa. Serves 4.

*Note: When seeding and chopping a fresh chili pepper, protect your hands with plastic gloves because the oils in the pepper can irritate your skin. Also, avoid direct contact with your eyes. When finished with the chili pepper, wash your hands thoroughly.

Nutrition information per serving: 268 cal., 40 g pro., 8 g fat, 1 mg chol., 135 mg sodium, 1,018 mg potassium, 1 g dietary fiber. U.S. RDA: 23% vit. A, 42% vit. C, 12% thiamine, 13% riboflavin, 83% niacin, 10% iron.

SPICED AND SMOKED RIBS

Coat the ribs with a spice rub before grilling. Then, during grilling, slather on either a molasses or a gingered teriyaki glaze—

- 4 cups hickory chips
- 4 pounds pork loin back ribs *or* meaty pork spareribs
- 1 tablespoon brown sugar
- 1 teaspoon five-spice powder
- ½ teaspoon salt
- ½ teaspoon paprika
- ¼ teaspoon celery seed
- ¼ teaspoon pepper

Molasses Glaze *or* Teriyaki Glaze (see recipes, *right*)

● **At least 1 hour before grilling,** soak the wood chips in enough water to cover them. Drain chips.
● **Meanwhile, cut the pork ribs** into serving-size pieces (portions with 3 to 4 ribs each). Place in a Dutch oven. Add enough *water* to cover ribs. Bring to boiling; reduce heat. Simmer, covered, for 30 minutes. Drain. Cool slightly.
● **Meanwhile, combine** brown sugar, five-spice powder, salt, paprika, celery seed, and pepper. When ribs are cool enough to handle, rub spice mixture over ribs.
● **In a covered grill arrange** preheated coals around a drip pan. Test for *slow* heat above the pan (see tip, *page 87*). Pour 1 inch of water into the drip pan. Place drained wood chips on top of coals. Place ribs on grill rack over the drip pan but not over the coals. Lower grill hood. Grill for 30 minutes.
● **Meanwhile, prepare** desired glaze. Brush glaze on ribs after the 30 minutes of grilling time. Grill for 15 to 20 minutes more or till ribs are tender, brushing with glaze occasionally. Makes 4 servings.

Nutrition information per serving with Molasses Glaze: 389 cal., 37 g pro., 18 g fat, 101 mg chol., 942 mg sodium, 795 mg potassium, 1 g dietary fiber. U.S. RDA: 13% vit. C, 85% thiamine, 36% riboflavin, 57% niacin, 14% iron.

MOLASSES GLAZE FOR RIBS

- ½ cup catsup
- 2 tablespoons light molasses
- 1 tablespoon lemon juice
- 1 tablespoon soy sauce

Several dashes bottled hot pepper sauce

● **In a small bowl stir together** catsup, molasses, lemon juice, soy sauce, and hot pepper sauce. Brush on ribs during the last 15 to 20 minutes of grilling. Makes about ¾ cup.

TERIYAKI GLAZE FOR RIBS

- ¼ cup unsweetened pineapple juice
- ¼ cup dry sherry
- ¼ cup soy sauce
- 2 tablespoons brown sugar
- 1 tablespoon cornstarch
- 2 teaspoons grated gingerroot *or* ½ teaspoon ground ginger
- 1 clove garlic, minced

● **In a small saucepan combine** pineapple juice, sherry, soy sauce, brown sugar, cornstarch, gingerroot, and garlic. Cook and stir over medium heat till mixture is thickened and bubbly. Cook and stir for 2 minutes more. Brush on ribs during last 15 minutes of grilling. Makes about ¾ cup.

GRILLED SUMMER VEGETABLES

Remember when a grilled vegetable meant a foil-wrapped potato nestled in the coals? This summer, try grilling most any vegetable right on the grill rack. Watch the grilling closely; a little charring on the vegetable is tasty, but don't overdo it—

Asparagus spears
Small carrots
Eggplant
Fennel
Sweet peppers
Leeks
New potatoes
Baby zucchini *or* **regular zucchini**
Scallopini squash
Olive oil, melted margarine, *or* **melted**
 butter

● **Before grilling,** rinse, trim, cut up, and precook vegetables as directed in the chart (*right*). To precook any one vegetable, in a saucepan bring a small amount of water to boiling; add desired vegetable and simmer, covered, for the time specified in chart. Drain well.

● **To grill,** generously brush vegetables with olive oil, margarine, or butter before grilling to prevent sticking to grill rack. (Lay vegetables perpendicular to bars on grill rack so vegetables don't fall into coals.) Cook vegetables on the grill rack directly over *medium-hot* coals (see tip, *page 87*) till tender and slightly charred, following the timings in chart and turning occasionally.

Nutrition information per serving (1 new potato, 1 baby carrot, 5 asparagus spears brushed with 1 tablespoon olive oil): 195 cal., 3 g pro., 14 g fat, 0 mg chol., 14 mg sodium, 487 mg potassium, 3 g dietary fiber. U.S. RDA: 91% vit. A, 46% vit. C, 14% thiamine, 13% niacin.

TIMINGS FOR GRILLED VEGETABLES

Vegetable	Preparation	Precooking time	Grilling time
Asparagus	Snap off and discard tough bases of stems. Precook, then tie asparagus in bundles with strips of cooked green onion tops.	3 to 4 minutes	3 to 5 minutes
Fresh baby carrots	Cut off carrot tops. Wash and peel.	3 to 5 minutes	3 to 5 minutes
Eggplant	Cut off top and blossom ends. Cut eggplant crosswise into 1-inch-thick slices.	Do not precook.	8 minutes
Fennel	Snip off feathery leaves. Cut off stems.	Precook whole bulbs for 10 minutes. Cut bulbs into 6 to 8 wedges.	8 minutes
Sweet peppers	Remove stem. Quarter peppers. Remove seeds and membrane. Cut peppers into 1-inch-wide strips.	Do not precook.	8 to 10 minutes
Leeks	Cut off green tops. Trim bulb roots and remove 1 or 2 layers of white skin.	10 minutes or till tender. Halve lengthwise.	5 minutes
New potatoes	Halve potatoes.	10 minutes or till almost tender.	10 to 12 minutes
Zucchini	Wash; cut off ends. Halve or quarter lengthwise into long strips.	Do not precook.	5 to 6 minutes
Scallopini squash	Rinse and trim ends.	Precook whole for 3 minutes.	20 minutes

FRESH GARDEN CHICKEN

So few ingredients, such a great taste!

  1   2½- to 3-pound broiler-fryer
      chicken, quartered *or* cut up
  1   cup bottled salsa
  2   tablespoons lime juice
  ½   cup finely chopped cucumber
  ¼   cup chopped green pepper
  1   tablespoon snipped fresh
      cilantro

● **Rinse chicken.** Pat dry with paper towels. Sprinkle chicken lightly with *salt* and *pepper.*

● **Grill chicken,** bone side up, on an uncovered grill directly over *medium* coals for 20 minutes (see tip, *right*).

● **Meanwhile, combine** salsa and lime juice. Turn chicken and grill for 15 to 25 minutes more or till tender and no longer pink, brushing often with about ½ cup of the salsa mixture during the last 10 to 15 minutes.

● **For vegetable sauce,** in a small saucepan combine remaining salsa mixture, cucumber, green pepper, and cilantro. Bring just to boiling. Remove from heat. Serve vegetable sauce with chicken. Makes 4 servings.

Fresh Garden Turkey: Prepare Fresh Garden Chicken as directed *except* use six 4- to 6-ounce *turkey breast tenderloin steaks* instead of chicken. Grill turkey over *medium* coals for 12 to 15 minutes, turning once. Brush on salsa mixture during the last 5 minutes of grilling.

Fresh Garden Hens: Prepare Fresh Garden Chicken as directed *except* use three 1- to 1½-pound *Cornish game hens,* halved lengthwise, instead of the chicken. Grill halved hens over *medium-hot* coals for 45 to 50 minutes, turning once (see tip, *right*). Brush on salsa mixture during the last 10 to 15 minutes of grilling.

Nutrition information per serving Fresh Garden Chicken: 294 cal., 31 g pro., 15 g fat, 99 mg chol., 510 mg sodium, 425 mg potassium, 0 g dietary fiber. U.S. RDA: 19% vit. C, 16% riboflavin, 72% niacin, 10% iron.

GREEK KABOBS WITH BULGUR PILAF

Kabobs are the original mix-and-match recipe. Vary your sticks-of-good-eating by changing the vegetables. Some denser vegetables such as carrots need a minute or two of precooking before grilling—

  ⅓   cup olive oil *or* cooking oil
  ⅓   cup lemon juice
  ⅓   cup water
  ¾   teaspoon dried oregano,
      crushed
  ½   teaspoon salt
  ¼   teaspoon pepper
  1   clove garlic, minced
  1   pound lean boneless leg of lamb
      or beef sirloin steak, cut into
      1-inch pieces
  4   small purple *or* white boiling
      onions
  1   small yellow summer squash, cut
      into ½-inch slices
  1   cup broccoli flowerets
  ½   cup fresh pea pods
  ½   medium sweet red *or* green
      pepper, cut into 1-inch squares
  ¾   cup bulgur wheat
  ½   cup sliced green onion
  1   medium tomato, chopped
  ¼   cup chopped walnuts

● **In a screw-top jar shake** together oil, lemon juice, water, oregano, salt, pepper, and garlic. Place lamb or beef in a plastic bag and set in a shallow dish. Pour marinade over meat; close bag. Chill 6 hours or overnight, turning once. Drain meat; reserve marinade.

● **Before grilling,** in a small saucepan cook onions, covered, in a small amount of boiling water for 2 minutes. Add squash slices and broccoli; continue cooking 2 minutes more. Drain.

● **Alternately thread** meat cubes, onions, squash, broccoli, pea pods, and sweet pepper pieces onto four 12-inch skewers. Reserve ¼ *cup* marinade. Add water to remaining marinade to equal 1½ cups. Transfer to a 1½-quart saucepan; bring to boiling. Add bulgur and green onion. Simmer, covered, for 5 minutes. Remove from heat.

● **Meanwhile,** tear off a 36x18-inch piece of heavy-duty foil. Fold in half to make an 18-inch square. Fold up sides, using fist to form pouch. Place bulgur mixture in pouch. Fold edges of foil to seal pouch securely, leaving space for steam to expand.

● **Brush kabobs** with reserved marinade. Grill both kabobs and bulgar mixture in foil pouch on an uncovered grill over *hot* coals (see tip, *below*) for 8 to 12 minutes or till meat is of desired doneness, brushing kabobs with the ¼ cup reserved marinade and turning both kabobs and foil pouch frequently.

● **Open foil** and stir in tomato and walnuts; toss to mix. Serve bulgur mixture with kabobs. Makes 4 servings.

Nutrition information per serving: 521 cal., 29 g pro., 30 g fat, 67 mg chol., 333 mg sodium, 767 mg potassium, 11 g dietary fiber. U.S. RDA: 33% vit. A, 172% vit. C, 33% thiamine, 35% riboflavin, 54% niacin, 31% iron.

Briquette Basics

Before you grill, light the coals and let burn about 20 minutes or till glowing. Then, spread the coals out for direct grilling or arrange around a drip pan for indirect grilling. Hold your hand, palm side down, above the coals at the height your food will be cooked. Then start counting the seconds, "one thousand one, one thousand two. . . ." If you need to withdraw your hand after two seconds, the coals are *hot;* after three seconds, they're *medium-hot;* after four seconds, *medium;* after five seconds, *medium-slow;* after six seconds, *slow.*

For indirect grilling: Start with hotter coals than needed for cooking, then arrange them around a drip pan. *Hot* coals provide *medium-hot* heat over the drip pan; *medium-hot* coals provide *medium* heat; *medium* coals provide *medium-slow* heat; and so on.

HONEY-ORANGE PORK CHOPS

Acini de pepe, used for the chop stuffing, is a very tiny, round pasta found in the pasta section of your supermarket. It's also called little peppercorns—

- 2 medium oranges
- 2 tablespoons honey
- 1 tablespoon Dijon-style mustard
- 2 tablespoons orange marmalade
- 2 tablespoons vinegar
- ¾ cup chicken broth
- ½ cup acini de pepe
- 4 green onions, thinly sliced
- ¼ teaspoon ground ginger
- ½ cup finely chopped celery
- 4 pork loin rib chops, cut 1¼ inches thick

● **Peel and section the oranges** over a bowl, reserving any juices; coarsely chop the orange sections. For glaze, in a small saucepan blend honey and Dijon-style mustard. Stir in orange marmalade and vinegar. Heat and stir mixture till the marmalade melts. Remove from heat; set saucepan aside.

● **For stuffing, in a saucepan** bring chicken broth to boiling; add acini de pepe, green onion, and ground ginger. Reduce heat; simmer, uncovered, about 5 minutes or till acini de pepe is tender. Remove from heat. Fold in orange sections, *2 tablespoons* reserved juice, *2 tablespoons* of the glaze, and celery.

● **Cut a pocket in each pork chop** by cutting from the fat side almost to the bone. Spoon 2 to 3 tablespoons of the stuffing into each chop. Fasten the pockets with wooden toothpicks. Spoon remaining stuffing onto a large sheet of double thickness foil and fold foil up into a pouch. Set pouch aside.

● **In a covered grill arrange** preheated coals around a drip pan. Test for *medium* heat above the pan (see tip, *page 87*). Place stuffed pork chops on the grill rack over the drip pan but not over the coals. Lower the grill hood and grill the chops for 15 minutes. Turn chops and brush with some of the glaze.

● **Place the foil pouch** of stuffing on grill next to chops. Cover and grill for 15 to 20 minutes more or till the chops reach desired doneness. Brush both sides of chops with the remaining glaze before serving. Serve chops with extra stuffing. Makes 4 servings.

Hot and steaming corn on the cob— a great go-along for Honey-Orange Pork Chops.

Honey-Apricot Pork Chops: Prepare Honey-Orange Pork Chops as directed *except* prepare the stuffing using ⅓ cup snipped *dried apricots* instead of the fresh oranges. Increase the chicken broth to *1 cup* to cook acini de pepe. For glaze, use *apricot preserves* in place of the orange marmalade. Stuff and grill pork chops as directed.

Nutrition information per serving Honey-Orange Pork Chops: *548 cal., 51 g pro., 23 g fat, 172 mg chol., 388 mg sodium, 861 mg potassium, and 2 g dietary fiber. U.S. RDA: 65% vit. C, 115% thiamine, 50% riboflavin, 86% niacin, 16% iron.*

STUFFED SIRLOIN WITH MIXED MUSHROOM SAUTÉ

The classic grilled steak with mushroom sauce gets even better with this delicious recipe. The exotic mushrooms taste rich and earthy—

Spinach Stuffing *or* Onion Stuffing (see recipes, *right*)
- 1 2-pound boneless beef top sirloin steak, cut 1½ inches thick
- 1½ cups sliced mixed fresh mushrooms (such as shiitake, oyster, and brown mushrooms)
- 1 tablespoon margarine *or* butter
- ¾ cup beef broth
- 2 teaspoons cornstarch
- 2 teaspoons Worcestershire sauce
- 2 tablespoons dry red wine
- 1 tablespoon snipped parsley

● **Prepare desired stuffing** for steak. To make a pocket in steak, use a sharp paring knife and make a short horizontal slit in one side of steak. Insert knife into slit, drawing from side to side to form a larger pocket in steak. Spoon stuffing into pocket. Close the pocket with wooden picks inserted diagonally.

● **For mushroom sauce,** in same skillet cook mushrooms in margarine or butter till tender. Combine beef broth, cornstarch, and Worcestershire sauce; carefully add to skillet. Cook and stir till thickened and bubbly; cook and stir 2 minutes more. Add wine and parsley. Keep warm while grilling steak.

● **Grill steak** directly over *medium-hot* coals (see tip, *page 87*) to desired doneness, turning once. (Allow 14 to 18 minutes for rare, 18 to 22 minutes for medium, or 24 to 28 minutes for well done.) Serve with mushroom sauce. Makes 6 to 8 servings.

Nutrition information per serving: *248 cal., 30 g pro., 11 g fat, 76 mg chol., 229 mg sodium, 551 mg potassium, 1 g dietary fiber. U.S. RDA: 31% vit. A, 12% thiamine, 24% riboflavin, 45% niacin, 18% iron.*

SPINACH STUFFING FOR STEAK

The horseradish adds just a little zip—

- ½ of a 10-ounce package frozen chopped spinach, thawed and well drained
- 1 tablespoon prepared horseradish
- ¼ teaspoon pepper

● **In a mixing bowl** stir together the spinach, horseradish, and pepper.

ONION STUFFING FOR STEAK

Double the recipe to serve extra cooked onions over the steak—

- 1 small onion, halved, sliced, and separated into rings
- 1 clove garlic, minced
- 1 tablespoon margarine *or* butter
- ¼ teaspoon lemon-pepper seasoning

● **In a large skillet cook** onion and garlic in margarine or butter till onion is tender. Stir in lemon-pepper seasoning.

COOK QUICK, EAT LEAN

Two Healthful Microwave Meals

ORIENTAL BEEF

Turn your microwave oven into a wok and stir up a delicious meal without adding extra fat —

- **⅔ cup couscous** *or* **1 cup quick-cooking rice**
- **½ cup reduced-calorie apricot preserves**
- **1 tablespoon sodium-reduced soy sauce**
- **½ teaspoon grated gingerroot**
- **⅛ teaspoon crushed red pepper**
- **¾ pound beef flank steak**
- **1 cup sliced fresh mushrooms**
- **1 medium green pepper, cut into strips (1 cup)**
- **1 medium sweet red pepper, cut into strips (1 cup)**
- **2 green onions, bias-sliced into 1-inch pieces**
- **2 tablespoons red wine vinegar**
- **2 teaspoons cornstarch**

Cook couscous or rice according to package directions on the range top, *except* omit margarine or butter and salt.

For sauce, stir together preserves, soy sauce, gingerroot, and crushed red pepper; set aside. Thinly slice steak on the bias into bite-size strips.

Place beef strips in a 1½-quart casserole. Cover and micro-cook on 100% power (high) for 5 or 6 minutes (low-wattage ovens: 8 to 9 minutes) or till meat is tender, stirring after 3 minutes. Remove meat and discard juices.

In the casserole place mushrooms, green and red pepper strips, and green onions. Pour sauce mixture over the vegetables. Toss gently till mixed. Cover and micro-cook on high for 4 to 5 minutes (low-wattage ovens: 7 to 8 minutes) or till pepper strips are crisp-tender, stirring after every minute.

Stir together vinegar and cornstarch, then add mixture to casserole. Stir in meat. Micro-cook, uncovered, on high for 3 to 4 minutes (low-wattage ovens: 5 to 6 minutes) or till mixture is thickened and bubbly, stirring after every minute. Serve with cooked couscous or rice. Makes 4 servings.

Nutrition information per serving: 366 cal. (25% from fat), 19 g pro., 49 g carbo., 10 g fat (saturated fat 4 g), 45 mg chol., 186 mg sodium, 488 mg potassium, and 2 g dietary fiber. U.S. RDA: 15% vit. A, 136% vit. C, 24% thiamine, 20% riboflavin, 38% niacin, 21% iron.

LIME-COD KABOBS

For extra color, thread both zucchini and yellow summer squash slices on the skewers—

- **¾ pound fresh** *or* **frozen cod steaks** *or* **halibut steaks, cut 1 inch thick**
- **¼ cup dry white wine**
- **¼ cup lime juice**
- **1 tablespoon olive oil**
- **1 small clove garlic, minced**
- **½ teaspoon dried basil, crushed**
- **¼ teaspoon dried oregano, crushed**
- **⅛ teaspoon salt**
- **⅛ teaspoon pepper**
- **1 medium zucchini, cut into ½-inch slices**

Thaw fish, if frozen. If necessary, remove skin. Cut fish into 1-inch cubes. For marinade, in a bowl mix wine, lime juice, oil, garlic, basil, oregano, salt, and pepper. Add fish; stir till coated. Cover

Oriental Beef, a complete meal, comes in at 366 calories per serving. The kabobs total even fewer calories—just 118.

and marinate at room temperature for 30 minutes, stirring gently twice.

Meanwhile, in a 1-quart casserole place squash and 1 tablespoon *water*. Cover and micro-cook on 100% power (high) for 2 minutes. Drain and let squash stand till cool enough to handle.

Drain fish, reserving marinade. On four 9-inch-long wooden skewers alternately thread fish cubes and squash. Place kabobs in a 12x7½x2-inch microwave-safe baking dish. Pour the reserved marinade over kabobs. Cover with vented microwave-safe plastic wrap. Micro-cook kabobs on high for 3 to 4 minutes or till fish just flakes with a fork, rearranging after 2 minutes by moving outside kabobs to center and turning kabobs over. Makes 4 servings.

Note: Recipe not recommended for low-wattage ovens; dish is too large.

Nutrition information per serving: *118 cal. (33% from fat), 15 g pro., 3 g carbo., 4 g fat (saturated fat 1 g), 36 mg chol., 119 mg sodium, 313 mg potassium, 1 g dietary fiber. U.S. RDA: 16% vit. C.*

JULY

BY JULIA MALLOY

Summer Harvest

RECIPES FRESH FROM THE GARDEN

PHOTOS: PETER KRUMHARDT

Dig in! It's time to take advantage of fresh produce from your garden, favorite supermarket, or a farmer's market. If you don't have the special varieties listed at the beginning of each recipe, try our recipes with market produce.

Serve *Best-of-the-Garden Platter* with *Creamy Salsa Dip* (in purple pepper) or *Lemon-Dill Dip* (in Sundrop squash).

Summer Harvest

Savor luscious summertime dishes using our fresh garden vegetables listed below.

CARROTS

Sweet ball-shape *Planet carrots* have a red-orange hue. Mini *Caramba carrots* mature at 3 inches.

LEEKS

When harvested young, tiny, tender *Varna leeks* can substitute for chives. Slice mature leeks for soups and sauces.

TOMATOES

Chello Yellow and *Sweet 100 Plus cherry tomatoes* deliver a zesty flavor. Medium-size meaty *Roma plum tomatoes* make great paste or sauce. Slice up larger, deep-red *Dona tomatoes* for salads.

Baby Carrots with Pineapple Glaze offers a touch of ginger.

Top this *Three-Tomato Tart* with large, juicy tomato slices and jewellike yellow and red cherry tomatoes.

Summer Harvest

EGGPLANT

Little Finger eggplants grow between 3 and 7 inches long. You can stew, stir-fry, pickle, or bake these miniature vegetables.

BEANS

Your hill of beans may yield green, spotted, striped, and even purple beans. *Royal Burgundy Purple Pods* turn green when they're cooked. Purple spots dot green *Selma Zebrina beans. Dragon Tongue beans* sport faint bronze stripes and turn pale yellow when cooked. Good ol' green means *Derby* or *Vernanden Haricots Verts beans.* Try these colorful varieties in any of your recipes that call for green beans.

Serve *Caponata,* an Italian appetizer, at room temperature with pita wedges and French bread.

Tarragon Bean Salad, with its vinaigrette dressing, totes along perfectly to a cookout.

Summer Harvest

PEPPERS

No longer just green, peppers now come in a rainbow of colors. *Lorelei peppers* taste similar to green bell peppers, only they're purple. *Quadrato D'Oro peppers* gleam gold with thick walls and sweet flesh. *Codice* wear a bright red skin. Another red pepper is *Super Cayenne,* a small but mighty hot pepper that makes a striking garnish.

SQUASH

Eat tender summer squash raw or cooked, as you would zucchini. Scalloped yellow *Sunburst squash* will yield a buttery fruit. Egg-shaped yellow *Sundrop squash* steams and microwaves beautifully.

Garden Vegetable Pasta Toss, made with fusilli pasta, combines succulent squash, leeks, and carrots.

Make *Green Bean Bundles in Sweet Pepper Sauce* with two different pepper colors: red and yellow.

SUNSET SALAD

Fresh garden choice: Quadrato D'Oro peppers; Salad Bowl, Buttercrunch, or Red Leprechaun lettuce; Roma or Dona tomatoes; Sweet 100 Plus and Chello Yellow cherry tomatoes; Varna leeks.

  ½ **teaspoon finely shredded orange peel**
  3 **tablespoons orange juice**
  2 **teaspoons snipped fresh chives**
  ½ **teaspoon honey**
  ⅛ **teaspoon salt**
  ⅛ **teaspoon pepper**
  2 **sweet yellow peppers, sliced into rings**
Lettuce leaves
  6 **to 9 plum tomatoes** *or* **2 to 3 medium tomatoes, sliced**
  1 **medium orange, sliced**
  1 **cup red cherry tomatoes, halved**
  ½ **cup yellow** *or* **red cherry tomatoes, halved (optional)**
Fresh young leeks *or* **chives (optional)**
Freshly ground pepper (optional)

● **For dressing,** in a small bowl stir together the orange peel, orange juice, the 2 teaspoons chives, honey, salt, and the ⅛ teaspoon pepper. Set aside.

● **In a skillet cook** yellow pepper rings, covered, in a small amount of boiling water for 1 to 2 minutes or till crisp-tender; drain and cool. Place pepper rings in a plastic bag set in a bowl. Add dressing; seal bag. Turn to coat. Chill, turning the bag occasionally.

● **To serve, line a large platter** with lettuce leaves. Arrange tomato and orange slices around the edge. Drain pepper rings, reserving dressing. Arrange the pepper rings in an overlapping circle inside tomatoes. Fill center with red cherry tomatoes. Drizzle with reserved dressing. If desired, garnish with yel-

low or red cherry tomatoes and a knot of leeks or chives and sprinkle with pepper. Makes 4 to 6 servings.

    Nutrition information per serving: *55 cal., 2 g pro., 13 g carbo., 0 g fat, 0 mg chol., 77 mg sodium, 384 mg potassium, and 3 g dietary fiber. U.S. RDA: 14% vit. A, 124% vit. C, 13% thiamine.*

A knot of young garden-fresh leeks crowns Sunset Salad.

Scalloped Sunburst squash adds a novel shape and buttery flavor to Green and Gold Stir-Fry.

GREEN AND GOLD STIR-FRY

Fresh garden choice: Varna leeks; Green Dwarf broccoli; Sunburst or Sundrop squash.

Nonstick spray coating
  1 **cup thinly sliced leeks**
  1 **tablespoon snipped fresh oregano** *or* **¼ teaspoon dried oregano, crushed**
  1 **clove garlic, minced**
  1 **to 2 tablespoons olive oil** *or* **cooking oil**
  ½ **teaspoon sesame oil**
  2 **cups broccoli flowerets**
  2 **cups yellow summer squash, cut into small wedges**
Lemon wedges
Fresh oregano (optional)

● **Spray a wok** or large skillet with nonstick coating. Preheat over medium heat. Add the leeks, oregano, and garlic. Stir-fry for 2 to 3 minutes or till leeks are tender. Remove mixture from the wok or skillet; set aside.

● **Add 1 tablespoon olive oil** or cooking oil and the sesame oil to the wok or skillet. Add the broccoli and the squash. Stir-fry for 3 to 4 minutes or till vegetables are crisp-tender, adding remaining oil if necessary. Return the leek mixture to the wok. Cook and stir till heated through. Transfer vegetable mixture to a large serving platter. Serve with lemon wedges. If desired, garnish with additional oregano. Makes 4 side-dish servings.

    Nutrition information per serving: *79 cal., 2 g pro., 9 g carbo., 5 g fat, 0 mg chol., 19 mg sodium, 337 mg potassium, and 3 g dietary fiber. U.S. RDA: 12% vit. A, 86% vit. C.*

TURKEY-STUFFED PEPPERS

Fresh garden choice: Quadrato D'Oro or Lorelei peppers; Varna leeks; Dona tomatoes.

> 2 large sweet yellow, red, *and/or* green peppers
> 12 ounces ground raw turkey
> 1 medium leek, thinly sliced (⅓ cup)
> 1 clove garlic, minced
> 1½ cups chopped tomatoes
> 1 cup sliced fresh mushrooms
> ¾ cup quick-cooking rice
> ¼ cup water
> 1 tablespoon snipped fresh parsley
> 1 tablespoon snipped fresh basil *or* ¾ teaspoon dried basil, crushed
> 1 teaspoon instant chicken bouillon granules
> Few dashes bottled hot pepper sauce
> 1 slice (1 ounce) Colby cheese, cut into 4 triangles

Keep cool in the kitchen; cook Turkey-Stuffed Peppers in your microwave oven.

● **Halve peppers lengthwise;** remove seeds and membrane. Arrange peppers, cut side down, in an 8x8x2-inch or 12x7x1½-inch microwave-safe baking dish. Cover with vented clear plastic wrap. Cook on 100% power (high) for 4 to 6 minutes (low-wattage oven: 7 to 9 minutes) or till crisp-tender, giving dish a half-turn once. Drain; set aside.
● **For filling,** in a 2-quart microwave-safe casserole crumble turkey. Add the leek and garlic. Cook, covered, on high for 5 to 6 minutes (low-wattage oven: 6 to 8 minutes) or till no pink remains and leek is tender, stirring once. Drain and return to casserole.
● **Add the tomatoes, mushrooms,** rice, water, parsley, basil, bouillon granules, and hot pepper sauce. Cook, covered, on high for 4 to 6 minutes (low-wattage oven: 6 to 8 minutes) or till rice is tender, stirring the vegetable mixture every 2 minutes.
● **Invert cooked pepper halves** in dish; fill with turkey-rice mixture. Cook, uncovered, on high for 2 to 3 minutes or till filling is heated through. Top each pepper with a cheese triangle. Serve immediately. Serves 4.

Nutrition information per serving: 282 cal., 20 g pro., 24 g carbo., 12 g fat, 51 mg chol., 332 mg sodium, 514 mg potassium, and 3 g dietary fiber. U.S. RDA: 42% vit. A, 171% vit. C, 24% thiamine, 23% riboflavin, 41% niacin, 11% calcium, 17% iron.

FREEZER TOMATO SAUCE

Spoon this chunky sauce over pasta, pizza, fish, or chicken—
Fresh garden choice: Roma tomatoes; Super Cayenne peppers.

> 6 pounds plum tomatoes
> 1½ cups chopped onion
> ½ cup chopped celery
> 3 large cloves garlic, minced
> 2 tablespoons olive oil *or* cooking oil
> 2 teaspoons sugar
> 1 to 2 teaspoons salt
> ½ teaspoon pepper
> 1 fresh red cayenne chili pepper, seeded and finely chopped (½ teaspoon) *or* ⅛ teaspoon ground red pepper (optional)
> 2 tablespoons snipped fresh oregano *or* 2 teaspoons dried oregano, crushed
> 1 to 2 tablespoons snipped fresh thyme *or* 1 to 2 teaspoons dried thyme, crushed

● **In a large kettle** bring 4 inches of *water* to boiling. Immerse tomatoes in boiling water for 1 minute. Drain in a colander; peel, seed, and chop tomatoes. (You should have 10 cups.)
● **In the same kettle cook** the onion, celery, and garlic in hot oil about 5 minutes or till tender. Add the tomatoes, the sugar, salt, pepper, and, if desired, red pepper. Bring to boiling; reduce heat. Simmer, uncovered, for 45 minutes, stirring occasionally. Add the oregano and the thyme. Simmer, uncovered, for 15 minutes more. Cool slightly.
● **In a food processor bowl** process sauce, one-fourth at a time, to desired texture. (Or, put sauce through a food mill.) Place sauce in a bowl set in ice water to cool quickly. Fill freezer containers; seal tightly, label, and freeze.
● **To thaw one portion,** remove from freezer container and place in a saucepan. Cook over medium heat till hot, stirring occasionally. Or, in a 1-quart microwave-safe casserole cook on 100% power (high) for 12 to 14 minutes, stirring occasionally. Serve hot tomato sauce over pasta. Makes 3 to 4 pints.

Nutrition information per ½ cup tomato sauce: 81 cal., 2 g pro., 14 g carbo., 3 g fat, 0 mg chol., 203 mg sodium, 556 mg potassium, and 4 g dietary fiber. U.S. RDA: 18% vit. A, 70% vit. C, 15% thiamine, 10% riboflavin, 11% niacin.

Freezer Tomato Sauce lets you savor Roma plum tomatoes long after the first frost.

BEST-OF-THE-GARDEN PLATTER

Serve the dips in hollowed peppers, squash, or tomatoes. Peppers pictured on page 91—

Fresh garden choice: Caramba carrots; Sunburst squash; Dragon Tongue, Vernandon Haricots Verts, Royal Burgundy Purple Pods, or Derby beans; Quadrato D'Oro, Lorelei, or Codice peppers; Chello Yellow or Sweet 100 Plus cherry tomatoes; County Fair cucumbers; Paros Swiss chard.

```
 8 to 12 baby carrots
 6 small yellow summer squash, cut
   into 1-inch pieces
16 to 24 snap beans, trimmed
 3 or 4 sweet yellow, purple, red
   and/or green peppers
 1 cup yellow and/or red cherry
   tomatoes
 1 medium cucumber
Fresh herbs or Swiss chard (optional)
Edible flowers (optional)
Creamy Salsa Dip
Chutney Dip
Lemon-Dill Dip
```

● **To trim carrots,** leave 1 to 2 inches of stem, if you like; do not peel. In a saucepan combine carrots, squash, beans, and a small amount of water. Bring to boiling; reduce heat. Simmer, covered, for 5 minutes; drain and cool. Cover and chill till serving time.

● **At serving time,** remove tops and seeds from sweet peppers; cut into rings or strips. Halve any large cherry tomatoes, and cut cucumber into strips or slices. On a platter arrange cooked vegetables, peppers, tomatoes, and cucumber. If desired, garnish with fresh herbs (dill and purple basil) and/or edible flowers (red and yellow nasturtiums). Serve with assorted dips. Makes 8 to 12 appetizer servings.

Creamy Salsa Dip: Stir together ½ cup *plain yogurt,* ½ cup *red salsa,* and ⅓ cup *reduced-calorie mayonnaise* or *salad dressing.* Cover and chill till serving time. Makes about 1¼ cups.

Chutney Dip: Stir together one 8-ounce carton *plain yogurt;* 1 *green onion,* chopped; 3 tablespoons *chutney,* snipped, and 1 teaspoon *curry powder.* Cover and chill till serving time. Makes about 1 cup.

Lemon-Dill Dip: Stir together ½ cup *low-fat dairy sour cream;* 3 ounces *cream cheese* or *Neufchâtel cheese,* softened; 1 tablespoon snipped *fresh dill* or 1 teaspoon *dried dillweed;* 1 teaspoon *lemon juice;* 2 cloves *garlic,* minced; ¼ teaspoon *onion powder;* and ⅛ teaspoon *salt.* Cover and chill till serving time. Stir in enough *milk* (1 to 2 tablespoons) to make of dipping consistency. Makes about ¾ cup.

Nutrition information per serving with 2 tablespoons Creamy Salsa Dip: 98 cal., 3 g pro., 14 g carbo., 4 g fat, 4 mg chol., 183 mg sodium, 544 mg potassium, and 4 g dietary fiber. U.S. RDA: 123% vit. A, 119% vit. C, 14% thiamine, and 11% riboflavin.

First there was carrot cake, now—Oatmeal-Carrot Cookies

OATMEAL-CARROT COOKIES

A soft and spicy cookie, with or without raisins—

Fresh garden choice: Caramba or Planet carrots.

```
¾ cup margarine or butter
1¾ cups all-purpose flour
¾ cup packed brown sugar
½ cup sugar
 1 egg
 1 teaspoon baking powder
½ teaspoon ground cinnamon
¼ teaspoon baking soda
¼ teaspoon ground cloves
 1 teaspoon vanilla
 2 cups rolled oats
 1 cup finely shredded carrots
½ cup raisins (optional)
```

● **In a large mixing bowl beat** margarine or butter with an electric mixer on medium to high speed for 30 seconds or till softened. Add about *half* of the flour, the brown sugar, sugar, egg, baking powder, cinnamon, baking soda, cloves, and vanilla. Beat till combined, scraping the sides of the bowl occasionally. Beat or stir in the remaining flour. Stir in the oats, carrots, and, if desired, raisins.

● **Drop dough** by rounded teaspoons 2 inches apart onto an ungreased baking sheet. Bake in a 375° oven for 10 to 12 minutes or till edges are golden. Remove from baking sheet. Cool on a wire rack. Makes about 4 dozen.

Nutrition information per cookie: 79 cal., 1 g pro., 12 g carbo., 3 g fat, 4 mg chol., 48 mg sodium, and 1 g dietary fiber. U.S. RDA: 13% vit. A.

BABY CARROTS WITH PINEAPPLE GLAZE

Fresh garden choice: Planet or Caramba carrots; Varna leeks.

    3 cups baby carrots (1 pound)
    3 medium leeks, sliced ½ inch
       thick (1 cup)
    2 tablespoons water
    1 6-ounce can (⅔ cup) unsweet-
       ened pineapple juice
    2 teaspoons cornstarch
    ½ teaspoon grated gingerroot *or*
    ⅛ teaspoon ground ginger
    ⅛ teaspoon ground nutmeg
    ⅛ teaspoon salt (optional)
Plain yogurt (optional)

● **To trim the carrots,** leave 1 to 2 inches of stem, if you like; do not peel. In a 2-quart microwave-safe casserole combine the carrots, leeks, and water. Micro-cook, covered, on 100% power (high) for 9 to 11 minutes or till crisp-tender, stirring once. Drain; cover to keep warm.
● **For glaze,** in a 2-cup microwave-safe measure combine the pineapple juice, cornstarch, gingerroot, nutmeg, and, if desired, salt. Cook, uncovered, on high for 2½ to 3½ minutes or till thickened and bubbly, stirring every minute till slightly thickened, then after every 30 seconds.
● **Pour the glaze** over carrots; stir to coat. If desired, garnish each serving with a dollop of plain yogurt. Makes 4 side-dish servings.

Nutrition information per serving: *92 cal., 2 g pro., 22 g carbo., 0 g fat, 0 mg chol., 45 mg sodium, 473 mg potassium, and 4 g dietary fiber. U.S. RDA: 399% vit. A, 30% vit. C, 15% thiamin, 10% niacin.*

Pastry For Single-Crust Pie

Use this pastry in any of the recipes that call for a single pastry crust, such as Three-Tomato Tart (at right)—

In a mixing bowl stir together 1¼ cups *all-purpose flour* and ¼ teaspoon *salt.* Cut in ⅓ cup *shortening* or *lard* till pieces are the size of small peas. Sprinkle 1 tablespoon *cold water* over part of the mixture; gently toss with a fork. Push to side of bowl. Repeat, using 2 to 3 more tablespoons *cold water,* till all is moistened. Form dough into a ball. Use as directed in your recipe.

THREE-TOMATO TART

Bake the crust ahead for this care-free appetizer—
Fresh garden choice: Dona, Chello Yellow, and Sweet 100 Plus tomatoes.

Pastry for Single-Crust Pie (see recipe at left)
    3 tablespoons grated Parmesan
       cheese
    2 slightly beaten egg whites
    1 cup low-fat ricotta cheese
    2 cloves garlic, minced
    1 tablespoon snipped fresh lemon
       thyme *or* thyme, *or* 1 teaspoon
       dried thyme, crushed
    2 large tomatoes, sliced
    5 yellow *or* red cherry tomatoes,
       sliced
    2 red cherry tomatoes, sliced
    1 tablespoon olive oil *or* cooking
       oil
    2 teaspoons snipped fresh lemon
       thyme *or* thyme, *or* ½ teaspoon
       dried thyme, crushed

● **Prepare pastry dough.** On a lightly floured surface, use a floured rolling pin to roll pastry into a circle about 12 inches in diameter. Transfer to a 10-inch tart pan; ease pastry into pan. Trim pastry even with rim of pan. Do not prick pastry. Line pastry shell with a double thickness of heavy-duty foil.
● **Bake pastry in a 450° oven** for 5 minutes. Remove foil. Bake for 5 to 7 minutes more or till pastry is nearly done. Remove from oven. Reduce oven temperature to 325°. Sprinkle tart shell with the Parmesan cheese.
● **Meanwhile, in a mixing bowl** combine the egg whites, ricotta cheese, garlic, and the 1 tablespoon thyme. Spread mixture evenly over pastry. Overlap large tomato slices in a circle around the edge. Arrange the yellow cherry tomatoes in a circle within the first tomato ring. Fill the center with red cherry tomatoes.
● **Stir together olive or cooking oil** and the 2 teaspoons thyme. Brush tomatoes with oil mixture.
● **Bake tart in a 325° oven** for 25 to 30 minutes or till nearly set. Serve warm or at room temperature. Store any leftovers in refrigerator. Serves 10 to 12.

Nutrition information per serving: *182 cal., 6 g pro., 15 g carbo., 11 g fat, 9 mg chol., 127 mg sodium, 142 mg potassium, and 1 g dietary fiber. U.S. RDA: 11% vit. C, 15% thiamine, 15% riboflavin, 12% calcium.*

GARDEN VEGETABLE PASTA TOSS

Be sure to wash your hands after handling the fresh chili peppers to rinse away irritating oils—
Fresh garden choice: Vernandon Haricots Verts or Derby beans; Varna leeks; Sundrop squash; Super Cayenne peppers.

    4 ounces fusilli, fettuccine, *or*
       linguine, broken in half
    ⅓ cup dry white wine
Nonstick spray coating
    1½ cups carrots cut into 2-inch-long
       strips
    1½ cups snap beans diagonally cut
       into 2-inch lengths
    ½ cup sliced leeks (½ inch thick)
    1 tablespoon snipped fresh basil
       or ½ teaspoon dried basil,
       crushed
    1 tablespoon snipped fresh dill *or*
       ½ teaspoon dried dillweed
    1 clove garlic, minced
    1½ cups yellow summer squash cut
       into 2-inch-long strips
    1 fresh red cayenne chili pepper,
       seeded and finely chopped (½
       teaspoon), *or* ⅛ teaspoon
       ground red pepper
    ½ cup finely shredded asiago *or*
       Parmesan cheese
Fresh red cayenne chili peppers
       (optional)

● **Cook pasta** according to package directions. Meanwhile, combine the wine, ¼ teaspoon *salt,* and ground red pepper (if using); set aside. Spray a wok with nonstick coating. Preheat over medium heat. Add the carrots, beans, leeks, basil, dill, and garlic. Stir-fry for 3 minutes.
● **Add squash, fresh red pepper** (if using), and 2 tablespoons *water.* Cover and cook for 5 to 6 minutes more or till vegetables are crisp-tender. Drain pasta; add to vegetables. Drizzle with wine mixture. Toss gently. Transfer to a serving platter. Sprinkle with cheese. If desired, garnish with additional red peppers. Makes 6 side-dish servings.

Nutrition information per serving: *149 cal., 7 g pro., 24 g carbo., 3 g fat, 5 mg chol., 246 mg sodium, 256 mg potassium, and 3 g dietary fiber. U.S. RDA: 125% vit. A, 17% vit. C, 17% calcium.*

GREEN BEAN BUNDLES IN SWEET PEPPER SAUCE

Fresh garden choice: Varna leeks; Vernandon Haricots Verts or Derby beans; Codice and Quadrato D'Oro peppers.

- 3 medium leeks (12 ounces)
- 40 snap beans (about 12 ounces)
- 2 tablespoons olive oil *or* cooking oil
- ¾ cup dry white wine
- 2 tablespoons snipped fresh basil *or* oregano
- ½ teaspoon salt
- 4 large sweet red peppers, cored, seeded, and chopped (about 4 cups)
- 2 large sweet yellow peppers, cored, seeded, and chopped (about 2 cups)
- Fresh basil *or* oregano sprigs (optional)

● **Rinse leeks** thoroughly under running water. Trim root and leaves from leeks, carefully separating 1 leaf (about 2 inches wide) from remaining leaves. In a large skillet cook leaf, uncovered, in boiling water about 1 minute or till tender and bright green. Remove leaf; drain on paper towels. When cool, cut leaf lengthwise into ¼-inch-wide strips.
● **For bean bundles,** trim ends and strings from beans. Gather beans into bunches of 5. Carefully tie each bundle with a cooled leek leaf strip. If necessary, trim ends of leek strip. Place bean bundles in a steamer basket. Steam over boiling water for 15 to 20 minutes or till beans are tender. Season with salt and pepper.
● **Meanwhile, for sauce,** chop white part of leeks (should have about 1 cup). In the same large skillet cook chopped leek in *1 tablespoon* hot oil about 5 minutes or till tender. Add the white wine, basil or oregano, and salt. Reduce heat; cook about 3 minutes or till most of the liquid has evaporated; set aside.
● **In another skillet,** cook red pepper in *1 tablespoon* hot oil about 10 minutes or till tender. Remove red pepper, reserving oil in skillet. In the reserved oil cook yellow pepper about 6 minutes or till tender.
● **In a blender container** or food processor bowl combine red pepper and ⅔ cup of the wine mixture. Cover and blend or process till smooth; set aside. In a clean blender container or food processor bowl combine the yellow pepper and the remaining wine mixture; cover and blend or process till smooth. Serve sauce warm or at room temperature with bundles. If desired, garnish with additional basil. Makes 4 side-dish servings.

Nutrition information per serving: *96 cal., 2 g pro., 13 g carbo., 4 g fat, 0 mg chol., 145 mg sodium, 324 potassium, and 3 g dietary fiber.*

TARRAGON BEAN SALAD

Make this a few hours before serving to keep the beans at their brightest—
Fresh garden choice: Derby, Vernandon Haricot Verts, or Dragon Tongue beans; Dona tomatoes.

- 3 cups snap beans (green *and/or* yellow) bias-sliced into 1½-inch lengths
- 2 tablespoons vinegar
- 2 tablespoons salad oil
- 1 shallot, finely chopped
- 2 teaspoons snipped fresh tarragon *or* ¼ teaspoon dried tarragon, crushed
- 1 teaspoon sugar
- ½ teaspoon dry mustard
- ¼ teaspoon salt
- 1 15-ounce can garbanzo beans, drained
- 1 medium tomato, coarsely chopped

● **Place a steamer basket** in a saucepan; add water till it almost touches bottom of steamer basket. Add beans and steam for 18 to 22 minutes or till crisp-tender; drain.
● **Meanwhile, for dressing,** in a screwtop jar combine the vinegar, salad oil, shallot, tarragon, sugar, dry mustard, and salt. Cover and shake well to mix.
● **In a salad bowl combine** the cooked beans, garbanzo beans, and tomato. Add dressing; toss gently to coat. Cover and chill about 4 hours, stirring once. Serve with a slotted spoon. Makes 4 side-dish servings.

Nutrition information per serving: *215 cal., 8 g pro., 28 g carbo., 9 g fat, 0 mg chol., 146 mg sodium, 468 mg potassium, and 7 g dietary fiber. U.S. RDA: 10% vit. A, 34% vit. C, 17% thiamine, 12% riboflavin, 19% iron.*

CAPONATA

Fresh garden choice: Little Finger eggplant; Sundrop or Sunburst squash; Dona tomatoes.

- 1 medium onion, sliced and separated into rings
- ¼ cup sliced celery
- 1 tablespoon olive oil *or* salad oil
- ¾ pounds unpeeled eggplant, cut into ½-inch pieces
- ½ pound yellow summer squash, cut into ½-inch cubes
- 1 small tomato, peeled, seeded, and chopped
- 2 tablespoons halved pimiento-stuffed olives
- 2 tablespoons red wine vinegar
- 1 tablespoon capers, rinsed and drained
- 1 tablespoon raisins (optional)
- 1 teaspoon sugar
- 1 tablespoon pine nuts *or* slivered almonds (optional)
- Toasted pita triangles *and/or* French bread slices

● **In a large skillet cook** onion and celery in hot oil till tender. Add eggplant, squash, tomato, olives, vinegar, capers, raisins (if desired), and sugar. Stir mixture to combine. Simmer mixture, covered, for 8 to 10 minutes or till eggplant and squash are tender. Simmer, uncovered, for 5 to 10 minutes more or till most of the liquid has evaporated. Season to taste with *salt* and *pepper.* Cool slightly.
● **If desired, add nuts.** Cool and serve at room temperature. *Or,* cover and chill overnight. Let stand at room temperature before serving. To serve, spoon mixture onto pita triangles and/ or French bread slices. Makes about 3½ cups (8 to 10 appetizer servings).

Nutrition information per serving: *86 cal., 3 g pro., 15 g carbo., 2 g fat, 0 mg chol., 153 mg sodium, 229 mg potassium, and 3 g dietary fiber. U.S. RDA: 11% vit. C, 13% thiamine.*

FAST-TO-FIX FAMILY FAVORITES
DINNER IN MINUTES

BY
LISA HOLDERNESS

Pair this chilled yellow pepper soup with a crisp summer salad.

For a care-free and refreshing supper, just toss together a hearty salad and pull the made-ahead soup out of the refrigerator.

CHILLED SWEET PEPPER SOUP

This soup makes enough for two meals. Dish up two servings and chill the rest, up to four days, to serve another time—

- 1 **tablespoon margarine** *or* **butter**
- 2 **medium carrots, chopped**
- 1 **large onion, chopped**
- 1¼ **cups chicken broth**
- 1 **sweet yellow pepper, chopped**
- 1 **3-ounce package cream cheese, cubed and softened**
- ½ **teaspoon salt**

Dash ground red pepper
Dash ground nutmeg

- ½ **cup milk** *or* **light cream**

Dairy sour cream (optional)

●**In a saucepan melt** margarine or butter. Add carrots and onion; cook, stirring occasionally, about 10 minutes or till vegetables are tender.

●**Stir in chicken broth;** bring to boiling over medium-high heat. Stir in yellow pepper. Reduce heat; cover and simmer for 15 minutes or till pepper is tender. Remove from heat and cool slightly. Stir in cream cheese, salt, red pepper, and nutmeg.

●**Transfer *half* of the mixture** to a blender container or food processor bowl; cover and blend or process till smooth. Transfer to a large bowl. Repeat. Cover and chill at least 4 hours.

●**To serve, stir** in the ½ cup milk. Ladle *half* the mixture into *two* soup bowls. Stir additional *milk* or *cream* into sour cream to thin slightly; drizzle atop soup. Serve with a salad from the Choose-Your-Own-Salad chart. Cover and chill remaining soup for up to 4 days. Makes 4 side-dish servings.

Nutrition information per serving: 164 cal., 5 g pro., 12 g carbo., 12 g fat, 26 mg chol., 635 mg sodium, 380 mg potassium, and 2 g dietary fiber. U.S. RDA: 216% vit. A, 53% vit. C.

CHOOSE-YOUR-OWN SALAD

Pull dinner together in minutes, then relax over a light soup-and-salad meal.

Mix and match your way to a super summer salad! Pick one or more ingredients from each category. (Use the amounts given for two main-dish salads.)

●**DELI MEATS:** *4 ounces thinly sliced and cut into strips*
Pastrami, roast beef, ham, smoked turkey, chicken
●**GREENS:** *2 cups, torn, of any combination*
Endive, iceberg lettuce, Bibb or Boston lettuce, spinach, watercress leaves, radicchio, sorrel
●**FRESH VEGETABLES:** *¾ cup—try an assortment!*
Halved cherry tomatoes, sliced yellow summer squash, peeled and sliced jicama, sprouts, peas, quartered and cooked tiny new potatoes
●**SALAD TOPPERS:** *About 3 tablespoons total*
Crumbled feta cheese, raisins, sunflower nuts, sliced olives, toasted sesame seed, sliced almonds, granola

Fix-ahead tip: *For more flavor, marinate the meat strips in 3 tablespoons of bottled Italian salad dressing. Cover and chill till salad time.*

At mealtime: *Toss greens and fresh vegetables with meat mixture. Sprinkle with salad toppings and serve with Chilled Sweet Pepper Soup. Makes 2 main-dish servings.*

Note: *For a time-saver, rinse and clean greens ahead of time. Prepare any vegetables needing to be rinsed, cooked, or sliced ahead of time also. Store cleaned greens and vegetables in plastic bags or storage containers with a paper towel to absorb excess liquid.*

AUGUST

GREAT FOOD
FOR FAMILY REUNIONS

Grandpa reminisces. Cousins get reacquainted. And everyone settles on the lawn with a generous plate of food. That's the heart of a family reunion.

BY LISA HOLDERNESS

Photographed at John Gardiner's Rancho Valencia Resort, Rancho Santa Fe, California

GREAT FOOD

3

2

1

2

J ust like your kitchen at home, the food table is where your loved ones will congregate at your next family reunion. Sampling every dish and swapping recipes is part of the fun. From kid-pleasing bar cookies to home-style casseroles, choose from our 20 recipes created especially for family gatherings. Whether serving 10 or 30, these recipes can be adjusted to fit your gang's appetite, and many can be made days ahead.

1 & 2. CHICKEN PINWHEELS WITH MUSTARD SAUCE: For midday grazing, set out ham-stuffed chicken spirals, a zippy mustard sauce, and fixin's for sandwiches.

3. APPLE AND MELON TOSS: A patch of pastel melon balls tops this nutty apple-and-yogurt salad. Serving as many as 50? No problem with this easy recipe.

4. STRAWBERRY PINEAPPLE-ADE: Make this triple-fruit sipper at the reunion site. Bring the cans of juice concentrate along and mix them with water before serving.

5. GRILLED BASIL BURGERS: To turn out a better-than-basic burger, mix in fresh basil for more flavor. Remember the pickles, onions, lettuce, and condiments, too.

6. SUCCOTASH SLAW: Go beyond plain coleslaw with just five ingredients. Fix a smoky bacon and vegetable salad that will bring everyone back for more.

7. ASPARAGUS BAKE: Here's a down-home casserole that's a crowd pleaser. Pair either asparagus or broccoli with the pasta, creamy mustard sauce, and crunchy topper.

8. 4-WAY BARS: Just one dough makes four different bar cookies—all in the same baking pan, all delicious. This way, folks can pick their favorite combination.

PHOTOGRAPHS: JOAN VANDERSHUIT. FOOD STYLIST: MABLE HOFFMAN

Summer salads, regional flavors, luscious desserts— there's something for everyone at a reunion.

GREAT FOOD

9

9. **TWO-BEAN AND RICE SALAD:** Spice it up. Chili peppers, cilantro, and a tangy dressing boost this bean salad above the rest.

10. **CINNAMON FRUIT COMPOTE:** Gorgeous layers of fruit piled high and drizzled with cinnamon syrup make a refreshing dessert you'll feel good about serving.

11. **TAMALE PIE:** Calling all grandparents, cousins, and especially kids for a heaping helping of this Mexican casserole.

12. **OATMEAL CARAMEL BARS:** These gooey chocolate, caramel, and nut bars will be a big hit. Fortunately, one recipe makes a bunch.

13. **STRAWBERRY-CHOCOLATE ALMOND TORTE:** Now you see it, now you don't. Eight luscious layers won't last long on your reunion table.

14. **NUTTY NIBBLE MIX:** Peanuts! Get your peanuts, pumpkin seeds, Chinese noodles, and other crunchy savories. But nibblers beware: This spiced-up party mix can be addicting.

GREAT FOOD

A potluck is more fun outdoors in the sunshine, where you have plenty of room to stretch and relax.

15

16

17

18

19

20

15. REUNION BREAD: Just as generations come together for a family reunion, the three rings of this bread hook together to make one giant loaf. Each ring is stuffed with a different savory filling; choose from sautéed onion, pesto and nut, and cheese and mustard.

16. MINIATURE FRUIT TARTS: Tiny, yes, but each bite-size dessert tart is full of ripe fruit flavor. Bake, fill, and chill tarts the night before or early on the morning of your reunion.

17. GARDEN-FRESH COUSCOUS SALAD: Salads, and lots of them, make a picnic. This colorful, summery salad will go fast, so you may want to fix a double batch.

18. AVOCADO-PAPAYA SALSA: There's more to salsa than tomatoes and heat. Spoon chunky, homemade fruit salsa atop grilled chicken, fish, or pork chops for a sweet and tangy accompaniment.

19. APRICOT WINE COOLERS: Mix and freeze these party coolers till frozen. Then, during the festivities, stir a bottle of carbonated water into the frozen mixture till slushy and relax with a tall glassful in hand.

20. SALMON AND GOUDA PÂTÉ: When the adults want something extra special to nibble on, try a savory appetizer pâté. Tote it to the reunion in the pan and turn it onto a platter just before serving.

August

SUCCOTASH SLAW

- 2 10-ounce packages frozen succotash (lima beans and corn)
- 8 cups shredded cabbage with carrot
- 4 slices bacon, crisp-cooked, drained, and crumbled
- ½ cup sliced radishes
- 1½ cups coleslaw dressing

● **Cook succotash** according to package directions; drain well and cool.

● **In a 2½-quart covered container** or large salad bowl combine cooled succotash, shredded cabbage with carrot, bacon, and radishes; cover. Chill up to 6 hours. To transport, place cabbage mixture and dressing (in separate containers) in a cooler with ice.

● **To serve, toss** together vegetables and dressing. Makes 15 servings.

For 30 servings: Double all of the ingredients.

Nutrition information per serving: 168 cal., 3 g pro., 17 g carbo., 11 g fat, 17 mg chol., 373 mg sodium, 229 mg potassium, and 3 g dietary fiber. U.S. RDA: 29% vit. A, 33% vit. C.

STRAWBERRY PINEAPPLE-ADE

- 1 6-ounce can frozen lemonade concentrate, thawed
- 1 6-ounce can frozen pineapple juice concentrate, thawed
- 1 6-ounce can frozen strawberry-flavored daiquiri mix concentrate, thawed
- 5 cups ice cold water

Ice cubes *or* ice ring
- 1 cup fresh strawberries, hulled and sliced

● **In a large pitcher,** punch bowl, or vacuum bottle, stir together lemonade concentrate, pineapple concentrate, and daiquiri concentrate. Add cold water, stirring gently. Add ice. Float berry slices on top. Makes 15 servings.

For 30 servings: Double all of the ingredients.

Nutrition information per 4-ounce serving: 72 cal., 0 g pro., 18 g carbo., 0 g fat, 0 mg chol., 5 mg sodium, 78 mg potassium, 0 g fiber. U.S. RDA: 21% vit. C.

CHICKEN PINWHEELS

Bake the pinwheels one day ahead. To tote, slice and pack in a storage container in a cooler with ice—

- 6 skinned, boneless large chicken breast halves (about 1½ pounds total)
- 1 tablespoon Dijon-style mustard
- ¾ teaspoon lemon-pepper seasoning
- ¼ teaspoon garlic powder
- ¼ teaspoon onion salt
- 6 thin slices boiled ham
Paprika
Leaf lettuce (optional)
- 32 slices rye party bread *or* other thin bread slices, cut into triangles
- 2 large tomatoes, thinly sliced and quartered
- 1 small cucumber, bias-sliced ¼ inch thick
- 1 recipe Mustard Sauce (see recipe, page 117)

● **Rinse chicken;** pat dry. Place *each* breast half, boned side up, between 2 pieces of plastic wrap. Working from the center to the edges, pound lightly with the flat side of a mallet to ¼-inch thickness. Remove plastic wrap.

● **Lightly spread each breast** with the Dijon-style mustard. Combine lemon-pepper seasoning, garlic powder, and onion salt. Sprinkle over mustard.

● **Place 1 ham slice** on each chicken breast, folding the ham to fit. Starting with a long edge, roll up chicken with ham inside. If necessary, secure with wooden toothpicks. Place rolls, seam side down, in a 12x7½x2-inch baking dish. Sprinkle with paprika.

● **Bake in a 350° oven** for 35 minutes or till chicken is no longer pink. Cool. Cover and chill up to 24 hours.

● **To serve, cut chicken rolls** into ¼-inch slices. Line a large serving platter with lettuce. Arrange chicken slices, bread, tomato, and cucumber on the platter. Serve with Mustard Sauce. Makes about 15 servings.

For 30 servings: Double all of the ingredients. Bake the chicken rolls in two 12x7½x2-inch baking dishes.

Nutrition information per serving with Mustard Sauce: 150 cal., 15 g pro., 9 g carbo., 7 g fat, 38 mg chol., 491 mg sodium, 200 mg potassium, and 0 g dietary fiber. U.S. RDA: 12% vit. C, 21% thiamine, 10% riboflavin, 42% niacin.

APPLE AND MELON TOSS

- 5 cups assorted melon balls (watermelon, cantaloupe, honeydew, Persian, *and/or* casaba)
- 1 8-ounce carton lemon yogurt
- 2 tablespoons orange juice *or* orange liqueur
- ½ of a 4-ounce container frozen whipped dessert topping, thawed
- 3 medium apples, cored and coarsely chopped (3 cups)
- ½ cup broken pecans

● **Store the melon balls** in a tightly covered 2-quart container. Chill till serving time.

● **In a 1½-quart covered container** stir together yogurt and juice or liqueur; fold in thawed dessert topping. Stir in chopped apples. Cover and chill for up to 4 hours.

● **Transport both containers** in a cooler with ice. To serve, spoon apple mixture onto platter; sprinkle broken pecans over apple mixture. Spoon melon balls over apple mixture, leaving apple mixture showing around the edges. Makes about 15 servings.

For 30 servings: Use 10 cups melon balls or *five 16-ounce packages* frozen melon balls, thawed and drained; *two 8-ounce cartons* lemon yogurt; ¼ cup orange juice or orange liqueur; *one 4-ounce container* frozen whipped dessert topping, thawed; 6 chopped apples; and 1 cup broken pecans. Arrange the salad on two platters or in a very large bowl.

For 50 servings: Use 16 cups melon balls or *eight 16-ounce packages* frozen melon balls, drained and thawed; *three 8-ounce cartons* lemon yogurt; ⅓ cup orange juice or orange liqueur; *one 8-ounce container* frozen whipped dessert topping, thawed; 10 apples; and 1½ cups broken pecans. Arrange the salad on two very large platters.

Nutrition information per serving: 92 cal., 2 g pro., 14 g carbo., 4 g fat, 1 mg chol., 27 mg sodium, 248 mg potassium, and 2 g dietary fiber. U.S. RDA: 14% vit. A, 11% vit. C.

GRILLED BASIL BURGERS

To make burgers ahead, wrap uncooked patties in freezer wrap and freeze for up to 3 months. The night before grilling, thaw in refrigerator—

       1 slightly beaten egg
    ⅔ cup chopped onion
    ½ cup grated Parmesan cheese
    ¼ cup snipped fresh basil *or*
       1 tablespoon dried basil, crushed
    ¼ cup catsup
       2 cloves garlic, minced
    ¼ teaspoon salt
    ¼ teaspoon pepper
       1 pound ground beef
       1 pound ground raw turkey
       8 hamburger buns, split and toasted
       8 tomato slices

● **In a mixing bowl combine** egg, onion, Parmesan cheese, basil, catsup, garlic, salt, and pepper. Add ground beef and turkey; mix well.

● **Shape meat mixture** into eight ¾-inch-thick patties. Wrap patties individually in plastic wrap if refrigerating or toting. To tote, pack the patties with ice in a cooler for up to 4 hours.

● **To grill, place patties** on the grill rack directly over *medium* coals. Grill for 15 to 18 minutes or till juices run clear, turning once. Serve patties on buns with fresh tomato slices. Makes 8 servings.

For 16 servings: Double all of the ingredients. Combine meat mixture in a large mixing bowl.

For 32 servings: Make two separate double batches of meat mixture.

Nutrition information per serving: 301 cal., 20 g pro., 28 g carbo., 12 g fat, 76 mg chol., 561 mg sodium, 350 mg potassium, and 2 g dietary fiber. U.S. RDA: 13% vit. C, 28% thiamine, 30% riboflavin, 34% niacin, 20% calcium, 18% iron.

ASPARAGUS BAKE

Assemble ahead and chill up to 24 hours. Bake 35 minutes or till hot—

       4 ounces broken spaghetti
       2 10-ounce packages frozen cut asparagus *or* broccoli
       1 10¾-ounce can condensed cream of celery soup
    ½ cup dairy sour cream *or* plain yogurt
    ¼ cup milk
       1 to 2 tablespoons Dijon-style mustard
       1 2-ounce jar diced pimiento, drained
    ¼ cup grated Parmesan cheese
       2 tablespoons fine dry bread crumbs
       1 tablespoon margarine *or* butter, melted

● **In a Dutch oven cook** spaghetti, uncovered, in boiling water for 6 minutes. Add asparagus or broccoli; return to boiling. Cook for 2 minutes more. Drain spaghetti and asparagus or broccoli.

● **In a large mixing bowl stir together** soup, sour cream or yogurt, milk, and mustard. Stir in spaghetti mixture, pimiento, and *3 tablespoons* of the Parmesan cheese. Spoon into a 12x7½x2-inch baking dish.

● **In a small mixing bowl stir together** fine dry bread crumbs, melted margarine or butter, and the remaining 1 tablespoon Parmesan cheese. Sprinkle over spaghetti mixture.

● **Bake in a 350° oven** for 30 to 35 minutes or till heated through. *Or,* use a microwave-safe dish and micro-cook on 100% power (high) for 7 to 9 minutes, rotating the dish after 4 minutes. Makes 10 servings.

For 20 servings: Double all of the ingredients. Combine in a 4-quart casserole. Bake, uncovered, in a 350° oven about 45 minutes or till hot. Do not bake in the microwave.

For 30 servings: Make one recipe for 10 servings and one recipe for 20 servings. Do not follow the microwave directions.

Nutrition information per serving: 134 cal., 5 g pro., 16 g carbo., 6 g fat, 11 mg chol., 351 mg sodium, 245 mg potassium, 1 g dietary fiber. U.S. RDA: 14% vit. A, 34% vit. C, 10% riboflavin.

TAMALE PIE

Need an easy dish with crowd appeal? This zesty casserole could be it—

       2 pounds lean ground beef
       2 medium green *and/or* red sweet peppers, seeded and chopped (2 cups)
       1 medium onion, chopped
       1 11-ounce can condensed nacho cheese soup
       2 2¼-ounce cans sliced pitted ripe olives, drained (1 cup)
       1 8-ounce jar mild chunky salsa (¾ cup)
    ¼ cup water
       2 8-ounce packages corn muffin mix
    ¾ cup shredded Cojack *or* Colby cheese (3 ounces)
Cherry tomatoes, quartered (optional)
Whole pitted ripe olives (optional)

● **In a 12-inch skillet cook** ground beef, peppers, and onion till meat is brown. Drain off fat.

● **Stir in** soup, sliced olives, salsa, and water. Bring to boiling; reduce heat. Simmer, uncovered, for 5 minutes. Remove from heat.

● **Meanwhile, prepare** corn muffin mix according to package directions. Spread *half* of the muffin batter into a greased 13x9x2-inch baking dish. Spoon the hot meat mixture over the muffin layer. Carefully spread the remaining corn muffin batter over the meat mixture.

● **Bake in a 350° oven** for 30 to 35 minutes or till muffin layer is golden. Top with cheese. If desired, garnish with tomatoes and whole olives. Cut into squares. Makes 12 to 15 servings.

For 30 servings: Double all ingredients and bake in two 13x9x2-inch baking dishes.

Nutrition information per serving: 397 cal., 23 g pro., 34 g carbo., 19 g fat, 74 mg chol., 773 mg sodium, 287 mg potassium, and 1 g dietary fiber. U.S. RDA: 26% vit. C, 19% thiamine, 25% riboflavin, 32% niacin, 14% calcium, 17% iron.

4-WAY BARS

- 1 cup margarine *or* butter
- 1 cup packed brown sugar
- 1 egg
- 2 teaspoons vanilla
- 2 cups all-purpose flour
- 3 tablespoons semisweet chocolate pieces, melted and cooled
- ¼ cup semisweet chocolate pieces
- ¼ cup tiny marshmallows
- ¼ cup chopped walnuts *or* pecans
- ⅓ cup creamy peanut butter
- ⅓ cup coarsely chopped candy-coated milk chocolate pieces
- ¼ cup seedless red raspberry preserves
- ¼ cup coarsely chopped almonds
- ¼ cup milk chocolate pieces
- ¼ cup coconut
- ¼ cup caramel ice-cream topping

● **In a large mixing bowl beat** margarine or butter with an electric mixer on medium to high speed for 30 seconds. Add brown sugar; beat till fluffy. Add egg and vanilla. Beat well. Stir in flour. Transfer *half* of the mixture to a 15x10x1-inch baking pan. Pat dough evenly into *half* of the pan crosswise.

● **Stir melted chocolate** into the remaining batter. Pat chocolate dough into the remaining half of the pan.

● **Bake in a 350° oven** for 15 minutes. Remove from oven. Sprinkle *half* of the chocolate crust with the ¼ cup semisweet chocolate pieces; let stand for 1 to 2 minutes. When softened, spread chocolate pieces evenly over *half* of the chocolate crust. Sprinkle marshmallows and walnuts over the melted chocolate; press lightly.

● **Carefully spread** peanut butter over the remaining chocolate crust (see photo, *above right*). Sprinkle with chopped candy-coated chocolate pieces. Press candy into peanut butter.

● **Spread the raspberry preserves** over *half* of the plain dough crust. Sprinkle preserves with almonds.

● **Sprinkle** milk chocolate pieces and coconut on remaining plain crust. Drizzle caramel ice-cream topping over chocolate pieces and coconut.

● **Bake in a 350° oven** for 5 minutes more. Cool on a wire rack for 10 minutes. Cut into small squares. Cool completely on the wire rack. Makes 48.

Nutrition information per serving: *121 cal., 2 g pro., 14 g carbo., 7 g fat, 5 mg chol., 59 mg sodium, 60 mg potassium, and 0 g dietary fiber.*

Spread peanut butter on chocolate dough.

CINNAMON FRUIT COMPOTE

Layer this colorful dessert in a large clear bowl for a centerpiece—

- 1½ cups white grape juice
- 2 tablespoons sugar
- 4 inches stick cinnamon
- 4 whole nutmegs
- 1 teaspoon finely shredded orange peel
- 2 cups strawberries, hulled and halved
- 3 medium nectarines, pitted and sliced
- 2 cups seedless green grapes
- 1 16-ounce can mandarin orange sections, drained
- 3 carambola (star fruit), sliced

● **In a small saucepan combine** grape juice, sugar, stick cinnamon, whole nutmegs, and orange peel. Cook over medium heat, stirring constantly, till sugar dissolves. Bring to boiling and reduce heat. Cover; simmer 5 minutes. Remove from heat. Cool 15 minutes. Remove cinnamon and nutmeg.

● **Meanwhile, in a large bowl layer** *half* of the strawberries, all of the nectarines, the grapes, the oranges, then the remaining strawberries, and lastly the carambola; cover and chill. For transporting, place grape juice mixture in a covered plastic container. To serve, pour juice mixture over fruit layers. (If outside, place bowl on ice till needed.) Makes about 15 servings.

For 30 servings: Double all of the ingredients and use two large bowls.

Nutrition information per serving: *69 cal., 1 g pro., 17 g carbo., 0 g fat, 0 mg chol., 3 mg sodium, 196 mg potassium, 2 g fiber. U.S. RDA: 44% vit. C.*

TWO-BEAN AND RICE SALAD

Short on time? Use an 8-ounce jar of Italian salad dressing in place of the Garlic Dressing—

- 3 cups cold cooked rice
- 1 15-ounce can pinto beans, rinsed and drained
- 1 15-ounce can black beans, rinsed and drained
- 1 10-ounce package frozen peas, thawed
- 1 cup sliced celery
- 1 medium red onion, chopped (½ cup)
- 2 4-ounce cans diced green chili peppers, drained
- ¼ cup snipped cilantro *or* parsley
- Garlic Dressing *or* one
- 8-ounce jar Italian salad dressing
- Cilantro sprigs (optional)
- Fresh whole chili peppers (optional)

● **In a 2½-quart covered container** combine cooked rice, pinto beans, black beans, peas, celery, onion, diced green chili peppers, and the ¼ cup cilantro or parsley.

● **Add the dressing** to the rice mixture; toss gently to mix. Cover and chill for up to 24 hours.

● **To serve, transfer** the chilled salad to a serving bowl. If desired, garnish with cilantro sprigs and whole chili peppers. Makes 16 servings.

For 30 servings: Double all of the ingredients.

Garlic Dressing: In a screw-top jar combine ⅓ cup *white wine vinegar,* ¼ cup *olive oil* or *salad oil,* 2 tablespoons *water,* ¾ teaspoon *salt,* ½ teaspoon *garlic powder,* and ½ teaspoon *pepper.* Cover and shake well to mix. Makes about ⅔ cup.

For 30 servings, double all of the ingredients.

Nutrition information per serving: *150 cal., 5 g pro., 24 g carbo., 4 g fat, 0 mg chol., 309 mg sodium, 255 mg potassium, and 5 g dietary fiber. U.S. RDA: 23% vit. C, 19% thiamine, 10% iron.*

STRAWBERRY-CHOCOLATE ALMOND TORTE

2 cups toasted slivered almonds
3 tablespoons all-purpose flour
4 teaspoons baking powder
6 eggs
1 cup sugar
1 8-ounce package cream cheese, softened
¾ cup sifted powdered sugar
½ teaspoon grated orange peel
1 6-ounce package semisweet chocolate pieces
1 8-ounce carton dairy sour cream
Milk
3 cups sliced strawberries

● **Combine** almonds, flour, and baking powder. Set aside. In a blender or food processor container combine eggs and sugar. Cover; blend or process till smooth. Add nut mixture. Cover; blend or process till smooth. Spread in 2 greased and floured 9x1½-inch round baking pans.

● **Bake in a 350° oven** for 20 to 25 minutes or till light brown. Cool on wire racks for 10 minutes. Remove from pans; cool thoroughly on racks.

● **For cream cheese filling,** in a small mixing bowl beat cream cheese with an electric mixer on medium-high speed till fluffy. Gradually add powdered sugar, beating well. Stir in orange peel.

● **For chocolate filling,** melt chocolate pieces over very low heat, stirring often. Remove from heat. Add sour cream; stir till smooth. Stir in milk (1 to 2 tablespoons) till frosting is of spreading consistency.

● **To assemble torte, split** cake layers horizontally. Place bottom of one split layer on serving plate. Spread with *half* of the cream cheese filling. Top with *1 cup* of the sliced strawberries. Place top of cake layer on strawberries. Spread with *half* of the chocolate filling, and another *1 cup* of the sliced strawberries. Repeat with remaining cake layers, fillings, and strawberries. If desired, garnish with additional whole strawberries and orange peel strips. Chill for 2 to 24 hours. Serves 12.

For 24 servings: Make 2 separate tortes, one at a time.

Nutrition information per serving: *458 cal., 11 g pro., 42 g carbo., 30 g fat, 136 mg chol., 200 mg sodium, 364 mg potassium, 4 g fiber. U.S. RDA: 21% vit. A, 36% vit. C, 10% thiamine, 35% riboflavin, 23% calcium, 12% iron.*

OATMEAL CARAMEL BARS

All you need is one bowl to mix—

1 cup margarine *or* butter
2½ cups all-purpose flour
2 cups packed brown sugar
2 eggs
2 teaspoons vanilla
1 teaspoon baking soda
3 cups quick-cooking rolled oats
1 6-ounce package (1 cup) semisweet chocolate pieces
½ cup chopped walnuts *or* pecans
24 vanilla caramels (7 ounces)
2 tablespoons milk

● **In a large mixing bowl beat** margarine or butter with an electric mixer on medium to high speed for 30 seconds. Add about *1 cup* of the flour, the brown sugar, eggs, vanilla, and the baking soda. Beat mixture till combined. Beat or stir in the remaining flour. Stir in the oats.

● **Press two-thirds** (about 3⅓ cups) of the dough into an ungreased 15x10x1-inch baking pan. Sprinkle with chocolate pieces and nuts.

● **In a medium saucepan combine** caramels and milk. Cook over low heat till caramels are melted. Drizzle caramel mixture over chocolate and nuts. Drop remaining *one-third* of the dough by teaspoons over the top.

● **Bake in a 350° oven** about 25 minutes or till top is light brown. Cool in pan on a wire rack. Cut into bars. To freeze, wrap the bars in moisture- and vaporproof wrap and freeze for up to 6 months. To serve, remove wrap and thaw at room temperature about 2 hours. Makes about 60 bars.

Nutrition information per bar: *126 cal., 2 g pro., 18 g carbo., 6 g fat, 7 mg chol., 63 mg sodium, 71 mg potassium, and 1 g dietary fiber.*

AVOCADO-PAPAYA SALSA

When buying papayas, look for yellow skin color on at least two-thirds of the fruit. A ripe papaya yields slightly to gentle pressure. Slightly green papayas will ripen at room temperature in three to five days—

2 medium avocados
1 small papaya
⅓ cup lime juice
2 medium tomatoes, chopped
2 green onions, sliced
2 tablespoons sugar
2 tablespoons olive oil *or* salad oil
1 tablespoon snipped parsley
1 tablespoon snipped fresh basil *or* 1 teaspoon dried basil, crushed
Several dashes bottled hot pepper sauce

● **Seed, peel, and chop** avocados and papaya. In a 1-quart container with a lid, toss avocados and papaya with lime juice. Add tomatoes, green onions, sugar, oil, parsley, basil, and hot pepper sauce. Cover and chill. Serve chilled salsa with grilled poultry, fish, or pork. Makes 4 cups (16 servings).

For 30 servings: Double all of the ingredients.

Nutrition information per 1/4 cup serving: *72 cal., 1 g pro., 6 g carbo., 6 g fat, 0 mg chol., 5 mg sodium, 236 mg potassium, 3 g fiber. U.S. RDA: 27% vit. C.*

APRICOT WINE COOLER

If the reunion is less than 30 minutes from your home, just remove the apricot mixture from the freezer right before leaving and it will be at a perfect serving temperature by the time you arrive. If you are traveling a longer distance, pack it in a cooler—

3 12-ounce cans apricot nectar
½ cup honey
3 tablespoons lemon juice
2 750-ml bottles dry white *or* rosé wine, chilled (8 cups)
Carbonated water, chilled (about 1 quart)

● **In a large mixing bowl combine** apricot nectar, honey, and lemon juice. Stir in wine. Transfer to one large or several smaller freezer containers. Seal, label, and freeze. Transport containers in a cooler packed with ice.

● **To serve, scrape** a large spoon across the frozen mixture to form a slush. If the mixture is too firm, let stand 10 to 20 minutes to thaw slightly. Spoon into 8-ounce glasses (about ¾ cup per glass). Add carbonated water to fill glasses. Makes 16 servings.

For 30 servings: Double all of the ingredients.

Nutrition information per serving: *132 cal., 0 g pro., 19 g carbo., 0 g fat, 0 mg chol., 32 mg sodium, 142 mg potassium, and 0 g dietary fiber. U.S. RDA: 10% vit. A.*

REUNION BREAD

Start a family tradition by hiding an almond in this festive bread. Whoever gets the hidden almond will have good luck this year, organize the next reunion, or head the clean-up committee! You decide what the almond means—

2½ to 3 cups all-purpose flour
2 packages active dry yeast
1½ cups milk
⅓ cup sugar
¼ cup margarine *or* butter
2 teaspoons salt
2 eggs
3 cups whole wheat flour
⅔ cup chopped onion
1 tablespoon margarine *or* butter
¼ cup pesto, purchased *or* homemade
2 tablespoons chopped walnuts
½ cup shredded Swiss cheese (2 ounces)
1 tablespoon Dijon-style mustard
1 whole almond
1 beaten egg white
Sesame seed
Caraway seed
Poppy seed

● **In a large mixing bowl** mix *2 cups* of the all-purpose flour and the yeast.
● **In a medium saucepan heat** and stir milk, sugar, the ¼ cup margarine or butter, and salt till warm (120° to 130°) and margarine almost melts.
● **Add milk mixture** and whole eggs to flour mixture. Beat with an electric mixer on low speed for 30 seconds, scraping constantly. Beat on high speed 3 minutes. Using a spoon, stir in whole wheat flour and as much remaining all-purpose flour as you can.
● **On a lightly floured surface,** knead in enough remaining all-purpose flour to make a moderately stiff dough that is smooth and elastic (6 to 8 minutes total). Shape into a ball. Place in a lightly greased bowl; turn once. Cover; let rise in a warm place till double (1 to 1½ hours).
● **Punch dough down.** Turn out onto a lightly floured surface. Cover and let rest 10 minutes.

● **Meanwhile, in a saucepan cook** the onion in the 1 tablespoon margarine or butter till tender; set aside. Combine pesto and walnuts; set aside. Combine cheese and mustard; set aside.
● **On a lightly floured surface, roll** dough into a 16x12-inch rectangle. Cut into three 16x4-inch strips.
● **Spread onion mixture** down the center of one strip, leaving the edges clear of filling. Spread pesto mixture down the center of another strip. Spread cheese mixture down the center of the remaining strip. Place one almond in the center of one strip.
● **Brush** the edges of the strips with egg white. Fold each strip over, enclosing filling and forming a rope. Pinch edges to seal.
● **Shape** one rope into a ring and place, seam side down, in center of a lightly greased large baking sheet. Form remaining 2 ropes into rings so they intertwine with the center ring, like the links of a chain, placing them seam sides down (see photo, *below*). Seal ends well. Cover and let rise in a warm place till almost double (45 to 60 minutes).
● **Brush** dough rings with beaten egg white. Sprinkle one ring with sesame seed, one with caraway seed, and one with poppy seed.
● **Bake in a 375° oven** about 25 minutes or till golden, covering with foil the last 10 minutes to prevent overbrowning. Cool on a wire rack. To freeze, wrap the loaf in freezer wrap and freeze for up to 3 months. To serve, thaw in package for 1 hour or heat in a 300° oven about 20 minutes. Makes 1 large loaf (30 servings).

Nutrition information per serving: 139 cal., 5 g pro., 21 g carbo., 5 g fat, 17 mg chol., 208 mg sodium, 117 mg potassium, 2 g dietary fiber. U.S. RDA: 16% thiamine, 13% riboflavin, 12% niacin.

Form two rings around center ring.

GARDEN-FRESH COUSCOUS SALAD

Couscous is a tiny pasta that cooks quickly and often is used in North African recipes. Look for it in your grocery store with the pasta or rice—

2 cups water
1 tablespoon instant chicken bouillon granules
1 10-ounce package couscous (1⅓ cups)
1 large carrot, shredded
1 large green pepper, cut into ½-inch squares
1 large zucchini, halved lengthwise and thinly sliced
1 large yellow summer squash, halved lengthwise and thinly sliced
1 cup cherry tomatoes, halved
1 8-ounce bottle Italian salad dressing

● **In a medium saucepan mix** 2 cups water and bouillon granules; bring to boiling. Add couscous. Remove from heat; cover and let stand for 5 minutes or till the liquid is absorbed. Transfer to a 2½-quart covered container.
● **Add** carrot, green pepper, zucchini, yellow summer squash, and cherry tomatoes; mix well. Add salad dressing; toss to coat. Cover and chill for 6 to 24 hours. Makes 15 servings.

For 30 servings: Double all of the ingredients.

Nutrition information per serving: 148 cal., 3 g pro., 18 g carbo., 9 g fat, 0 mg chol., 305 mg sodium, 121 mg potassium, and 1 g dietary fiber. U.S. RDA: 24% vit. A, 15% vit. C.

NUTTY NIBBLE MIX

Make this savory snack up to a week ahead. Store in an airtight container—

- ⅓ cup margarine *or* butter
- 1 tablespoon soy sauce
- ¾ teaspoon chili powder
- ⅛ teaspoon garlic powder
- ⅛ teaspoon ground red pepper
- 3 cups bite-size corn and rice square cereal
- 1 3-ounce can chow mein noodles
- 1 cup peanuts
- 1 cup shelled raw pumpkin seeds

● **In a small saucepan mix** margarine or butter, soy sauce, chili powder, garlic powder, and red pepper. Cook and stir till margarine or butter melts.

● **In a roasting pan mix** cereal, chow mein noodles, peanuts, and pumpkin seeds. Drizzle margarine mixture over noodle mixture; toss to coat.

● **Bake in a 300° oven** for 30 minutes, stirring every 10 minutes. Spread on foil to cool. Store in an airtight container. Makes 12 to 15 servings.

For 30 servings: Double all of the ingredients and use 2 medium roasting pans or 1 large pan.

Nutrition information per serving: 242 cal., 7 g pro., 15 g carbo., 19 g fat, 0 mg chol., 292 mg sodium, 199 mg potassium, and 2 g dietary fiber. U.S. RDA: 19% thiamine, 11% riboflavin, 27% niacin, 15% iron.

MUSTARD SAUCE

This easy-to-mix spread doubles as a zippy sauce for roast beef, grilled pork, or burgers—

- ¼ cup dairy sour cream
- ¼ cup mayonnaise *or* salad dressing
- 1 tablespoon Dijon-style mustard
- 1 teaspoon prepared horseradish (optional)

● **In a small bowl stir together** sour cream, mayonnaise or salad dressing, mustard, and, if desired, horseradish. Cover and chill till serving time. Makes ½ cup.

For 30 servings: Double all of the ingredients.

Nutrition information per teaspoon: 23 cal., 0 g pro., 0 g carbo., 2 g fat, 2 mg chol., 34 mg sodium, 4 mg potassium, and 0 g dietary fiber.

MINIATURE FRUIT TARTS

Some pastry shells may bake into uneven shapes. If this happens, split the shells so the top half is even all the way around. Then, trim the bottom half so the sides are even. When you assemble the tart, it will stand upright—

- 1 17¼-ounce package (2 sheets) frozen puff pastry, thawed
- 1 beaten egg white
- ½ cup finely chopped pecans and 1 tablespoon sugar; *or* ½ cup pearl sugar
- ⅓ cup orange juice
- 1½ teaspoons light corn syrup
- 1 teaspoon cornstarch
- 1 8-ounce carton lemon yogurt
- 1 4½- *or* 5-ounce container vanilla pudding (⅔ cup)
- 2 cups assorted fresh fruit (such as peeled, thinly sliced, and halved peaches; thinly sliced and halved nectarines; thinly sliced plums *and/or* strawberries; *and/or* fresh raspberries)

● **On a lightly floured surface, roll** pastry slightly to flatten creases. Cut puff pastry circles and diamonds using 2-inch pastry cutters. Place on an ungreased baking sheet. Brush pastry rounds with egg white. Stir together pecans and the 1 tablespoon sugar. Sprinkle pecan mixture over pastry shapes. *Or,* use the pearl sugar instead of nut mixture.

● **Bake in a 375° oven** for 12 to 14 minutes or till puffed and golden. Transfer pastries to a wire rack. Cool.

● **Meanwhile,** mix orange juice, corn syrup, and cornstarch. Cook and stir over medium heat till mixture is thickened and bubbly. Cook and stir for 2 minutes more. Transfer to a small bowl. Cover; cool to room temperature.

● **Combine** yogurt and pudding. Split pastry rounds horizontally. Spread about *1 teaspoon* of the yogurt mixture on the bottom half of each round. Arrange fresh fruit atop yogurt mixture. Brush the fruit with orange juice mixture. Replace tops. Cover and chill for 1 to 24 hours. To tote, arrange the tarts in single layers in shallow, covered, plastic containers or in baking pans. Cover the pans with foil. Stack the pans in a cooler. Makes about 45.

Nutrition information per tart: 71 cal., 1 g pro., 7 g carbo., 4 g fat, 0 mg chol., 63 mg sodium, 33 mg potassium, and 0 g dietary fiber.

SALMON AND GOUDA PÂTÉ

Try this colorful appetizer featuring a creamy layer of smoke-flavored cheese spread sandwiched between two spicy layers of salmon spread—

- 1 7-ounce round smoke-flavored Gouda cheese, peeled and shredded
- 1 3-ounce package cream cheese, cubed
- 3 tablespoons milk
- ¼ cup margarine *or* butter
- ⅓ cup mayonnaise *or* salad dressing
- ¼ cup finely chopped green onion
- 2 tablespoons lemon juice
- ¼ teaspoon garlic salt

Several dashes bottled hot pepper sauce

- 1 pound cooked salmon *or* one 14-ounce can *and* one 7½-ounce can salmon, drained, flaked, and skin and bones removed
- ⅓ cup toasted sliced almonds

Lettuce leaves
Lemon slices
Assorted breads and crackers

● **In a small mixer bowl place** Gouda and cream cheese. Let soften. Add milk. Beat with an electric mixer on medium speed till mixed. Set aside.

● **In a large mixer bowl beat** margarine or butter with an electric mixer till fluffy. Beat in mayonnaise or salad dressing, green onion, lemon juice, garlic salt, and hot pepper sauce. Add salmon; beat till combined.

● **Line bottom and sides of** an 8x4x2-inch loaf pan with plastic wrap. Sprinkle almonds in the bottom of pan. Carefully spoon in *half* of the salmon mixture; spread evenly. Spread cheese mixture atop salmon layer. Spread with the remaining salmon mixture. Cover and chill for 6 to 24 hours.

● **To serve, unmold** onto a lettuce-lined serving platter. Remove plastic wrap. Garnish with lemon slices. Serve with breads and crackers. Makes 16 to 20 servings.

For 30 servings: Double all of the ingredients and spoon into two 8x4x2-inch loaf pans.

Nutrition information per serving of pâté: 177 cal., 10 g pro., 1 g carbo., 15 g fat, 34 mg chol., 218 mg sodium, 173 mg potassium, and 0 g dietary fiber. U.S. RDA: 14% vit. A, 14% niacin, and 14% calcium.

SEPTEMBER

OUR AWARD-WINNING **HOME OF THE YEAR** page 67

Better
Homes
and Gardens

SEPTEMBER 1990

Quick!

WHAT'S FOR DINNER?
Easy spur-of-the-moment meals

LANDSCAPING
Making a
barren yard
beautiful

**ROOM
ARRANGING
MADE EASY**
page 93

$1.95

BY
JULIA
MALLOY

THE NEW PANTRY

20 Ingredients for Today's Streamlined Cooking

Everything you need for tonight's dinner is on your shelf. And for tomorrow night, and the next. With the BH&G® food editors' pantry plan, it's easy. Our top-20 list of foods to keep on hand fits family-style cooking for the '90s: bold flavors, good nutrition, and convenience. Turn the pages for great recipes made from these foods. For more about our pantry, see *page 128*.

1 Colorful sweet peppers

2 Broccoli

3 Pears

4 Low-fat cheese

5 Low-fat yogurt

6 Lean ground beef or turkey

7 Boneless chicken breasts or turkey cutlets

8 Fresh or frozen fish fillets

9 Assorted pastas

10 Instant or quick-cooking brown rice

11 Refrigerated pizza dough

12 Frozen fruit juice concentrates

13 Loose-pack frozen vegetables

14 Stewed tomatoes

15 Ripe olives

16 Sodium-reduced or regular canned soups

17 Canned beans

18 Dried mushrooms

19 Almonds

20 Nonstick spray coating

RECIPES FROM THE
NEW PANTRY

GARLIC BREAD TWISTS

See recipe, page 127.

BROCCOLI-CHEESE STROMBOLI

See recipe, page 127.

TWO-WAY MINESTRONE

- 12 ounces fresh or frozen fish fillets (cod, pike, or orange roughy) or boneless, skinless, chicken breast halves or turkey breast tenderloin steaks
- 2 14½-ounce cans reduced-sodium or regular chicken broth
- 1 15-ounce can beans (garbanzo or kidney), rinsed and drained
- 1 cup loose-pack frozen mixed vegetables
- 1 medium onion, chopped (½ cup)
- ½ cup cavatelli or other small pasta (shells, wheels, or macaroni)
- 1 teaspoon dried basil or thyme, crushed
- ¼ teaspoon pepper
- 1 14½-ounce can Italian-style stewed tomatoes

• **Thaw fish,** if frozen. Remove skin, if present. Cut fish or poultry into 1-inch pieces.

• **In a large saucepan stir** together the chicken broth, beans, frozen vegetables, onion, pasta, basil or thyme, and pepper. Bring to boiling; reduce heat. Simmer, covered, for 10 minutes.

• **Stir in the undrained** tomatoes. Add fish or poultry. Return to boiling; reduce heat. Simmer, covered, till fish flakes easily or poultry is no longer pink, stirring once. For fish, allow 2 to 3 minutes; for poultry, allow 4 to 5 minutes. Makes 4 servings.

Nutrition information per serving: 317 cal., 27 g pro., 46 g carbo., 4 g fat, 35 mg chol., 1,063 mg sodium, 778 mg potassium, and 7 g dietary fiber. U.S. RDA: 39% vit. A, 27% vit. C, 316% thiamine, 297% riboflavin, 59% niacin, 41% iron.

FETTUCCINE WITH PEPPER SAUCE

Colorful peppers brighten the easy soup-based sauce. For microwave directions, turn to page 127—

Nonstick spray coating

1½ **cups broccoli flowerets *or* 1 medium pear, cored and chopped**

1 **medium sweet red, yellow, *or* green pepper, cut into ¾-inch squares**

1 **medium onion, chopped (½ cup)**

1 **tablespoon cooking oil**

12 **ounces boneless, skinless chicken breast halves *or* turkey breast tenderloin steaks, cut into strips**

1 **10¾-ounce can reduced-sodium *or* regular condensed cream soup (chicken, celery, *or* broccoli)**

½ **cup water**

1 **teaspoon dried basil, crushed**

½ **cup shredded low-fat cheese (cheddar *or* Swiss) (2 ounces)**

8 **ounces fettuccine *or* other noodle (spinach, carrot, *or* whole wheat), cooked, drained, and kept warm**

● **Spray a cold large skillet** with nonstick coating. Preheat skillet over medium heat. Stir-fry the broccoli or pear, sweet pepper, and onion for 3 to 4 minutes; remove from skillet. Add oil to skillet. Add poultry; stir-fry for 3 to 4 minutes or till no longer pink.

● **Add condensed soup,** water, and basil to the skillet; mix thoroughly. Stir in the sweet pepper mixture. Bring to boiling; reduce heat. Add cheese; cook and stir till cheese is almost melted. Serve over hot cooked pasta. Makes 4 servings.

Nutrition information per serving: 495 cal., 35 g pro., 54 g carbo., 15 g fat, 64 mg chol., 530 mg sodium, 555 mg potassium, and 6 g dietary fiber. U.S. RDA: 51% vit. A, 113% vit. C, 29% thiamine, 27% riboflavin, 84% niacin, 11% calcium, 15% iron.

SPICY FILLETS WITH YOGURT SAUCE

Pan-fry, micro-cook, broil, or grill this entrée in 20 minutes. For microwave, broiling, and grilling directions, turn to page 128—

- **1 pound fresh *or* frozen fish fillets (snapper, cod, haddock, *or* orange roughy) *or* boneless, skinless chicken breast halves *or* turkey breast tenderloin steaks**
- **2 teaspoons curry powder *or* chili powder**
- **¼ teaspoon garlic salt**
- **¼ teaspoon onion salt**
- **¼ teaspoon pepper**
- **1 tablespoon cooking oil**
- **½ cup plain yogurt**
- **¼ cup toasted sliced *or* slivered almonds *or* sliced pitted ripe olives**

● **Thaw fish,** if frozen. Remove skin, if present. In a small bowl combine the curry or chili powder, garlic salt, onion salt, and pepper. Rub seasoning mixture onto both sides of fish or poultry.

● **In a large skillet cook** fish or poultry in hot oil till fish flakes easily or poultry is no longer pink, turning once. For fish, allow 4 to 6 minutes for each ½ inch of thickness; for poultry, allow 8 to 10 minutes total. To serve, top each serving of fish or poultry with yogurt and almonds or olives. Makes 4 servings.

Nutrition information per serving: 195 cal., 25 g pro., 4 g carbo., 9 g fat, 42 mg chol., 203 mg sodium, 573 mg potassium, and 1 g dietary fiber. U.S. RDA: 14% riboflavin, 23% niacin, and 14% calcium.

123

A boldly colored and flavored stir-fry encourages your whole family to eat vegetables.

CHICKEN AND PEAR STIR-FRY

- **6** dried mushrooms
- **¾** cup cold water
- **3** tablespoons frozen fruit juice concentrate (orange, apple, *or* pineapple)
- **2** tablespoons soy sauce
- **2** teaspoons cornstarch
- **¼** teaspoon ground ginger
- **¼** teaspoon ground cinnamon
- **⅛** to **¼** teaspoons ground red pepper
- **¼** cup sliced *or* slivered almonds
- **1** tablespoon cooking oil
- **2** medium sweet red, orange, yellow *and/or* green peppers, cut into thin 2-inch-long strips
- **2** medium pears, thinly sliced
- **12** ounces boneless, skinless chicken breast halves *or* turkey breast steaks, cut into 1-inch pieces

Hot cooked brown rice

● **Soak mushrooms** for 30 minutes in warm water. Drain and squeeze mushrooms; thinly slice, discarding stems.

● **For sauce,** combine cold water, juice concentrate, soy sauce, cornstarch, ginger, cinnamon, and ground red pepper; set aside.

● **Preheat a wok** over medium-high heat. Stir-fry almonds 1 minute to toast; remove.

● **Add oil.** Stir-fry mushrooms, peppers, and pears about 1½ minutes or till crisp-tender; remove. Add poultry; stir-fry about 3 minutes or till no longer pink. Push to side.

● **Stir sauce;** add to center. Cook and stir till thickened. Cook for 1 minute more. Stir in pear mixture and poultry; heat through. Stir in almonds. Serve over rice. Serves 4.

Nutrition information per serving: 390 cal., 25 g pro., 50 g carbo., 11 g fat, 54 mg chol., 575 mg sodium, 577 mg potassium, 7 g fiber. U.S. RDA: 62% vit. C, 81% niacin, 21% thiamine, 23% riboflavin, 12% iron.

PHOTOGRAPHS: SCOTT LITTLE; FOOD STYLIST: JANET HERWIG

Dinner can be as simple as a satisfying sandwich, preferably one that's made from freshly baked bread and served warm.

GREEK-STYLE POCKETS

Turn pizza dough into bread pockets; stuff with a spiced meat filling—

- 1 **pound lean ground beef** *or* **ground raw turkey**
- 1 **14½-ounce can stewed tomatoes**
- ½ **teaspoon ground allspice** *or* **cinnamon**
- ¼ **teaspoon garlic salt**
- ¼ **teaspoon pepper**
- 1 **10-ounce package refrigerated pizza dough**

Nonstick spray coating
- ½ **cup plain yogurt**
- 2 **tablespoons thinly sliced green onion**

● **For filling,** in a large saucepan cook meat till no longer pink. Drain off fat. Stir in *undrained* tomatoes, allspice, garlic salt, and pepper. Bring to boiling; reduce heat. Cover; simmer 15 minutes, stirring often. Uncover; simmer about 10 minutes more or till most of the liquid has evaporated, stirring often.

● **Meanwhile, cut pizza** dough crosswise into 4 equal portions. On a lightly floured surface, roll each piece into a 7-inch round from center to edge. Spray a cold large skillet with coating. Cook dough rounds, one at a time, over low heat 2 minutes on each side or till light brown (they may shrink).

● **Combine yogurt and onion.** Spoon filling onto each dough round. Top with yogurt mixture. Fold and secure with wooden toothpicks. Serves 4.

Nutrition information per serving: 462 cal., 34 g pro., 41 g carbo., 16 g fat, 93 mg chol., 742 mg sodium, 614 mg potassium, and 2 g dietary fiber. U.S. RDA: 24% vit. C, 34% thiamine, 47% riboflavin, 59% niacin, 12% calcium, 31% iron.

NEW PANTRY

CHILI CHICKEN AND BROWN RICE

Round out this fix-and-forget one-dish meal with steamed broccoli—

- **1 pound boneless, skinless chicken breast halves *or* turkey breast tenderloin steaks, cut into 6 portions**
- **1 tablespoon cooking oil**
- **1 medium onion, chopped (½ cup)**
- **1 small green *and/or* sweet yellow *or* red pepper, chopped (½ cup)**
- **1 clove garlic, minced**
- **1 14½-ounce can Mexican-style, Italian-style, *or* plain stewed tomatoes, cut up**
- **1 14½-ounce can reduced-sodium *or* regular chicken broth**
- **1¾ cups quick-cooking *or* instant brown rice**
- **Several dashes bottled hot pepper sauce**
- **½ cup shredded low-fat cheese (cheddar *or* Monterey Jack) (2 ounces)**
- **Sliced pitted ripe olives**
- **Plain yogurt**

● **In a large skillet cook poultry** in hot oil about 2 minutes on each side or till brown; remove and set aside. In the same skillet, cook the onion, pepper, and garlic till tender but not brown. Drain off fat. Stir in the *undrained* tomatoes, broth, *uncooked* rice, and hot pepper sauce. Bring to boiling; remove from heat and spoon mixture into a 12x7½ x2-inch baking dish. Arrange chicken on top of rice mixture.

● **Bake, covered, in a 350° oven** for 30 to 35 minutes or till rice is done. Sprinkle with cheese. Let stand, uncovered, about 5 minutes or till cheese is melted. Sprinkle with olives; top with yogurt. Makes 6 servings.

Nutrition information per serving: 391 cal., 26 g pro., 49 g carbo., 10 g fat, 55 mg chol., 401 mg sodium, 322 mg potassium, 2 g dietary fiber. U.S. RDA: 22% vit. A, 28% vit. C, 24% thiamine, 25% riboflavin, 11% niacin, 10% iron.

HEARTY RICE SKILLET

A meatless main dish that cooks in less than 20 minutes—

- **1 15-ounce can beans (black, garbanzo, *or* kidney), rinsed and drained**
- **1 14½-ounce can stewed tomatoes, cut up**
- **2 cups loose-pack frozen mixed vegetables**
- **1 cup water***
- **¾ cup quick-cooking *or* instant brown rice***
- **½ teaspoon dried thyme *or* dillweed, crushed**
- **Several dashes bottled hot pepper sauce (optional)**
- **1 10¾-ounce can reduced-sodium *or* regular condensed tomato soup**
- **⅓ cup toasted slivered almonds**
- **½ cup shredded low-fat cheese (mozzarella *or* cheddar) (2 ounces)**

● **In a large skillet stir** together beans, *undrained* tomatoes, vegetables, water, *uncooked* rice, thyme or dillweed, and, if desired, hot pepper sauce. Bring to boiling; reduce heat. Simmer, covered, for 12 to 14 minutes or till rice is tender. Stir in soup; heat through. Stir in almonds. Top with cheese. Serve immediately. Makes 4 main-dish servings.

***Note:** If using instant brown rice, use only ⅔ cup water.

Nutrition information per serving: 456 cal., 19 g pro., 73 g carbo., 12 g fat, 10 mg chol., 748 mg sodium, 824 mg potassium, and 14 g dietary fiber. U.S. RDA: 66% vit. A, 48% vit. C, 43% thiamine, 35% riboflavin, 37% niacin, 27% calcium, 23% iron.

BROCCOLI-CHEESE STROMBOLI

A cheesy, pizzalike filling wrapped in refrigerated pizza dough. Pictured on page 121—

    6 dried mushrooms
    8 ounces lean ground beef,
       ground pork, *or* ground raw
       turkey
    1 medium onion, chopped (½ cup)
    1 14½-ounce can Italian-style *or*
       plain stewed tomatoes
    ½ cup chopped broccoli
    ½ teaspoon Italian seasoning,
       crushed
    ¼ teaspoon pepper
    ¼ cup chopped sweet red *or*
       green pepper
    ¼ cup sliced pitted ripe olives
Nonstick spray coating
    1 10-ounce package refrigerated
       pizza dough
    1 cup shredded low-fat mozzarella
       cheese (4 ounces)
Milk
Sesame seed *or* poppy seed

● **Soak dried mushrooms** for 30 minutes in enough warm water to cover. Squeeze to drain thoroughly. Thinly slice mushrooms, discarding stems.
● **For filling,** in a medium skillet cook the meat and onion till meat is no longer pink and onion is tender. Drain fat. Stir in the *undrained* tomatoes, broccoli, Italian seasoning, and pepper. Bring to boiling; reduce heat. Simmer, uncovered, about 15 minutes or till most of the liquid has evaporated, stirring occasionally. Stir in the red or green pepper, olives, and mushrooms. Cool slightly.
● **Spray a 15x10x1-inch** baking pan with nonstick coating; set aside. On a lightly floured surface, roll the pizza dough into a 14x12-inch rectangle. Cut the dough into four 7x6-inch rectangles. Down the center of *each* rectangle, spoon *one-fourth* of the meat mixture. Then sprinkle with cheese. Moisten the dough edges with milk. Bring the long edges together over filling; stretch and pinch to seal. Fold the ends up and over the seam and seal.

● **Arrange rolls,** seam side down, on the prepared baking sheet. If desired, use hors d'oeuvre cutters to make 2 or 3 cutouts in tops or prick tops with a fork. Brush the tops with milk; sprinkle with sesame seed or poppy seed. Bake, uncovered, in a 375° oven for 25 to 30 minutes or till light brown. Makes 4 servings.
Microwave directions: Prepare mushrooms as above. In a 2-quart microwave-safe casserole combine crumbled meat and onion. Micro-cook, covered, on 100% power (high) for 3 to 5 minutes or till no pink remains and onion is tender, stirring once. Drain well. Stir in *drained* tomatoes, broccoli, Italian seasoning, and pepper. Cook, uncovered, on high for 2 to 4 minutes or till heated through. Continue as above.
Nutrition information per serving: 430 cal., 28 g pro., 44 g carbo., 15 g fat, 62 mg chol., 931 mg sodium, 608 g potassium, and 1 g dietary fiber. U.S. RDA: 26% vit. A, 36% vit. C, 328% thiamine, 321% riboflavin, 69% niacin, 27% calcium, 43% iron.

GARLIC BREAD TWISTS

Serve these easy breadsticks with Two-Way Minestrone, other soups, or salads. Pictured on page 120—

Nonstick spray coating
    1 10-ounce package refrigerated
       pizza dough
    1 egg white
    1 tablespoon water
    ¼ teaspoon garlic powder
Grated Parmesan cheese, sesame
    seed, *or* poppy seed

● **Spray a baking pan** with nonstick coating; set aside. Remove dough from package; do not unroll dough. Cut pizza dough roll crosswise into 12 slices. Unroll each slice. Cut each strip of dough in half crosswise. Twist each strip, then place on a baking sheet.
● **In a small bowl stir** together egg white, water, and garlic powder. Brush egg white mixture onto dough. Sprinkle with Parmesan, sesame seed, or poppy seed. Bake in a 375° oven for 12 to 15 minutes or till golden brown. Serve warm. Makes 24 breadsticks.

To freeze: Place breadsticks in a freezer container; seal tightly, label, and freeze for up to 8 months. To reheat, arrange breadsticks on a baking sheet; bake in a 350° oven for 5 to 10 minutes or till heated through.
Nutrition information per breadstick: 34 cal., 1 g pro., 5 g carbo., 1 g fat, 0 mg chol., 70 mg sodium, 10 mg potassium, and 0 g dietary fiber.

FETTUCCINE WITH PEPPER SAUCE

For picture, regular cooking directions, and nutrient content, turn to page 122—

    1½ cups broccoli flowerets *or* 1 pear,
        cored and chopped
     1 medium sweet red, yellow, *or*
        green pepper, cut into squares
     1 medium onion, chopped
    12 ounces boneless, skinless chick-
        en breast halves *or* turkey breast
        tenderloin steaks, cut into strips
     1 10¾-ounce can reduced-sodium
        or regular condensed cream
        soup (chicken, celery, *or*
        broccoli)
     1 teaspoon dried basil, crushed
     ½ cup shredded low-fat cheese
        (cheddar *or* Swiss) (2 ounces)
Hot cooked fettuccine *or* other
    noodle (spinach, carrot, *or* whole
    wheat) (8 ounces uncooked)

● **In a 2-quart** microwave-safe casserole combine the broccoli or pear, sweet pepper, onion, and 2 tablespoons *water.* Micro-cook, covered, on 100% power (high) for 4 to 6 minutes (low-wattage oven: 6 to 8 minutes) or till crisp-tender, stirring once during cooking. Drain vegetables and set aside.
● **Add poultry strips** to same casserole. Micro-cook, covered, on high for 4 to 6 minutes (low-wattage oven: 5 to 7 minutes) or till poultry is no longer pink, stirring once. Drain.
● **Stir in the condensed soup,** ½ cup *water,* and basil. Stir in vegetable mixture. Cook, uncovered, on high for 3 to 5 minutes (low-wattage oven: 5 to 7 minutes) or till bubbly, stirring once. Add cheese; stir till melted. Serve over hot cooked pasta. Makes 4 servings.

SPICY FILLETS WITH YOGURT SAUCE

Serve with sliced peppers and pears, as pictured on page 123. You'll find stove-top cooking directions and nutrition information there, too—

- 1 **pound fresh *or* frozen fish fillets (snapper, cod, haddock, *or* orange roughy) *or* boneless, skinless chicken breast halves, *or* turkey breast tenderloin steaks**
- 2 **teaspoons curry powder *or* chili powder**
- ¼ **teaspoon garlic salt**
- ¼ **teaspoon onion salt**
- ¼ **teaspoon pepper**
- ½ **cup plain yogurt**
- ¼ **cup toasted sliced almonds *or* sliced pitted ripe olives**

● **Thaw fish,** if frozen. Remove skin, if present. In a bowl combine the curry or chili powder, garlic salt, onion salt, and pepper; rub onto both sides of fish or poultry.

Microwave directions: In an 8x8x2-inch microwave-safe baking dish arrange coated fish or poultry with thicker portions toward edges. Turn under any thin portions to obtain an even thickness of about ½ inch.

Cover dish with vented microwave-safe plastic wrap. Micro-cook on 100% power (high) till fish flakes easily or poultry is no longer pink, rearranging once. For fish, allow 4 to 7 minutes; for poultry, allow 6 to 8 minutes. To serve, drizzle with yogurt. Top with almonds or olives. Makes 4 servings.

Broiling directions: On a greased unheated rack of a broiler pan arrange coated fish or poultry. Tuck under any thin edges. Broil 4 to 5 inches from heat till fish flakes easily or poultry is no longer pink, turning once. For fish, allow 4 to 6 minutes for each ½ inch of thickness; for poultry, allow 12 to 15 minutes total. To serve, top fish or poultry with yogurt and almonds or olives. Makes 4 servings.

Grilling directions: In a well-greased grill basket arrange coated fish or poultry. Place fish or poultry on grill rack directly over *medium-hot* coals. Grill, uncovered, till fish flakes easily or poultry is no longer pink, turning once. For fish, allow 4 to 6 minutes for each ½ inch of thickness; for poultry, allow 15 to 18 minutes total. To serve, top with yogurt and almonds or olives. Makes 4 servings.

The New Pantry

Our pantry of 20 ingredients promises convenience, good nutrition, and bold flavors. Here are some more reasons to keep your kitchen stocked with these foods.

Sweet peppers: Today's array of pepper colors brightens your cooking.

Broccoli: These bushy stalks boast of fiber and vitamins A and C. Broccoli and its cruciferous cousins, such as cabbage and brussels sprouts, may help prevent heart disease and some forms of cancer.

Pears: No longer a fall fruit, juicy pears are available all year.

Low-fat cheeses: You'll find more types of cheeses available in low-fat form. Look for shredded or sliced.

Low-fat plain yogurt: Remember when yogurt was a health food? Now it's a healthful cooking staple.

Lean ground beef or turkey: A family favorite for decades, ground beef has leaned up. To be called lean, beef can have no more than 10 percent fat by weight. Turkey, as an option, is gaining a following.

Boneless, skinless chicken breasts or turkey cutlets: These cut the fat from family meals and save you time.

Fresh or frozen fish fillets: Another quick-cooking, lean entrée.

Pasta: It's nutritious, fast-cooking, and you can do lots with it.

Quick-cooking or instant brown rice: Cook rice in 10 minutes or less.

Refrigerated pizza dough: No rising or thawing, this handy dough makes more than pizza. Use it as a crust, wrapper, pocket bread, or for breadsticks.

Frozen fruit juice concentrate: Pick from a growing number of flavors.

Loose-pack frozen vegetables: Exciting new unseasoned combinations take the ho-hum out of vegetables.

Stewed tomatoes: This kitchen basic now comes plain, no salt added, or seasoned—Italian, Mexican, or Cajun.

Ripe olives: The popularity of Mediterranean and Mexican cooking makes black olives a pantry essential.

Canned soups: Lower sodium alternatives keep this standby in step with today's tastes.

Canned beans: With the protein in beans, you often can cut back or eliminate meat in cooking.

Dried mushrooms: Soak this flavorful Oriental import to use in recipes calling for mushrooms.

Almonds: Go nuts—a toasty sprinkle dresses up almost anything, adding protein and monounsaturated fat.

Nonstick spray coating: One squirt eliminates the mess of greasing dishes and the added fat.

Our Staple Ingredients

When we created our recipes for the New Pantry, we counted on your having the following ingredients already on hand:

milk
eggs
cornstarch
flour
cooking oil
onions and onion salt
garlic, garlic salt or powder
soy sauce
bottled hot pepper sauce
black and red pepper
salt
sesame or poppy seed
dried herbs (such as basil, oregano, thyme, dillweed, and Italian seasoning)
spices (such as ginger, cinnamon, allspice, paprika, chili powder, and curry powder)

RECIPE BY REQUEST: KIWI LIME PIE

A tortelike pie—layers of tender pastry, jelly, and lemon-lime custard. Fix a day ahead and chill.

Now that kiwi fruit is mainstream, this recipe is even more popular than when we first ran it in 1980.

KIWI LIME PIE

- ¾ cup sugar
- ⅓ cup all-purpose flour
- 1¾ cups milk
- 3 beaten eggs
- ¼ cup margarine *or* butter
- 2 teaspoons finely shredded lime peel
- ¼ cup lime juice
- 1 8-ounce carton lemon yogurt
- Few drops green food coloring
- Pastry for Double-Crust Pie
- ¼ cup apple jelly
- Whipped cream
- 2 kiwi fruit, peeled and sliced
- 1 *or* 2 limes, sliced

In a saucepan combine sugar, flour, and ⅛ teaspoon *salt.* Stir in milk. Stir over medium heat till bubbly. Reduce heat; cook and stir for 2 minutes more. Remove from heat. Stir *1 cup* of the hot mixture into eggs. Return to saucepan; cook and stir till thickened. Cook and stir for 2 minutes more. *Do not boil.* Remove from heat. Stir in margarine, lime peel, and juice. Fold in yogurt. Tint with food coloring. Cover surface with plastic wrap; cool.

On a floured surface, roll *half* of the pastry into a 12-inch circle. Line a 9-inch pie plate with pastry. Trim and flute edge; prick pastry. Bake in a 450° oven 10 to 12 minutes. Cool. Divide remaining pastry in half. Roll each half into a circle ⅛ inch thick; cut an 8¾-inch circle out of one portion and an 8-inch circle out of the other. Place circles on a baking sheet; prick. Bake in a 450° oven 10 minutes. Cool.

Brush the pastry shell with some jelly. Place about *1 cup* of the custard in shell. Cover with 8-inch pastry; brush with jelly. Spread with *1¼ cups* custard. Top with 8¾-inch pastry. Top with remaining jelly and custard. Cover; chill pie overnight. To serve pie, garnish with whipped cream, kiwi fruit slices, and lime slices. Serves 8.

Pastry for Double-Crust Pie: Stir together 2 cups *all-purpose flour* and 1 teaspoon *salt.* Cut in ⅔ cup *shortening.* Sprinkle 1 tablespoon *water* over part of the mixture; gently toss with a fork. Push to side of bowl. Repeat till all is moistened (6 to 7 tablespoons of water total). Form dough into a ball.

Nutrition information per serving: 528 cal., 10 g pro., 66 g carbo., 26 g fat, 108 mg chol., 440 mg sodium.

YOU FEEL A CHILL FROM THAT FIRST BRISK OCTOBER EVENING, AND YOU WELCOME BACK YOUR WOOL SWEATERS, A CRACKLING FIREPLACE, AND THE HEARTY FOODS OF FALL. COMFORTING FAVORITES SUCH AS POT ROAST AND VEGETABLES, SIMMERING SOUPS, AND HOME-BAKED BREADS COME TO MIND. CELEBRATE THE SEASON WITH THESE AND OTHER SOUL-SOOTHING RECIPES, FEATURED ON THE FOLLOWING PAGES.

BY LISA HOLDERNESS

TASTES OF AUTUMN

MAPLE-GLAZED POT ROAST AND VEGETABLES WITH MINI GRUYERE PUFFS.

RED CABBAGE WITH FENNEL
Fall-fresh fennel, with its mellow licorice flavor, pairs exquisitely with pork, beef, or game.

CHOUCROUTE GARNI
Savor the tangy sauerkraut, sausage, and apples in this easy French country dish.

LEEK AND PEPPER SPOON BREAD
When Southerners yearn for comfort food, this corn-pudding-style bread satisfies.

133

TASTES OF AUTUMN

PORK MEDAILLONS WITH BRANDY CREAM
Imagine tender, juicy pork drizzled with a silky, rich sauce. This one's worth serving on a special occasion.

WILD RICE AND CRANBERRY PILAF
This hearty pilaf, spiked with dried cranberries and almonds, cozies up to the Pork Medaillons.

AMARETTO COMPOTE
Light, simple desserts can be elegant, too. Red pears and dried fruit in amaretto sauce is proof.

SWEET-POTATO PEAR PIE
Experience two of autumn's most treasured harvests, sweet potatoes and pears, baked in a pecan pastry crust.

**CARAMEL
ALMOND TORTE**
*What an irresistible
dessert—almond cake
layered with caramel
filling and lavishly
spread with whipped
cream and caramel.*

GUIDE TO FALL PRODUCE

Apples: When shopping for apples, remember that the varieties are truly different. For pie baking or sauce making, top choices this time of year include Golden Delicious, Jonathan, Rome Beauty, Newtown Pippin, and Winesap. For snacking or salad making, try McIntosh, Red Delicious, Cortland, Empire, or Golden Delicious.

Firm texture is key when selecting apples. Those that yield to slight pressure on the skin are probably mealy or mushy inside. Also check for smooth skin that is relatively bruise free.

Keep apples chilled in a vented plastic bag. Those stored at room temperature lose flavor and juiciness and become mealy.

Cranberries: Enjoy fresh cranberries from mid-September through December. These tart fruits vary in color from vibrant to dark red. Look for glossy, plump, and firm berries. Those that appear dull or shriveled are past their prime.

Chill cranberries in their original package or loosely covered for up to two months. Plan to buy extra during peak season to freeze for year-round use. Simply freeze in the package for up to a year. You needn't thaw the berries to use.

Guide to Fall Produce

Fennel: Fennel is in season from October through April. Look for firm, white fennel bulbs with rigid, crisp stalks. Bright green leaves are also a key to freshness.

You can store fennel, unwashed, in a plastic bag for up to one week. Before using, trim the stalks to within 1 inch of the bulb and discard the outer stalks. Halve the fennel bulb and remove the tough core from the base of the bulb.

Snip the green fennel leaves and use as a seasoning for sauces, salad dressings, and soups and stews. Or, use them as a garnish.

Grapes: Table grapes are in the markets year-round. When buying grapes, choose those found in clusters with plump, well-colored berries on pliable, green stems. Soft, wrinkled grapes or those with bleached areas around the stem are beyond their peak. Grapes should keep for several days, unwashed and chilled in a plastic bag.

Jerusalem artichokes: These tubers, also called sunchokes, are related to the sunflower plant. Raw, the Jerusalem artichoke has a nutty flavor. Cooked, it tastes more like an artichoke. Jerusalem artichokes are available fall through winter and will keep about a week if stored in a plastic bag in the refrigerator.

Parsnips: These creamy white, slightly sweet, carrot-shaped root vegetables mainly are available during the late fall and winter months. Small- to medium-width roots usually have the best flavor and texture. Other signs of quality include firm, well-shaped, smooth roots that are free of blemishes. To store, wrap tightly in plastic wrap and refrigerate for up to two weeks. Before cooking, wash and peel away the outer skin. Many parsnips are wax coated to extend storage.

Pears: Most varieties can be used for both cooking and eating fresh. Cooking favorites tend to be Bartlett, Bosc, and Nelis varieties. You will enjoy Anjou, Comice, Forelle, and Seckel for eating fresh. Pears are harvested green because they do not mature well on the tree. Place pears in a paper bag and let them stand a few days at room temperature. Ripe pears should yield to gentle pressure at the stem end. When just ripe, enjoy them right away or chill till needed.

Persimmons: This Oriental fruit comes in two main varieties, Hachiya and Fuyu. Both are orange but the Hachiya (the more common) is acorn shaped, large, soft when ripe, and very sweet. The Fuyu tends to be smaller, rounded, tannin-free, and crisp like an apple. Look for both varieties from September through December.

To ripen either variety, store at room temperature in a loosely closed paper bag. Then store in the refrigerator and use as soon as possible. Enjoy both varieties, unpeeled, eaten out of your hand or cut up in salads. You can wrap ripe persimmons in freezer wrap and freeze for up to three months to use them out of season.

Pomegranates: Between September and December, look for pomegranates about the size of a small grapefruit. They should be reddish-green in color. The heavier the fruit, the better, as this is a sign of juiciness. The inside of this unusual fruit is filled with a wealth of translucent, vivid red pouches (called arils), each encompassing a tiny seed. It is these sweet, juicy arils that you scoop out and savor. You can freeze the arils for later use or keep the pomegranate whole and chill for up to three months.

Squash: Although some winter squash varieties may be found all year, most primarily are available from September through March. Some of the more common varieties include acorn, butternut, banana, hubbard, and pumpkin. Look for squash with hard, thick shells that feel heavy for their size. When buying pumpkins for cooking, pick those smaller in size. To store squash, keep all varieties whole and unwrapped in a cool (50 degrees F.), dry, dark place for up to two months.

Sweet potatoes: Is it a sweet potato or a yam? Actually, these names are used interchangeably in American markets. Shop for firm, smooth-skinned yams, free from blemishes. Store in a cool (50 degrees F.), dry, well-ventilated spot for up to two months or at room temperature for a week. *Do not refrigerate uncooked potatoes.* In most locations, sweet potatoes are available all year, with the summer months yielding the lowest supply.

Swiss chard: A member of the beet family, Swiss chard is grown for its lush, full-flavored leaves. Pick leaves that are fresh and free from bruises and store for up to three days, unwashed, in the refrigerator. Swiss chard is most plentiful fall through spring. Fresh Swiss chard tastes wonderful in salads. It also can be added to soup or served cooked like spinach.

Turnips: A close relative to cabbage, this mild-flavored root has existed for centuries. From October through March is the peak season for turnips, although you may find turnips available year-round. Look for turnips that are about 2 to 3 inches in diameter, firm to the touch, and fairly heavy. Avoid those with bruised or decayed areas. Keep them chilled for up to one week. Before using, wash and cut off the outer skin.

Rutabagas: Often rutabagas and turnips are used interchangeably, although the rutabaga is larger and stronger flavored. Yellow rutabagas usually have a bronze-colored skin and the white variety has a green skin.

Shop for this root vegetable from October through March. Select firm, unblemished rutabagas 3 to 4 inches in diameter and refrigerate for up to one week. Before cooking, peel the wax-coated skin down to the inner flesh of the root.

MAPLE-GLAZED POT ROAST AND VEGETABLES

- 1 2½- to 3-pound beef chuck pot roast *or* boneless beef round rump roast
- 1 tablespoon cooking oil
- ½ cup maple *or* maple-flavored syrup
- 1 teaspoon finely shredded orange peel
- ½ cup orange juice
- 2 tablespoons white wine vinegar
- 1 tablespoon Worcestershire sauce
- ½ teaspoon salt
- ¼ teaspoon pepper
- 1 bay leaf
- 5 medium carrots *or* parsnips, peeled and cut into 3-inch pieces (or, use a combination of both)
- 2 small onions, cut into wedges
- 2 stalks celery, bias sliced into 2-inch pieces
- 1 medium acorn squash
- ¼ cup water
- 2 tablespoons cornstarch

● **Trim excess fat** from roast. In a Dutch oven brown roast on all sides in hot oil; drain fat. Combine maple syrup, orange peel, orange juice, vinegar, Worcestershire sauce, salt, pepper, and bay leaf. Pour over roast. Bring to boiling; reduce heat. Cover and simmer over low heat for 1¼ hours.
● **Add carrots or parsnips,** onions, and celery to meat mixture. Cover and simmer for 15 minutes. Meanwhile, rinse squash; cut horizontally into ¾-inch-thick slices. Halve slices. Discard seeds and stem. Add squash; cover and simmer 10 to 15 minutes more or till meat and vegetables are tender. Remove the meat and vegetables from pan, discarding bay leaf. Cover and keep warm.
● **Measure pan juices,** reserving 1¾ cups. Return reserved juices to pan. Combine water and cornstarch; stir into pan juices. Cook and stir till thickened and bubbly. Cook and stir for 2 minutes more. Spoon atop meat and vegetables. Makes 8 servings.
Nutrition information per serving: 380 cal., 28 g pro., 34 g carbo., 15 g fat, 90 mg chol., 246 mg sodium, 827 mg potassium, and 4 g dietary fiber. U.S. RDA: 163% vit. A, 37% vit. C, 29% thiamine, 25% riboflavin, 26% niacin, 11% calcium, 25% iron.

CHOUCROUTE GARNI

Precooked potatoes and sausage speed this easy one-skillet dish to your table—

- 8 ounces fully cooked Polish sausage *or* fully cooked smoked bratwurst, bias sliced into 3-inch chunks
- 2 slices bacon, cut up
- ⅓ cup chopped onion
- 1 clove garlic, minced
- ⅓ cup dry white wine
- 2 teaspoons brown sugar
- 1 teaspoon caraway seed
- ¼ teaspoon pepper
- ⅛ teaspoon ground cloves
- 1 16-ounce can sauerkraut, rinsed and drained
- 1 16-ounce can sliced potatoes, drained
- 8 ounces fully cooked ham, cut into ½-inch cubes
- 2 medium green *or* red apples, cored and cut into 8 wedges each

● **If desired,** cut 2 or 3 horizontal slits in each sausage chunk so that the chunk remains intact but is easier to break apart for eating. Set aside.
● **In a 10-inch skillet cook** bacon, onion, and garlic till onion is tender but not brown. Drain. Stir in wine, brown sugar, caraway seed, pepper, and ground cloves. Add sauerkraut and potatoes. Top with Polish sausage or bratwurst and ham.
● **Bring the mixture to boiling;** reduce heat. Cover and simmer for 20 minutes. Add apple wedges and cook about 8 minutes more or till apples are tender. Makes 4 main-dish servings.
Nutrition information per serving: 439 cal., 26 g pro., 34 g carbo., 22 g fat, 74 mg chol., 1,842 mg sodium, 863 mg potassium, and 5 g dietary fiber. U.S. RDA: 44% vit. C, 80% thiamine, 24% riboflavin, 47% niacin, 25% iron.

RED CABBAGE WITH FENNEL

For more about fennel, an anise-flavored vegetable, see the Guide to Fall Produce on page 139—

- 2 medium fennel bulbs
- 1 clove garlic, minced
- 2 tablespoons margarine *or* butter
- 1 cup water
- 2 tablespoons white vinegar *or* lemon juice
- 1½ teaspoons instant chicken bouillon granules
- ¼ teaspoon onion salt
- ¼ teaspoon white pepper
- ¼ cup red wine vinegar
- ¼ cup water
- 6 cups coarsely shredded red cabbage
- 4 teaspoons cornstarch
- 2 tablespoons water

● **Remove green tops** from fennel. Rinse; pat dry. Snip enough to make *2 teaspoons*. Reserve remaining tops for a garnish. Cut bulbs into wedges.
● **In a medium saucepan cook** garlic in hot margarine or butter 1 minute. Add fennel bulbs, the 1 cup water, vinegar or lemon juice, the 2 teaspoons snipped fennel tops, bouillon granules, onion salt, and white pepper. Bring to boiling; reduce heat. Cover and simmer for 12 to 14 minutes or till fennel wedges are tender.
● **In a large saucepan** bring red wine vinegar and the ¼ cup water to boiling. Add red cabbage. Cover and cook for 8 to 12 minutes or till cabbage is tender. Drain. Transfer to a serving platter.
● **Remove fennel bulbs** from liquid with a slotted spoon; place atop red cabbage. Combine cornstarch and the 2 tablespoons water; add to fennel cooking liquid. Cook and stir till thickened and bubbly. Cook and stir for 2 minutes more. Pour sauce over cabbage and fennel. Garnish with remaining fennel tops. Serves 4 to 6.
Nutrition information per serving: 106 cal., 3 g pro., 12 g carbo., 6 g fat, 0 mg chol., 598 mg sodium, 520 mg potassium, and 2 g dietary fiber. U.S. RDA: 92% vit. A, 113% vit. C, 10% thiamine, and 12% calcium.

SWEET POTATO-PEAR PIE

Give pie a whole new look by preparing this dessert in a springform pan. You can substitute a 9-inch round cake pan, if needed, and serve this unique pie from the pan—

- 1 cup all-purpose flour
- ¾ cup finely ground pecans
- 2 tablespoons brown sugar
- ½ teaspoon salt
- ⅓ cup shortening
- 3 tablespoons cold water
- 2 small pears, peeled, cored, and thinly sliced, *or* one 16-ounce can pear slices, drained
- 2 tablespoons granulated sugar
- 1 tablespoon all-purpose flour
- 1 18-ounce can vacuum-packed sweet potatoes *or* one 16-ounce can pumpkin
- 3 beaten eggs
- 1¼ cups milk
- ¾ cup packed brown sugar
- 1 teaspoon ground cinnamon
- ¼ teaspoon salt

● **In a medium mixing bowl combine** the 1 cup flour, ground pecans, the 2 tablespoons brown sugar, and the ½ teaspoon salt. Cut in shortening till pieces are the size of small peas. Sprinkle *1 tablespoon* of the water over part of the mixture; gently toss with a fork. Push to side of bowl. Repeat till all is moistened. Form dough into a ball.

● **On a lightly floured surface, roll** dough from center to edges, forming an 11-inch circle. Ease pastry into a 9-inch springform pan and pat in place with your fingers. Pastry should cover bottom of pan and 1½ inches up sides. Trim edges, if necessary. Set aside.

● **Toss pear slices** with granulated sugar and the 1 tablespoon flour; arrange in pastry shell.

● **Drain and mash sweet potatoes.** In a large mixing bowl combine sweet potatoes or pumpkin, eggs, milk, the ¾ cup brown sugar, cinnamon, and the ¼ teaspoon salt.

● **Place pastry shell** with pears on oven rack; carefully pour in sweet potato filling. Bake in a 375° oven for 55 to 60 minutes or till a knife inserted near the center comes out clean.

● **Cool on a wire rack** for 15 minutes; loosen crust from sides of pan. Cool 30 minutes more; remove sides of pan.

Cool completely. Chill to store. If desired, top with whipped cream and chopped pecans. Makes 8 servings.

Nutrition information per serving: 439 cal., 7 g pro., 62 g carbo., 19 g fat, 83 mg chol., 287 mg sodium, 473 mg potassium, and 4 g dietary fiber. U.S. RDA: 71% vit. A, 32% vit. C, 28% thiamine, 26% riboflavin, 12% niacin, 13% calcium, 14% iron.

APPLE BUTTER MUFFINS

To keep on top of busy mornings, freeze a batch of these muffins. To defrost, place two muffins on a paper towel. Microcook, uncovered, on 100% power (high) for 50 to 60 seconds—

- 1¾ cups all-purpose flour
- ⅓ cup sugar
- 2 teaspoons baking powder
- 1 teaspoon apple pie spice* *or* pumpkin pie spice
- ¼ teaspoon salt
- 1 beaten egg
- ¾ cup milk
- ¼ cup cooking oil
- ⅓ cup apple butter
- ⅓ cup chopped pecans
- 2 tablespoons sugar

● **In a medium mixing bowl combine** flour, the ⅓ cup sugar, baking powder, apple pie spice or pumpkin pie spice, and the salt. Make a well in the center.

● **Combine the egg, milk, and oil;** add all at once to flour mixture. Stir just till moistened.

● **Lightly grease muffin cups** or line with paper bake cups. Spoon a rounded *tablespoon* of batter into each muffin cup. Top each with a rounded *teaspoon* of apple butter and then with the remaining batter.

● **Combine pecans** and the 2 tablespoons sugar; sprinkle atop the batter. Bake in a 400° oven about 20 minutes or till golden. Remove from pans; serve warm. Makes 12 muffins.

*For the apple pie spice, you can substitute ½ teaspoon *ground cinnamon*, ¼ teaspoon *ground nutmeg*, ⅛ teaspoon *ground allspice*, and a dash *ground ginger*.

Nutrition information per muffin: 187 cal., 3 g pro., 27 g carbo., 8 g fat, 19 mg chol., 106 mg sodium, 83 g potassium. U.S. RDA: 18% thiamine.

You'll find a tasty pocket of apple butter nestled inside each fresh-baked muffin.

AMARETTO COMPOTE

Red-skinned pears, one of the newer varieties, give this warm fruit medley a rich fall look—

- 2 cups water
- 1 cup dried, pitted prunes
- ½ cup dried apricots
- 2 medium pears (preferably red skinned), cored and sliced into wedges (1½ cups)
- 1 cup amaretto
- ¼ cup sugar
- 1 teaspoon shredded lemon peel

● **In a medium saucepan combine** the water, prunes, and apricots. Bring to boiling. Remove from heat and let stand for 15 minutes. Drain, reserving ½ cup of the liquid.

● **In the same saucepan combine** the reserved liquid, pears, amaretto, sugar, and lemon peel. Bring to boiling; reduce heat. Cover and simmer for 8 to 10 minutes or till pears are crisp-tender. Stir in prunes and apricots; heat through. Spoon into 4 individual serving dishes. Serve warm. Serves 4.

Nutrition information per serving: 446 cal., 2 g pro., 88 g carbo., 1 g fat, 0 mg chol., 8 mg sodium, 597 mg potassium, and 7 g dietary fiber. U.S. RDA: 24% vit. A, 10% riboflavin, 10% niacin, 11% iron.

PORK MEDAILLONS WITH BRANDY CREAM

Look to the harvest dinner menu box (right) to see this impressive entree as part of a complete meal—

- 1 2- to 2½-pound boneless pork loin roast
- Pepper
- ⅓ cup chicken broth
- 1 tablespoon chopped shallot *or* green onion
- ¼ cup whipping cream
- ¼ cup brandy *or* cognac
- ½ cup unsalted butter, cut into small pieces and softened
- 1 tablespoon lemon juice
- ¼ teaspoon salt
- ⅛ teaspoon white pepper
- 12 3-inch chives (optional)

● **Rub pork roast with pepper.** Place on a rack in a shallow baking pan; insert a meat thermometer. Roast in a 325° oven till the meat thermometer registers 160° (allow 26 to 31 minutes per pound).
● **Meanwhile, for sauce,** in a medium saucepan combine chicken broth and shallot or green onion. Bring to boiling; reduce heat. Cover and simmer 2 minutes. Add whipping cream and brandy. Simmer, uncovered, over medium heat 10 minutes or till sauce is reduced to ⅓ cup. Remove from heat. Strain sauce; return sauce to pan.
● **Add butter to sauce,** one piece at a time, stirring constantly with a wire whisk. Stir in lemon juice, salt, and white pepper.
● **To serve, slice** meat across the grain into 18 slices. Place 3 slices on each dinner plate; spoon sauce atop meat. If desired, top with chives. Serves 6.

Nutrition information per serving: 446 cal., 29 g pro., 4 g carbo., 34 g fat, 149 mg chol., 210 mg sodium, 415 mg potassium, and 0 g dietary fiber. U.S. RDA: 23% vit. A, 83% thiamine, 33% riboflavin, 48% niacin.

An Elegant Harvest Dinner Menu
Pork Medaillons with Brandy Cream
Wild Rice and Cranberry Pilaf
Sourdough or French bread
Steamed baby pattypan squash
Fumé Blanc or Chardonnay wine
Amaretto Compote
Coffee and Tea

For a special autumn dinner, enjoy this complete menu, including complementary wine selections. The pork medaillons and the pilaf can share the same oven, since they both cook at the same oven temperature. Steam the squash easily by cutting it into halves and micro-cooking, covered, in 2 tablespoons water till crisp-tender. While the pork and pilaf are cooking, use the range top to make the brandy cream and Amaretto Compote. Serve the compote with purchased tea cookies, if desired.

WILD RICE AND CRANBERRY PILAF

More varieties of dried fruits are available to sweeten your cooking—

- ¾ cup wild rice
- 3 cups chicken broth
- ½ cup pearl barley
- ¼ cup snipped dried cranberries, apricots, *and/or* cherries
- ¼ cup currants
- 1 tablespoon margarine *or* butter
- ⅓ cup sliced almonds, toasted

● **Rinse rice** with cold water; drain. In a saucepan combine rice and chicken broth. Bring to boiling; reduce heat. Cover; simmer 10 minutes. Remove from heat. Stir in barley; cranberries, apricots, and/or cherries; currants; and margarine or butter. Spoon rice mixture into a 1½-quart casserole.
● **Bake, covered,** in a 325° oven for 55 to 60 minutes or till rice and barley are tender and liquid is absorbed, stirring once. Fluff rice mixture with a fork; stir in almonds. Makes 6 side-dish servings.

Nutrition information per serving: 223 cal., 8 g pro., 36 g carbo., 6 g fat, 1 mg chol., 415 mg sodium, 306 mg potassium, and 5 g dietary fiber. U.S. RDA: 13% riboflavin, 25% niacin.

LEEK AND PEPPER SPOON BREAD

Spoon bread puffs as it bakes just like a soufflé. Serve it steaming hot from the oven, with a spoon, of course—

- 1 medium leek, thinly sliced
- ½ cup chopped sweet red pepper
- 2 tablespoons margarine *or* butter
- 2 cups milk
- 1½ cups yellow cornmeal
- 3 beaten egg yolks
- 1 cup cream-style cottage cheese
- 1 cup shredded provolone cheese *or* Swiss cheese
- 1 8½-ounce can cream-style corn
- ½ teaspoon salt
- 3 egg whites

● **In a large saucepan cook** leek and red pepper in hot margarine or butter for 4 minutes. Combine the milk and cornmeal; add to the saucepan. Cook, stirring constantly, till mixture is very thick and pulls away from sides of pan. Remove from heat.
● **In a mixing bowl combine** egg yolks, cottage cheese, provolone or Swiss cheese, corn, and salt. Stir into cornmeal mixture in saucepan.
● **In a medium mixer bowl beat** egg whites with an electric mixer on high speed till stiff peaks form (tips stand straight). Fold into cornmeal mixture. Spoon mixture into a greased 2-quart casserole. Bake in a 350° oven 55 to 60 minutes or till a knife inserted near the center comes out clean. Serve immediately. Makes 8 side-dish servings.

Nutrition information per serving: 287 cal., 14 g pro., 32 g carbo., 11 g fat, 99 mg chol., 540 mg sodium, 278 mg potassium, and 3 g dietary fiber. U.S. RDA: 26% vit. A, 26% vit. C, 25% thiamine, 34% riboflavin, 14% niacin, 27% calcium, 10% iron.

CARAMEL ALMOND TORTE

    6 **egg yolks**
1½ **cups sugar**
    ½ **cup apple cider** *or* **apple juice**
    2 **teaspoons vanilla**
    1 **teaspoon baking powder**
    ½ **teaspoon ground cinnamon**
    6 **egg whites**
    2 **cups graham cracker crumbs**
    1 **cup ground almonds**
Caramel Sauce
Caramel Cream Cheese Filling
Sweetened Whipped Cream

● **In a small mixer bowl combine** egg yolks, *1 cup* of the sugar, the apple cider or juice, vanilla, baking powder, and cinnamon. Beat with an electric mixer on medium speed about 3 minutes or till light and fluffy. Wash the beaters thoroughly.

● **In a large mixer bowl beat** egg whites on medium speed till soft peaks form (tips curl). Beat on high speed, slowly adding remaining sugar, till stiff peaks form (tips stand straight).

● **Fold the egg yolk mixture** into the egg white mixture. Fold cracker crumbs and almonds into egg mixture, *one-fourth* at a time.

● **Divide batter evenly** among 3 well-greased and floured 8-inch round baking pans. (If necessary, use two 8-inch pans. Refrigerate *one-third* of the batter while the first 2 layers are baking. Bake remaining layer as directed.)

● **Bake in a 325° oven** for 25 to 30 minutes or till cake springs back when lightly touched near the center. Cool on a wire rack for 10 minutes. Loosen sides; remove cake layers from pans. Cool thoroughly on wire racks.

● **Place one cake layer** on a cake plate; spread with *half* of the Caramel Cream Cheese Filling. Top with second layer; spread with the remaining filling. Top with last layer. Frost the top and sides with the Sweetened Whipped Cream. Drizzle with the remaining Caramel Sauce. Makes 12 to 14 servings.

Caramel Sauce: In a small saucepan combine ⅔ cup packed *brown sugar* and 1 tablespoon *cornstarch*. Add ¼ cup *apple cider* or *apple juice* and ¼ cup *margarine* or *butter*. Cook and stir over medium heat till thickened and bubbly. Cook and stir for 2 minutes more. Remove from heat. In a small bowl beat 1 *egg yolk;* gradually stir in ½ cup of the hot brown sugar mixture. Return the egg mixture to the saucepan. Cook and stir till bubbly; reduce heat. Cook and stir for 2 minutes more. Remove from heat; cover and cool. Makes ¾ cup.

Use ½ *cup* of the Caramel Sauce for the Caramel Cream Cheese Filling. Use remaining sauce to drizzle atop the Sweetened Whipped Cream. If necessary, thin the remaining Caramel Sauce with 1 to 2 teaspoons *apple cider* or *apple juice* to make a topping of drizzling consistency.

Caramel Cream Cheese Filling: In a bowl beat one 8-ounce package *cream cheese* till fluffy. Gradually beat in ½ *cup* of the Caramel Sauce.

Sweetened Whipped Cream: In a small chilled mixing bowl combine 1 cup *whipping cream*, 2 tablespoons *sugar*, and ½ teaspoon *vanilla*. Beat till mixture mounds slightly and soft peaks form. Makes 2 cups.

Nutrition information per serving: *503 cal., 8 g pro., 60 g carbo., 27 g fat, 172 mg chol., 294 mg sodium, 244 mg potassium, and 1 g dietary fiber. U.S. RDA: 34% vit. A, 26% riboflavin, 13% calcium, 10% iron.*

MINI GRUYÈRE PUFFS

A cross between popovers and cream puffs, these little puffs get their marvelous rich flavor from Gruyère cheese, a nutty, creamy, yet firm cheese from Switzerland—

    1 **cup water**
    ½ **cup margarine** *or* **butter**
    ¾ **teaspoon dried basil, crushed**
    ¼ **teaspoon garlic salt**
    ⅛ **teaspoon ground red pepper**
    1 **cup all-purpose flour**
    4 **eggs**
    ½ **cup shredded Gruyère** *or* **Swiss cheese (2 ounces)**
    2 **tablespoons grated Parmesan cheese**

● **In a medium saucepan combine** water and margarine or butter. Add basil, garlic salt, and red pepper. Bring to boiling. Add flour all at once, stirring vigorously. Cook and stir till mixture forms a ball that doesn't separate. Remove from heat. Cool 5 minutes.

● **Add eggs, one at a time,** beating with a spoon after each addition till smooth. Stir in Gruyère cheese.

● **On a greased baking sheet drop** dough by rounded tablespoons into 18 equal mounds, about 2 inches apart. Sprinkle with Parmesan cheese.

● **Bake in a 400° oven** 30 to 35 minutes or till golden. Turn off oven; let puffs stand in oven 10 minutes. Serve hot. Makes 18 puffs.

Nutrition information per puff: *103 cal., 3 g pro., 6 g carbo., 7 g fat, 51 mg chol., 118 mg sodium, 29 mg potassium. U.S. RDA: 12% vit. A.*

For a memorable autumn afternoon with friends, serve cups of hot cider.

BRANDIED CIDER SIPPER

For a spicier sipper, let the spice bag steep in the cider for several minutes after heating through—

    1 quart apple cider *or* apple juice
    3 tablespoons honey
    2 tablespoons lemon juice
    4 whole cloves
    1 whole nutmeg
    1 2-inch-piece stick cinnamon
    ¼ to ⅓ cup brandy
    6 cinnamon stick stirrers (optional)
    6 lemon slices, halved (optional)

●**In a medium saucepan combine** apple cider or apple juice, honey, and lemon juice.

●**For spice bag, place** the cloves, nutmeg, and cinnamon in a double thickness of cheesecloth. Bring the corners of the cheesecloth together and tie the cheesecloth around the spices with a string. Add spice bag to cider mixture.

●**Cover and heat through** but *do not boil.* Remove spice bag and discard. Stir in brandy.

●**Serve the warm cider** in mugs. If desired, garnish with cinnamon stick stirrers and lemon slices. Makes six 6-ounce servings.

Nutrition information per serving: 135 cal., 0 g pro., 32 g carbo., 0 g fat, 0 mg chol., 6 mg sodium, 211 mg potassium, and 0 g dietary fiber.

HARVEST SQUASH AND APPLE SOUP

    ½ cup chopped onion
    1 small carrot, sliced (⅓ cup)
    1¾ cups apple cider *or* apple juice
    1 teaspoon instant chicken
       bouillon granules
    1 teaspoon lemon juice
    ¼ teaspoon ground ginger
    ¼ teaspoon white pepper
    2 cups cooked, mashed acorn
       squash* *or* one 16-ounce can
       pumpkin
    1 cup milk *or* light cream
Dairy sour cream (optional)
Snipped chives (optional)

●**In a large saucepan cook** onion and carrot in apple cider or juice, covered, for 12 minutes or till very tender. *Do not drain.* Add bouillon granules, lemon juice, ginger, and pepper.

●**Transfer to a blender container** or food processor bowl. Add mashed squash; blend or process till smooth. Return squash mixture to saucepan.

Add milk or light cream. Bring to boiling, stirring constantly. Reduce heat; cover and simmer for 5 to 10 minutes or till flavors are blended, stirring once or twice.

●**If desired, top each serving** with 3 small dollops of sour cream. To make the design in the photo *below,* start in the center of each dollop and pull a wooden skewer or pick through the soup just far enough to make little spokes. If desired, garnish with snipped chives. Makes 4 to 6 side-dish servings.

*To cook acorn squash, wash, quarter, and remove seeds from two 1-pound acorn squash. Place squash in a large saucepan with 1 cup *water.* Bring to boiling and reduce heat. Cover and simmer for 20 to 25 minutes or till squash is tender.

Or, to micro-cook the squash, wash, halve, remove seeds, and prick the skin. Place squash halves, skin side up, and 3 tablespoons *water* in a 12x7½x2-inch microwave-safe dish. Cover with vented plastic wrap. Micro-cook, covered, on 100% power (high) for 12 to 15 minutes or till tender, rearranging once. Drain.

Nutrition information per serving: 166 cal., 4 g pro., 37 g carbo., 2 g fat, 6 mg chol., 273 mg sodium, 822 mg potassium, and 4 g dietary fiber. U.S. RDA: 50% ₁vit. A, 28% vit. C, 26% thiamine, 12% riboflavin, 10% niacin, 18% calcium, 10% iron.

Enjoy a smooth and tangy blend of autumn's bounty in a homemade soup.

A Much Improved!

Lean eye of round paired with a low-fat Dijon sauce.

Fingers pointed to red meat when nutrition experts first recommended that we eat less fat. Was our long love affair with steak over? The message to beef producers was clear: lean up or lose out. They responded by cutting fat in several ways:

Updated farming. Beef today has less fat than beef of 20 years ago because of new production methods.

More trimming. Butchers now trim outside fat to ¼ inch or even less. That's a big change from the days of steaks that were framed with ½ inch or more of fat.

Better labeling. Many stores now mark lean cuts and include nutrition information, too. Look for the cuts labeled rump, round, sirloin, chuck, arm, and shank.

Revised grades. In 1987, the "Good" grade of beef was renamed *Select*. Because it has less marbling (intramuscular fat), USDA Select beef usually provides fewer calories than Prime or Choice grades, but it may not be as tender as Prime or Choice when cooked to well done.

A NEW BRAND OF BEEF

You may notice branded beef, such as Coleman, in your market, claiming to be leaner and more *natural* than unbranded. Natural beef usually, but not always, comes from cattle raised without antibiotics or added hormones.

NEW REPORT CARD GIVES BEEF A BETTER GRADE

COOKING LEAN BEEF

Any cut of lean beef needs quick cooking to stay tender and juicy—about one-third the traditional cooking time. The *Better Homes and Gardens*® Test Kitchen recommends cooking lean beef to rare or medium-rare doneness. Our taste testers found that branded and Select cuts cooked this way had similar flavor and tenderness. Try this lean roast beef and see.

BEEF WITH DIJON SAUCE

The lower-fat mustard sauce is based on thickened broth instead of the fat drippings that are usually used in gravy— Place one 2- to 3-pound *beef eye round roast* on a rack in a roasting pan. Insert a meat thermometer. Roast in a 325° oven to desired doneness, allowing 1 to 1¾ hours for rare (140°) or 1¾ to 2¼ hours for medium (160°) doneness.

For sauce, combine 1 cup *beef broth,* 1 tablespoon *cornstarch,* 1 tablespoon *Dijon-style mustard,* 1 teaspoon *honey,* and 1 teaspoon *Worcestershire sauce.* Cook and stir till thickened and bubbly. Cook and stir for 2 minutes more. Slice roast; serve with sauce. Top with snipped fresh chives. Makes 8 to 10 servings.

Nutrition information per serving: *166 cal., 25 g pro., 2 g carbo., 6 g fat, 59 mg chol., 215 mg sodium, 354 mg potassium. U.S. RDA: 13% riboflavin, 26% niacin, 10% iron.*

LEAN BEEF'S NUTRITION SCORE

All beef provides important nutrients: protein, iron, zinc, thiamine, and vitamin B$_{12}$. The amount of cholesterol, calories, and fat varies by the cut, grade, and amount of fat trimmed away. Prices vary greatly, too.

Sirloin Steak	Calories	Fat (g)	Cholesterol (mg)	Average Price/lb.
Coleman Natural	157	4.9	74	$7.47
Golden Trim	135	3.5	70	4.52
PureLean (Kohler)	134	2.9	70	6.49
USDA Choice	172	6.8	76	3.19
USDA Select	158	5.3	76	2.99

These figures are for a 3-ounce broiled beef sirloin steak. The branded meats were totally trimmed. The Choice and Select cuts had a ¼-inch fat cover, trimmed after cooking.
Sources: Applied Microbiological Services Inst.; Industrial Lab.; USDA Handbook 8.

BY BRENDA McDOWELL AND LISA PIASECKI

The JOY of
HOLIDAY

Even if you love to cook, preparing for the holidays can turn into a last-minute frenzy. To ease the rush and keep the joy in holiday baking, try our streamlined recipes on the following pages. You'll discover appetizers and sweets for parties, breads and cookies for gift giving, and luscious desserts for festive holiday dinners. Each recipe offers make-ahead steps, storage hints, and serving ideas. And if your time is too short for baking ahead, you can make and serve these recipes the same day.

BAKING
15 Fabulous Recipes You Can Make Ahead

BY JULIA MALLOY

FESTIVE
FINGER FOOD

*Cook now, play later. Be ready for a
spur-of-the-moment party by making and
freezing a few goodies ahead. When those
red-cheeked revelers appear at your door,
warm them with some quick-serve foods.
They'll delight in these appetizers that are
both sweet and savory.*

CHERRY-NUT
PINWHEELS

HERBED CHEESE TARTS

CURRIED SHRIMP
PHYLLO BUNDLES

ONION-BACON ROLLS

PUMPKIN-NUT GINGERBREAD

HOMEMADE GIFTS

In this age of mail-order convenience, why make a gift yourself? Because the pleasure that comes from lovingly baking and wrapping a food gift can't be bought. And the appreciation from those receiving your homemade gifts is such a worthwhile reward for your goodwill. This year, rediscover the simple joy of doing it yourself— the tantalizing aroma of baking will kindle your holiday spirit.

APRICOT-ALMOND WREATHS

WHOLE WHEAT
SPICE COOKIES

TREASURED DESSERTS

The whole family is anticipating that traditional holiday feast, complete with time-honored desserts. You can satisfy everyone's expectations and your own creativity by updating classic recipes just a bit. For ideas, start with our sweet selection that mixes the best of old and new.

RUM-RAISIN STEAMED PUDDING

THE JOY OF HOLIDAY BAKING

HONEY-PISTACHIO TART

RIBBON-OF-CRANBERRY
CHEESECAKE

On the November Cover

The recipes pictured on page 146 include variations of Cream Cheese Sugar Cookies (*below*), Shape-Up Cookies (*page 158*), and Slice-and-Bake Cookies (*page 157*). For dough shapes and colors, turn to our list of Cookie Decorating Ideas on page 157. To decorate, use Sugar Glaze, Butter Frosting, and various decorative candies or candied fruit.

CREAM CHEESE SUGAR COOKIES

To make the delicate dough easier to shape, be sure to use butter, then chill the dough and roll it out half at a time—

- ½ cup butter
- 1 3-ounce package cream cheese, softened
- 2 cups all-purpose flour
- ⅔ cup sugar
- 1 egg
- ½ teaspoon baking powder
- ½ teaspoon vanilla
- ¼ teaspoon almond extract
- 1 egg (optional)
- 1 tablespoon cooking oil (optional)

Sugar (optional)

● **In a large mixer bowl combine** butter and cream cheese. Beat with an electric mixer on medium to high speed for 30 seconds. Add *half* of the flour, the ⅔ cup sugar, 1 egg, baking powder, vanilla, and almond extract; beat till combined. Beat or stir in remaining flour. Divide in half. Cover and chill for 1 to 2 hours or till firm.

● **On a lightly floured surface,** roll *one portion* of the chilled dough to ¼-inch thickness. Using cookie cutters, cut into desired shapes. If desired, decorate before baking, following the Cookie Decorating Ideas on *page 157*. Transfer cutouts to an ungreased cookie sheet. If desired, stir together the remaining egg and the oil; brush over dough and sprinkle with sugar.

● **Bake in a 350° oven** for 8 to 10 minutes or till edges are light brown and cookies are slightly puffed. Transfer cookies to a wire rack; cool thoroughly. If desired, decorate after baking, following the Cookie Decorating Ideas on *page 157*. Makes 32.

Striped Cookies: Prepare dough as above; divide into 3 portions. Add desired food coloring paste to each portion, following directions for coloring dough on *page 157*. Cover; chill.

Divide each portion of dough into fourths. On a well-floured surface, roll each fourth of dough into a 12-inch rope. Place 4 ropes next to each other, alternating colors. Press ropes together slightly so each rope is about ¼ inch thick. Using a sharp knife, cut crosswise into 6 cookies. Place on a greased baking sheet. Repeat with remaining dough. Bake in a 350° oven for 10 to 12 minutes or till edges are light brown. Cool on a wire rack. Makes 18.

Cherry-Nut Pinwheels: Prepare and chill dough as above. On a lightly floured surface, roll *one portion* of the chilled dough into a 10-inch square, ⅛ inch thick. With a sharp knife, cut into sixteen 2½-inch squares. Arrange ½ inch apart on an ungreased cookie sheet. Drop 1 teaspoon of *Cherry-Nut Filling* (see recipe, *right*) in the center of *each* dough square. Cut 1-inch slits diagonally from each corner toward filling. Fold every other tip over to cover filling, forming a pinwheel (see photo, *page 148*). Place a *candied cherry* or *pecan half* in the center of each square; press lightly to seal. Brush with the egg mixture; sprinkle with the sugar. Bake and cool as above. Repeat with the remaining dough and filling.

Cherry-Nut Starbursts: Prepare and chill dough as above. On a lightly floured surface, roll *one portion* of the dough into a 10-inch square, ⅛ inch thick. Cut cookies with a 2-inch round cookie cutter. Using a small star-shaped cutter, cut stars from centers of *half* the rounds. Arrange plain rounds ½ inch apart on ungreased cookie sheet. Place a scant teaspoon of *Cherry-Nut Filling* (see recipe, *right*) in center of each plain round. Top with a cutout round. Seal edges with a fork. Brush with egg mixture; sprinkle with sugar. Bake and cool as above. Repeat with remaining dough and filling.

Stained Glass Cookies: Cut out cookie dough shapes. Arrange cutouts on a foil-lined cookie sheet. Using smaller cookie cutters, cut out small shapes from each dough shape. Fill cutouts with finely crushed *colored hard candies*. Brush with egg mixture; sprinkle with sugar. Bake and cool.

Glazed Cookies: Prepare cookie circles as above, *except* do not brush with egg or sprinkle with sugar. Glaze or dip, following Cookie Decorating Ideas on *page 157*, or use one of the following ideas.

Web Cookies: Glaze cookies with *Sugar Glaze* (see recipe, *page 156*). Add a few drops *paste food coloring* to some Sugar Glaze. Using a fine paintbrush, draw 3 concentric circles with colored Sugar Glaze on glazed cookies. With the dull edge of a table knife, draw 4 evenly spaced lines through circles from center to edge, wiping the knife after drawing each line. Then draw 4 more evenly spaced lines through the circles from edge to center, wiping the knife after drawing each line.

Painted Cookies: Glaze cookies with *Sugar Glaze* (see recipe, *page 156*). Add a few drops *paste food coloring* to some Sugar Glaze. Paint designs of dots or stripes on glazed cookies with colored Sugar Glaze.

To refrigerate: Store unglazed and unfrosted cookies, covered, in the refrigerator for up to 1 week.

To freeze: Arrange cooled, unglazed, and unfrosted cookies in a single layer in a freezer container. Cover tightly, seal, label, and freeze for up to 8 months. To thaw, let stand at room temperature for 30 minutes.

Nutrition information per plain cookie: *81 cal., 1 g pro., 10 g carbo., 4 g fat, 17 mg chol., 39 mg sodium, 15 mg potassium, and 0 g dietary fiber.*

CHERRY-NUT FILLING

Use this red-and-green filling for Cherry-Nut Pinwheels or Starbursts—

- ½ cup chopped candied cherries *and/or* diced mixed candied fruits and peels
- ⅓ cup chopped pecans *or* walnuts
- ⅓ cup snipped pitted whole dates
- 1 tablespoon light corn syrup
- ¼ teaspoon ground allspice

● **In a small bowl combine** chopped candied cherries and/or fruits and peels, chopped pecans or walnuts, snipped dates, corn syrup, and allspice. Makes 1 cup filling.

Make-Ahead Hints

The Joy of Holiday Baking recipes are designed for you to bake ahead and freeze. When the busy holidays arrive, just pull the cookies out and enjoy. To make sure your frozen goodies taste as good as the day you made them, package them properly. Wrap them in a moisture- and vaporproof wrap, such as freezer paper or freezer plastic wrap. Or, put them in a container that can withstand freezer temperatures.

Seal your package or container tightly to avoid the possibility of freezer burn. If taping, use a freezer tape. Label your packages with the recipe title, the quantity, reheating directions, and the date you froze it or the date by which it should be used. Be sure to use a waterproof marker, wax crayon, or ballpoint pen.

Bring corners together and twist.

CURRIED SHRIMP PHYLLO BUNDLES

When phyllo dough is left uncovered, it dries out quickly. That's why our Test Kitchen suggests working with three squares at a time while keeping the remaining phyllo covered with a damp paper towel or cloth—

- ⅓ cup plain yogurt
- ¼ cup coconut
- ¼ cup finely chopped unsalted peanuts
- 2 tablespoons chopped chutney
- 1 teaspoon curry powder
- ½ teaspoon grated gingerroot *or* ¼ teaspoon ground ginger
- 1 4½-ounce can tiny shrimp, drained
- 6 sheets frozen phyllo dough (16x12 inches), thawed
- ½ cup margarine *or* butter, melted

● **For filling,** in a small mixing bowl stir together yogurt, coconut, peanuts, chutney, curry powder, and gingerroot or ginger. Gently stir in shrimp.
● **Unfold phyllo dough.** Place *one* sheet of phyllo dough on a waxed-paper-lined cutting board. Cover remaining sheets with a damp paper towel or cloth. Generously brush with *some* of the margarine or butter. Top with another sheet of phyllo, then brush with *more* of the margarine. Repeat with a third sheet of phyllo and margarine.

● **Using a sharp knife, cut** the stack of buttered phyllo sheets into twelve 4-inch squares. Place about *2 teaspoons* of the filling in the center of *each* square. For each bundle, bring the 4 corners together; pinch and twist slightly.
● **Repeat with remaining phyllo** dough, margarine or butter, and filling to make 24 bundles total. Arrange bundles on an ungreased parchment- or foil-lined baking sheet.
● **Bake, uncovered, in a 375° oven** for 18 to 20 minutes or till golden. Serve immediately. Makes 24 bundles.

To freeze: Prepare phyllo bundles as directed, *except* do not bake. Freeze the unbaked bundles on a baking sheet. Transfer to a storage container; seal, label, and freeze. To serve, place frozen bundles on a parchment- or foil-lined baking sheet. Bake, uncovered, at 375° for 18 to 20 minutes or till golden.

Nutrition information per bundle: *76 cal., 2 g pro., 6 g carbo., 5 g fat, 8 mg chol., 91 mg sodium, 34 mg potassium, and 0 g dietary fiber.*

HERBED CHEESE TARTS

Combine three cheeses to create one superb filling—

Nonstick spray coating
- ⅓ cup fine dry bread crumbs *or* finely crushed zwieback
- 1 8-ounce package cream cheese, softened
- ¾ cup cream-style cottage cheese
- ½ cup shredded Swiss cheese
- 1 tablespoon all-purpose flour
- ¼ teaspoon dried basil, crushed
- ⅛ teaspoon garlic powder
- 2 eggs
Dairy sour cream (optional)
Sliced or slivered pitted ripe olives, red caviar, *or* chives (optional)
Roasted red pepper *or* pitted ripe olive cutouts* (optional)

● **For crust,** spray twenty-four 1¾-inch muffin cups with nonstick spray coating. Sprinkle the bread crumbs or crushed zwieback onto the bottom and sides of muffin cups to coat. Shake pans to remove excess crumbs. Set aside.
● **In a small mixer bowl combine** cream cheese, cottage cheese, Swiss cheese, flour, basil, and garlic powder. Beat with an electric mixer on medium speed just till fluffy. Add eggs; beat on low speed just till combined. *Do not overbeat.*
● **Fill *each* crumb-lined muffin cup** with *1 tablespoon* of the cheese mixture. Bake in a 375° oven for 15 minutes or till centers appear set. (Tarts will puff during baking, then deflate as they cool.) Cool in pans on wire racks for 10 minutes. Remove from pans. Cool thoroughly on wire racks.
● **To serve, spread tops** with sour cream. Garnish with olives, caviar, chives, and/or red pepper and olive cutouts. Makes 24 tarts.

To refrigerate: Bake and cool tarts as directed, *except* do not spread with sour cream or top with garnish. Cover and chill in the refrigerator for up to 48 hours. Let tarts stand at room temperature for 30 minutes before serving. Spread with sour cream and garnish as directed.

To freeze: Bake and cool tarts as directed, *except* do not spread with sour cream or garnish. Freeze tarts, uncovered, on the wire rack about 1 hour or till firm. Transfer to a freezer container or bag. Seal, label, and place in the freezer. To thaw, let stand, loosely covered, at room temperature about 2 hours or in the refrigerator overnight. Spread with sour cream and garnish as directed.

*Decorative cutouts: Use tiny hors d'oeuvre cutters to cut leaves, stars, or other decorative shapes out of the roasted red peppers and pitted ripe olives.

Nutrition information per tart: 62 cal., 3 g pro., 2 g carbo., 5 g fat, 31 mg chol., 76 mg sodium, 28 mg potassium, 0 g dietary fiber.

ONION-BACON ROLLS

These rolls are similar to Lithuanian Laṣinuočiai (La-SHEE-no-i-chay), but they're made with frozen bread dough instead of the more traditional home-made dough—

    1   12-ounce package sliced bacon
    1   large onion, chopped (1 cup)
    ½   cup chopped green pepper
    ½   teaspoon dried dillweed
    ¼   teaspoon pepper
    1   16-ounce loaf frozen bread
        dough, thawed
Milk
Poppy seed, fennel seed, *or* sesame
    seed

● **For filling,** in a skillet cook bacon till crisp; remove bacon, reserving *1 table-spoon* drippings. Drain bacon on paper towels; crumble when cool.
● **In the same skillet cook** onion, green pepper, dillweed, and pepper in reserved bacon drippings till onion is tender but not brown. Cool. Stir in crumbled bacon.
● **Divide bread dough** into 30 portions. Roll *each* portion into a ball; roll or pat each ball into a 3-inch circle. Place a scant *1 tablespoon* of the filling in the center of each circle. Bring up dough edges around the filling; seal the edges together.
● **Arrange filled rolls,** seam side down, on a greased baking sheet. Brush with milk. Sprinkle with poppy seed, fennel seed, or sesame seed.
● **Bake, uncovered, in a 375° oven** for 15 to 20 minutes or till rolls are golden. Serve warm. Makes 30 rolls.
    To freeze: Prepare and bake rolls as directed above. Cool thoroughly on a wire rack. Transfer rolls to a freezer container. Seal, label, and freeze for up to 4 months. To reheat, arrange frozen rolls on an ungreased baking sheet. Bake, uncovered, in a 375° oven about 15 minutes or till rolls are heated through.
    Nutrition information per roll: *75 cal., 3 g pro., 7 g carbo., 4 g fat, 6 mg chol., 169 mg sodium, 42 mg potassium, 0 g dietary fiber. U.S. RDA: 10% thiamine.*

LAYERED CHOCOLATE-PEANUT DIAMONDS

To make even diamonds, measure with a ruler and mark with toothpicks before cutting—

    ⅓   cup margarine *or* butter
    ¼   cup peanut butter
    1¼ cups all-purpose flour
    ¾   cup packed brown sugar
    1   8-ounce package cream cheese,
        softened
    ¼   cup honey
    2   tablespoons brown sugar
    2   tablespoons all-purpose flour
    2   eggs
    1½ cups finely chopped peanuts
    1   6-ounce package (1 cup) semi-
        sweet chocolate pieces

● **In a small mixer bowl combine** margarine or butter and peanut butter; beat with an electric mixer on medium to high speed for 30 seconds. Add about *half* of the 1¼ cups flour and the ¾ cup brown sugar; beat till combined. Beat or stir in the remaining half of the 1¼ cups flour.
● **Press mixture evenly** into a 13x9x2-inch baking dish. Bake in a 350° oven about 15 minutes or till light brown.
● **In a small mixer bowl combine** cream cheese, honey, the 2 tablespoons brown sugar, and the 2 tablespoons flour; beat on medium speed till combined. Add eggs; beat just till combined. Stir in *1 cup* of the peanuts. Pour over baked crust. Bake about 15 minutes more or till set.
● **Sprinkle chocolate pieces** over top; bake about 2 minutes more or till softened. Place the dish on a wire rack. Spread melted chocolate pieces over top. Sprinkle with remaining peanuts. Cool thoroughly on wire rack. Cut into diamonds or bars. Refrigerate or freeze as directed. Makes 42 bars.
    To refrigerate: Cover the cooled bars and store in the refrigerator for up to 1 week.
    To freeze: Arrange cooled bars in a single layer in a freezer container. Cover tightly, seal, label, and freeze for up to 8 months. To thaw, let stand at room temperature for 1 hour.
    Nutrition information per bar: *133 cal., 3 g pro., 13 g carbo., 8 g fat, 16 mg chol., 68 mg sodium, 92 mg potassium, and 1 g dietary fiber.*

SUGAR GLAZE

Three ingredients for sweet success—

    2   cups sifted powdered sugar
    1   tablespoon light corn syrup
    2   to 3 tablespoons milk

● **In a small bowl stir together** powdered sugar, corn syrup, and enough of the milk to make a glaze of drizzling consistency. Makes ⅔ cup.

CHOCOLATE GLAZE

So quick, so easy!

    1   6-ounce package (1 cup) semi-
        sweet chocolate pieces
    2   tablespoons shortening

● **In a small heavy saucepan heat** chocolate pieces and shortening over low heat till melted, stirring often. Makes ⅔ cup.
    Microwave directions: In a 2-cup measure combine chocolate pieces and shortening. Cook, uncovered, on 100% power (high) for 2 to 2½ minutes or till soft enough to stir till smooth.

COOKIE PAINT

    1   egg yolk
    ¼   teaspoon water
Liquid food coloring

● **In a small mixing bowl beat** together egg yolk and water. Divide among 3 or 4 small bowls. Add 2 or 3 drops of food coloring to each bowl and mix well. Brush over cookies before baking. Makes 2 tablespoons paint.

BUTTER FROSTING

⅓ cup butter *or* margarine
4½ cups sifted powdered sugar
¼ cup milk
1½ teaspoons vanilla
Milk

● **In a bowl beat** butter or margarine till fluffy. Gradually add 2 cups of the powdered sugar, beating well. Slowly beat in the ¼ cup milk and vanilla.
● **Slowly beat in** remaining powdered sugar. Beat in additional milk, if needed, to make a frosting of spreading consistency. If desired, tint with food coloring.

Chocolate Butter Frosting: Prepare as above, *except* beat ½ cup unsweetened cocoa powder into butter; reduce powdered sugar to 4 cups.

SLICE-AND-BAKE COOKIES

Make a bunch of different cookies like those on page 146. The picture on pages 150-151 shows the variation, Whole Wheat Spice Cookies—

1 cup margarine *or* butter
2¼ cups all-purpose flour
½ cup sugar
½ cup packed brown sugar
1 egg white
Chopped nuts *or* colored sugar
(optional)

● **In a large mixer bowl beat** margarine or butter with an electric mixer on medium to high speed for 30 seconds or till softened. Add about *half* of the flour, the sugar, brown sugar, and egg white. Beat till combined. Beat or stir in remaining flour.
● **Shape dough** into two 7-inch rolls. If desired, coat the rolls in nuts or colored sugar. Wrap and chill the rolls in the refrigerator about 4 hours or till firm enough to slice.
● **Cut chilled dough** into ¼-inch-thick slices. Arrange slices 1 inch apart on an ungreased cookie sheet. Bake in a 375° oven about 8 minutes or till golden. Remove from cookie sheet; cool.
● **Decorate cookies** as desired, following Cookie Decorating Ideas, *right*. Makes about 54 cookies.

Kaleidoscope Cookies: Prepare dough as directed; divide into 3 portions before shaping. Prepare 3 colored doughs, following the directions for coloring dough *right*. Shape each dough portion into two 7-inch-long logs. Combine 3 different colored doughs into one roll; repeat to make two tri-colored 7-inch-long rolls. Wrap and continue as directed.

Whole Wheat Spice Cookies: Prepare dough as directed, *except* use only 1½ cups *all-purpose flour*, ¾ cup *whole wheat flour*, 1 teaspoon *ground cinnamon*, ¼ teaspoon *ground cloves*, and ¼ teaspoon *ground allspice* or *ground nutmeg*. Bake and cool as above. To decorate, dip or drizzle cookies with *Sugar Glaze* and/or *Chocolate Glaze* (see recipes, *page 156*). Place on waxed paper. If desired, immediately top with chopped *walnuts* or *chocolate-flavored sprinkles*. Let stand till glaze is set.

To refrigerate dough: Shape dough into rolls and wrap as directed. Store in the refrigerator for up to 1 week. Slice and bake as directed.

To freeze dough: Shape dough into rolls as directed. Wrap in moisture- and vaporproof wrap. Seal, label, and freeze for up to 6 months. To thaw, let stand at room temperature till soft enough to slice. Slice and bake cookies as directed.

To freeze cookies: Shape and bake cookies as directed, *except* do not decorate. Place cookies in a freezer container. Seal, label, and freeze for up to 8 months. To thaw, let stand at room temperature for 1 hour. Decorate, if desired, as directed.

Nutrition information per cookie: *64 cal., 1 g pro., 8 g carbo., 3 g fat, 0 mg chol., 42 mg sodium, 15 mg potassium, and 0 g dietary fiber.*

Cookie Decorating Ideas

Shape and decorate the cookies as shown on *page 146* or design your own. These ideas will work on our Cream Cheese Sugar Cookies, Slice-and-Bake Cookies, and Shape-Up Cookies (see recipes on *pages 154, 157,* and *158*).

To decorate before baking: Top cookie dough with chocolate pieces, cut-up candied cherries, small decorative candies, colored sugar, crushed hard candies, chopped nuts, or coconut. You also can paint unbaked dough with colored Cookie Paint (see recipe, *page 156*).

To decorate after baking: Dip, drizzle, or frost cookies with Sugar or Chocolate Glaze or Butter Frosting (see recipes, *page 156* and *left*). If desired, top with chocolate pieces, raisins, dried fruit, cut-up candied cherries, small decorative candies, chocolate sprinkles, colored sugar, crushed hard candies, chopped nuts, or coconut.

To color dough: After mixing the plain dough, divide it into as many portions as you'd like to color. Add a few drops food coloring (paste or liquid) to each dough portion. Work food coloring into dough. Chill or shape as directed.

To marbleize dough: Prepare the dough; divide in half. Color *half* of the dough. Combine the plain and colored doughs. Work doughs with hands until the desired marbled effect is achieved. Shape as directed.

For patchwork dough: Prepare dough; divide and color with several colors. Pinch off generous teaspoons of different colored doughs. Press pieces together to seal edges. Shape as directed in each recipe.

For quilt dough: Prepare dough as directed for each recipe; divide in half. Color *half* of the dough. Shape as directed in the recipe. Using smaller cookie or hors d'oeuvre cutters or a knife, remove small cutout shapes from within cookie dough shapes. Fill cutout holes with the same shape of the different colored dough. Bake as directed.

For dipped cookies: After baking and cooling, dip parts of cookies into plain or colored Sugar Glaze or Chocolate Glaze. If desired, let dry and dip into another color of glaze.

For frosted cookies: After baking and cooling the cookies, frost each with Butter Frosting (see recipe, *left*).

To drizzle cookies: After baking and cooling, drizzle plain, dipped, or frosted cookies with plain or colored Sugar Glaze or Chocolate Glaze (see recipes on *page 156*).

For cookie sandwiches: Spread bottom of one cookie with Butter Frosting, fruit preserves, or jelly. Top with same shape cookie to make a sandwich. To show off the filling, the top cookie can be smaller than the bottom cookie or the top cookie can have the center cut out.

To paint cookies: After shaping dough, paint with Cookie Paint (see recipe, *page 156*), using a clean brush for each color. Bake as directed for each recipe.

Chilling Cookie Dough

The firmness of a cookie dough after chilling depends on whether you use butter or margarine. Doughs made with butter generally will be firmer.

To chill, place dough in refrigerator for recommended time or in freezer for about one-third of the refrigerator chilling time. (Do not freeze cookie dough made with butter as the dough will become too firm to slice.) Expect dough to be softer if you use 100-percent corn oil margarine instead of regular margarine. And do not use spread, diet, or soft-style margarine products in doughs, because your cookies may not turn out.

SHAPE-UP COOKIES

Use this dough to create a variety of cookie shapes and characters, as pictured on page 146—

- 1 cup butter
- ⅔ cup sugar
- ⅔ cup light corn syrup
- 1½ teaspoons vanilla
- 1 beaten egg
- 4 cups all-purpose flour
- 2 teaspoons baking powder

● **In a saucepan combine** the butter, sugar, and corn syrup. Cook and stir over medium heat till butter is melted and sugar is dissolved. Pour into a mixing bowl. Stir in vanilla. Cool mixture for 5 minutes.

● **Add egg; mix well.** In a bowl stir together flour and baking powder. Add dry ingredients to egg mixture; mix well. Divide dough into 2 or more portions. If desired, color dough following directions for coloring dough on *page 157.* Cover and chill dough at least 2 hours or overnight.

● **Shape dough** into 1-inch balls. Roll in additional sugar. Arrange on an ungreased baking sheet about 2 inches apart. Bake in a 350° oven for 8 to 10 minutes or till edges are firm. Cool on wire racks. Makes 64 cookies.

Shape-Up Spiced Cookies: Prepare dough as directed, *except* substitute *molasses* or *dark corn syrup* for light corn syrup and use only 1½ teaspoons *baking powder.* Add 1½ teaspoons *ground cinnamon*, 1 teaspoon *ground ginger*, ½ teaspoon *ground cloves,* and ¼ teaspoon *baking soda* to the dry ingredients.

Shape-Up Chocolate Cookies: Prepare dough as directed, *except* decrease the butter to ⅔ cup and melt 2 squares (2 ounces) *unsweetened chocolate* with the butter mixture in the saucepan.

Nut Prints: Before baking, imprint tops of dough balls with *nut halves* or *candied fruit.* Bake and cool as directed. If desired, drizzle with *Chocolate Glaze* (see recipe, *page 156*).

Kiss Prints: Immediately after baking, press a *chocolate kiss* or *pastel cream mint heart* or *kiss* in the center of each hot cookie.

Thumbprints: Roll balls of dough in beaten *egg white* then in chopped *nuts.* Press center of each cookie with thumb. Bake and cool as directed. Before serving, fill center with *jam* or *jelly* or piped *Butter Frosting* (see recipe, *page 157).*

Twist Shapes: Prepare dough as directed; divide into 2 or 3 portions. Add paste food coloring, if desired, following directions for coloring dough on *page 157.* Using ½ *tablespoon* dough for *each* rope, shape dough into 6-inch-long ropes. If desired, roll ropes in *colored sugar.* Twist 2 or 3 different colored ropes together. Form into circles, canes, coils, or sticks. Bake and cool as directed. Decorate as desired.

Cookie Characters: Shape desired color doughs into characters, such as clowns, elves, pigs, or lions. Decorate with desired candies, dried fruit, nuts, glazes, or frostings.

Cookie Elves: Use plain, pink, and green dough. Shape one 2-inch ball of green dough into the body and legs. For head, roll plain dough into a 1-inch ball; place on an ungreased baking sheet. For arms, shape plain dough into 2x½-inch-thick logs; put in place at shoulders, with hands on hips. For feet, roll pink dough into two ½-inch rounds; put in place and pinch to shape. For vest, flatten 2x½-inch balls of pink dough, and cover chest of elf. For hat, shape one ½-inch ball of green dough into a triangle; attach to top of head. For bells on shoes, place one tiny ball of plain dough on each foot. For nose, use a tiny ball of pink dough. With a toothpick, draw eyes and mouth. Bake at 350° for 10 to 12 minutes or till done. Cool on a wire rack. Frost hat, vest, and legs with *Sugar Glaze* (see recipe, *page 156)* drizzled from a spoon.

Pigs: Using pink dough, shape into a 2-inch ball. Flatten slightly on an ungreased baking sheet. For ears, pinch and flatten dough to shape. For nose, roll dough into a ¼-inch ball; flatten slightly. Place nose on face and prick 2 holes with a toothpick to make nostrils. Use silver decorative candies for eyes. Bake as directed.

Lions: Use yellow, pink, and orange doughs. Shape yellow dough into a 2-inch ball; flatten slightly on an ungreased baking sheet. For mane, use a clean garlic press to press orange cookie dough on top of the yellow circle. For mouth, shape pink dough. For nose, roll orange dough into a tiny ball. For eyes, use silver decorative candies. For whiskers, use chocolate-flavored sprinkles. Bake as directed.

Clowns: Use orange, purple, pink, and plain doughs. Shape plain dough into a 2-inch ball; flatten slightly on ungreased baking sheet. For hair and hat, shape orange dough. For collar, fasten purple dough under neck in a fan design. For mouth, shape pink dough. Use silver decorative candies for eyes and a red candy for a nose.

Nutrition information per cookie: *73 cal., 1 g pro., 11 g carbo., 3 g fat, 11 mg chol., 36 mg sodium, 11 mg potassium, and 0 g dietary fiber.*

Raising Yeast Dough

Yeast dough raises best in a place that is 80° to 85° F. and free of drafts, such as an unheated oven. Simply place the bowl of dough on one rack and a large pan of hot water on the rack underneath.

To see if the dough has risen enough and is ready for shaping, press two fingers ½ inch into the dough. If the indentation remains when you remove your fingers, the dough is ready for the next step.

APRICOT-ALMOND WREATHS

4¼ to 4¾ cups all-purpose flour
1 package active dry yeast
1 teaspoon ground cardamom *or* ground cinnamon
¼ teaspoon ground nutmeg
1⅓ cups orange juice
¼ cup sugar
3 tablespoons margarine *or* butter
½ teaspoon salt
2 eggs
1 cup snipped dried apricots
½ cup chopped toasted almonds
Milk
Orange Glaze
Snipped dried apricots (optional)

● **In a large mixer bowl stir** together *2 cups* of the flour, the yeast, cardamom or cinnamon, and nutmeg; set aside.
● **In a small saucepan heat** and stir orange juice, sugar, margarine or butter, and salt just till warm (120° to 130°) and margarine or butter is almost melted. Add to flour mixture. Add eggs. Beat with an electric mixer on low to medium speed for 30 seconds, scraping sides of bowl constantly. Beat on high speed for 3 minutes. Stir in the 1 cup apricots and the almonds. Using a spoon, stir in as much of the remaining flour as you can.
● **Turn dough out** onto a lightly floured surface. Knead in enough of the remaining flour to make a moderately stiff dough that is smooth and elastic (6 to 8 minutes). Shape into a ball. Place in a lightly greased bowl; turn once to grease surface. Cover; let rise in a warm place till double (about 1¼ hours). (See tip, *page 158.*)
● **Punch dough down;** turn out onto a lightly floured surface. Divide into 6 portions. Cover; let rest 10 minutes.
● **Roll each portion** into an evenly thick rope 20 inches long. Lay 2 ropes side by side and 1 inch apart; twist together loosely. Join ends to form a circle. Place on a lightly greased baking sheet. Repeat with remaining ropes. Cover; let rise till nearly double (about 45 minutes).
● **Brush dough with milk.** Bake in a 350° oven for 20 to 25 minutes or till golden. Cool on wire racks. Drizzle with Orange Glaze. If desired, top with additional snipped apricots. Makes 3 wreaths, 12 servings each.

Orange Glaze: In a bowl combine ½ cup *powdered sugar* and ¼ teaspoon *vanilla.* Stir in enough *orange juice* to make a glaze of drizzling consistency (2 to 3 teaspoons). Makes ⅔ cup.

To freeze: Shape and bake bread as directed; cool. Do not glaze. Wrap in moisture- and vaporproof wrap. Seal, label, and freeze for up to 3 months. To thaw, let stand, loosely covered, at room temperature for 2 to 3 hours. If desired, top with Orange Glaze and snipped apricots.

Nutrition information per serving with Orange Glaze: *102 cal., 3 g pro., 18 g carbo., 2 g fat, 12 mg chol., 45 mg sodium, 107 mg potassium, and 1 g dietary fiber. U.S. RDA: 13% thiamine, 10% riboflavin.*

PUMPKIN GINGERBREAD LOAVES

2 cups all-purpose flour
½ cup packed brown sugar
2 teaspoons baking powder
1 teaspoon ground cinnamon
½ teaspoon baking soda
1 cup canned pumpkin
½ cup molasses
2 eggs
⅓ cup margarine *or* butter
¼ cup milk
1 tablespoon grated gingerroot *or* 1 teaspoon ground ginger
⅓ cup finely chopped walnuts
2 tablespoons sugar

● **Grease bottom and sides** of four 4½x2½x1½-inch loaf pans. Set aside.
● **Stir** together *1 cup* of the flour, the brown sugar, baking powder, cinnamon, and baking soda. Add pumpkin, molasses, eggs, margarine or butter, milk, and gingerroot or ginger.
● **Beat with an electric mixer** on low to medium speed for 30 seconds or till combined. Beat on medium to high speed 2 minutes, scraping sides of bowl occasionally. Add remaining flour; beat 2 minutes or till mixed. Divide batter evenly among pans.
● **For topping, stir together** walnuts and sugar; sprinkle evenly over batter. Bake in a 350° oven for 40 to 50 minutes or till a toothpick inserted near the center of each loaf comes out clean. Cool loaves in pans on wire racks for 10 minutes. Remove from pans. Cool thoroughly on wire racks. Makes 4 loaves, 8 servings each.

To freeze: Wrap each loaf tightly in moisture- and vaporproof wrap. Seal, label, and freeze for up to 6 months. To thaw, let stand, loosely covered, at room temperature for 1 hour. Or, to micro-thaw, place 1 unwrapped loaf on a microwave-safe paper towel. Micro-cook, uncovered, on 30% power (medium-low) for 1 to 1½ minutes.

Nutrition information per serving: *89 cal., 2 g pro., 14 g carbo., 3 g fat, 14 mg chol., 61 mg sodium, 100 mg potassium, and 0 g dietary fiber. U.S. RDA: 25% vit. A.*

CRANBERRY-HAZELNUT BREAD

1½ cups all-purpose flour
1 teaspoon ground cinnamon
½ teaspoon baking powder
¼ teaspoon baking soda
¼ teaspoon ground cloves
1 cup dried cranberries, dried cherries, *or* snipped pitted whole dates
⅓ cup dried blueberries *or* raisins
⅓ cup chopped hazelnuts *or* pecans
2 eggs
¾ cup packed brown sugar
½ cup orange juice
⅓ cup cooking oil
Brandy

● **Grease bottom and sides** of four 4½x2½x1½-inch loaf pans. Set aside.
● **In a large mixing bowl stir** together flour, cinnamon, baking powder, baking soda, and cloves. Add cranberries, cherries, or dates; blueberries or raisins; and hazelnuts or pecans.
● **In a medium mixing bowl beat** eggs; stir in brown sugar, orange juice, and cooking oil. Stir into fruit mixture. Spoon about ¾ cup of the batter into *each* pan, stirring batter often.
● **Bake loaves in a 300° oven** about 40 minutes or till a toothpick inserted near the center of each loaf comes out clean. Cool loaves in pans on wire racks for 10 minutes. Remove from pans. Cool thoroughly on wire racks.
● **Wrap loaves** in brandy-moistened 100% cotton cheesecloth; over-wrap with foil. To mellow flavors, store in the refrigerator for up to 8 weeks. Remoisten cheesecloth with about 1 tablespoon brandy once a week or as needed. Makes 4 loaves, 8 servings each.

Nutrition information per serving: *94 cal., 1 g pro., 15 g carbo., 3 g fat, 13 mg chol., 18 mg sodium, 54 mg potassium.*

DOUBLE-OAT BUBBLE BREAD

Cut the wait for freshly baked bread by partially baking before freezing—

1½ cups water
¾ cup regular rolled oats
4½ to 5 cups all-purpose flour
2 packages active dry yeast
¾ cup milk
¼ cup margarine *or* butter
2 tablespoons sugar
1 teaspoon salt
2 eggs
1½ cups oat bran
⅓ cup molasses
Rolled oats, poppy seeds, *or* sesame seeds

● **In a medium saucepan bring** water to boiling; add the ¾ cup rolled oats. Reduce heat; simmer, uncovered, about 8 minutes or till water is nearly absorbed by the oats. Cover saucepan. Let stand for 10 minutes. Uncover and cool cooked oats to lukewarm.
● **In a large mixer bowl stir** together *1½ cups* of the flour and the yeast; set mixture aside.
● **In a small saucepan heat** and stir milk, margarine or butter, sugar, and salt just till warm (120° to 130°) and margarine or butter is almost melted. Add to flour mixture. Add eggs. Beat with an electric mixer on low speed for 30 seconds, scraping sides of bowl constantly. Beat on high speed for 3 minutes. Using a spoon, stir in the cooled oat mixture, oat bran, and molasses. Stir in as much of the remaining flour as you can.
● **Turn the dough out** onto a lightly floured surface. Knead in enough of the remaining flour to make a moderately stiff dough that is smooth and elastic (6 to 8 minutes total). Shape into a ball. Place in a lightly greased bowl; turn once. Cover; let rise in a warm place till double (about 1 hour). (See tip, *page 158*.)
● **Punch dough down;** turn out onto a lightly floured surface. Divide dough in half. Cover and let rest for 10 minutes. Divide *each* dough half into 9 portions for square or round loaves or 10 portions for rectangular loaves. Shape dough into balls. Place 9 or 10 balls in *each* of two greased 8x8x2-inch baking pans, 8x1½-inch round baking pans, or 9x5x3-inch loaf pans. Cover; let rise till nearly double (30 to 40 minutes).

● **Brush top of risen dough** with water; sprinkle with rolled oats, poppy seeds, or sesame seeds. Bake in a 375° oven for 30 to 35 minutes or till bread sounds hollow when tapped, covering with foil the last 10 minutes to prevent overbrowning, if necessary. Remove from pans and cool on a wire rack. Makes 2 loaves, 9 or 10 servings each.

Mini Double-Oat Loaves: To make 4 smaller loaves, prepare dough and let rise once as directed. Divide dough into 4 portions, making 10 balls from each portion. Arrange 10 balls in each of four 7½x3½x2-inch loaf pans. Let rise and bake as directed.

To freeze: Prepare, shape, and let dough rise as directed above. Do not brush with water or top with oats, poppy seed, or sesame seed. Bake untopped loaves in a 300° oven about 25 minutes or till loaves just start to brown. Remove from pans and cool on wire racks. Transfer loaves to freezer bags. Seal, label, and freeze for up to 3 months.

To thaw, partially uncover loaves; let stand at room temperature for 15 minutes. Remove wrapping; place loaves on a greased baking sheet. Brush with water; sprinkle with oats, poppy seeds, or sesame seeds. Bake, uncovered, in a 375° oven about 20 minutes (15 minutes for smaller loaves) or till bread sounds hollow when tapped, covering with foil the last 10 minutes to prevent overbrowning, if necessary. Remove from pans; cool on wire racks.

Nutrition information per roll: *202 cal., 6 g pro., 37 g carbo., 4 g fat, 25 mg chol., 162 mg sodium, 183 mg potassium, and 3 g dietary fiber. U.S. RDA: 39% thiamine, 22% riboflavin, 17% niacin, 14% iron.*

CHEDDAR CHEESE BOWS

6¾ to 7¼ cups all-purpose flour
3 cups shredded cheddar, Swiss, *or* Monterey Jack cheese
2 packages quick-rising active dry yeast
2½ cups milk
½ cup sugar
1 teaspoon salt
2 eggs
Milk
Finely shredded fresh Parmesan cheese *or* grated Parmesan cheese

● **In a large mixer bowl combine** *3 cups* of the flour, the cheese, and yeast; set mixture aside.
● **In a medium saucepan heat** and stir the 2½ cups milk, the sugar, and salt just till warm (120° to 130°). Add to flour mixture. Add eggs. Beat with an electric mixer on low to medium speed for 30 seconds, scraping sides of bowl constantly. Beat on high speed for 3 minutes. Using a spoon, stir in as much remaining flour as you can.
● **Turn the dough out** onto a lightly floured surface. Knead in enough of the remaining flour to make a moderately stiff dough that is smooth and elastic (6 to 8 minutes total). Shape into a ball. Place in a lightly greased bowl; turn once to grease surface. Cover and let rest for 10 minutes.
● **Turn the dough out** onto a lightly floured surface. Divide dough into 4 portions. Roll each portion into a 12-inch square. Cut each square into twelve 12x1-inch strips.
● **On lightly greased** or foil-lined baking sheets, shape each strip into a bow. Hold 1 end of each strip in each hand. Bring the ends up and around so the center of the strip forms 2 loops. Bring ends of strip together at the center of the loops, crisscrossing the ends and leaving about 1½ inches of the strip for the bow's tails. Twist ends together once. Press dough together at center. Cover; let rise in a warm place till nearly double (20 to 30 minutes).
● **Brush rolls** with additional milk; sprinkle with Parmesan cheese. Bake in a 375° oven 12 minutes or till golden. Cool on wire racks. Makes 48.

To refrigerate: Prepare and shape dough as directed, *except* do not allow dough to rise or bake. Cover dough with oiled waxed paper. Refrigerate up to 24 hours. Before baking, let bows rise, loosely covered, at room temperature 30 minutes. Brush with milk; top with Parmesan cheese. Bake as directed.

To freeze: Prepare and shape as directed, *except* do not allow dough to rise or bake. Cover bows tightly with moisture- and vaporproof wrap. Seal, label, and freeze for up to 4 months.

Before baking, let bows stand, loosely covered, at room temperature for 1¼ hours to thaw and rise. Brush with milk and top with Parmesan cheese. Bake as directed.

Nutrition information per bow: *112 cal., 4 g pro., 16 g carbo., 3 g fat, 18 mg chol., 102 mg sodium, 55 mg potassium, and 1 g dietary fiber. U.S. RDA: 15% thiamine, 13% riboflavin.*

RUM-RAISIN STEAMED PUDDING

    1 egg
    3 slices white bread, torn into
        pieces
  ¾ cup dairy eggnog
  ¾ cup all-purpose flour
  ¾ teaspoon baking soda
  ½ teaspoon ground nutmeg
  ⅔ cup packed brown sugar
  ½ cup margarine *or* butter,
        cut up
    2 tablespoons rum *or* brandy
    2 cups raisins
  ½ cup chopped walnuts
Sugared Orange Peel Curls
        (optional)
    3 tablespoons rum *or* brandy
        (optional)
Rum Hard Sauce (optional)

● **Lightly beat** egg, using a fork. Add bread and eggnog; let stand about 3 minutes or till softened. Meanwhile, in another bowl stir together flour, baking soda, and nutmeg; set aside.
● **Stir bread mixture** to break up. Stir in sugar, margarine, and the 2 tablespoons rum. Stir in raisins and nuts. Add flour mixture; stir till combined.
● **Lightly grease** a 6-cup mold or heat-safe mixing bowl. Pour bread mixture into prepared mold or bowl. Cover with foil, pressing foil tightly against rim of mold or bowl. Place mold, foil side up, on a rack in a deep kettle. Add *boiling water* to the kettle till water reaches 1 inch above the bottom of the mold. Cover the kettle. Bring water to a gentle boil.
● **Steam about 2½ hours** or till a wooden skewer inserted near the center of the pudding comes out clean, adding more boiling water as necessary during cooking.
● **Carefully remove mold** or bowl from kettle. Cool on a wire rack for 10 minutes. Invert pudding onto a serving platter; remove the mold or bowl. If desired, garnish pudding with Sugared Orange Peel Curls (see recipe *right*). If desired, in a saucepan heat the 3 tablespoons rum or brandy till hot. Ignite with a long match and pour over pudding. Serve after flame goes out. If desired, serve with Rum Hard Sauce (see recipe *right*). Makes 8 to 10 servings.

    To refrigerate: Prepare and steam pudding as directed above; unmold and wrap tightly in foil. Store in the refrigerator for up to 2 weeks. To reheat,

place the foil-wrapped pudding on a baking sheet. Bake in a 350° oven about 40 minutes or till pudding is heated through. Serve as directed.

    Sugared Orange Peel Curls: Cut long strips of orange peel. Curl the strips. Place them in a small bowl of sugar, coating them well. Remove coated peel from bowl and let stand on waxed paper to dry. Store in a cool, dry place for up to 1 week.

    Rum Hard Sauce: In a small mixer bowl combine 1 cup sifted *powdered sugar* and ¼ cup *margarine* or *butter*. Beat with an electric mixer on medium speed for 3 to 5 minutes or till combined. Beat in 1 tablespoon *rum* or *brandy*. Spoon sauce into a serving bowl. Cover and chill about 3 hours or till firm. Makes ⅔ cup.

    Nutrition information per serving without sauce: *464 cal., 6 g pro., 70 g carbo., 19 g fat, 41 mg chol., 299 mg sodium, 489 mg potassium, and 3 g dietary fiber. U.S. RDA: 22% vit. A, 25% thiamine, 19% riboflavin, 12% niacin, 12% calcium, 14% iron.*

HONEY-PISTACHIO TART

  ½ cup sugar
  ¼ cup honey
  ¼ cup water
  1½ cups chopped toasted pistachio
        nuts *or* pecans
  ½ cup mixed dried fruit bits *or*
        raisins
  ½ cup milk
    2 tablespoons margarine *or* butter
    2 cups all-purpose flour
  ⅔ cup margarine *or* butter, cut up
    1 egg
  ¼ cup cold water
    1 beaten egg yolk
Whipped cream (optional)

● **For filling,** in a medium saucepan combine sugar, honey, and the ¼ cup water. Bring to boiling, stirring gently till sugar is dissolved. Reduce heat to medium-low; boil gently about 15 minutes or till mixture turns a light caramel color, stirring occasionally.
● **Stir in the toasted nuts,** fruit bits or raisins, milk, and the 2 tablespoons margarine or butter. Return to boiling. Boil gently over low heat about 5 minutes more or till slightly thickened, stirring occasionally. Set aside to cool to room temperature.

● **Meanwhile, for dough,** place flour in a bowl. Using a pastry cutter or fork, cut in the ⅔ cup margarine till pieces are the size of small peas. In a bowl beat egg; stir in the ¼ cup cold water. Add egg mixture to flour mixture. Toss with a fork till moistened. Divide dough in half; form each half into a ball. Wrap and chill till filling is cool.
● **On a lightly floured surface,** flatten 1 dough portion at a time with hands and roll into an 11-inch circle. To transfer pastry, wrap 1 dough circle around the rolling pin; unroll onto a 9x1½-inch flan pan, quiche dish, or cake pan. Ease dough into pan, being careful not to stretch pastry. Let dough hang over edges. Spread filling evenly over crust. Top with remaining dough circle. Trim dough ½ inch beyond edge of pan. Fold edges over toward center of tart, pressing to seal well. Brush egg yolk over dough. With the tines of a fork, gently make crisscross patterns in the surface of dough (see photo *below*). Prick top.
● **Bake in a 375° oven** 40 to 45 minutes or till golden. Cool. If using a flan pan, remove sides. If desired, serve with whipped cream. Serves 8 to 12.

    To freeze: Prepare as directed, up to and including brushing dough with egg yolk. Do not bake. Freeze for 30 minutes. Wrap tightly in moisture- and vaporproof wrap; seal, label, and freeze for up to 3 months. To serve, unwrap and bake in a 375° oven for 50 to 55 minutes or till crust is golden brown. Cool and serve as directed.

    Nutrition information per serving: *544 cal., 10 g pro., 59 g carbo., 32 g fat, 55 mg chol., 238 mg sodium, 414 mg potassium, and 3 g dietary fiber. U.S. RDA: 36% vit. A, 45% thiamine, 24% riboflavin, 18% niacin, 19% iron.*

Using a fork, lightly score the tart across the top.

APPLE-FIG PIE

Look for light Calimyrna figs or dark Mission figs—

½ cup sugar
1 tablespoon cornstarch
1 teaspoon purchased *or* Home-made Apple Pie Spice*
6 ounces dried figs (stems removed), finely chopped (1 cup)
1 cup cold water
2 tablespoons honey
1 teaspoon finely shredded lemon peel
2 tablespoons lemon juice
4 cups thinly sliced, peeled, cooking apples (about 1½ pounds)
1 15-ounce package folded refrigerated unbaked piecrusts (2 crusts), at room temperature
1 egg
1 tablespoon water
Whipped cream (optional)

● **For filling,** in a large saucepan stir together sugar, cornstarch, and spice. Stir in figs, the 1 cup water, honey, lemon peel, and lemon juice. Cook and stir till thickened and bubbly. Remove from heat; gently stir in apples.

● **Line a 9-inch pie plate** with one of the pastry crusts. Pour filling into pie plate; spread evenly. Trim pastry to edge of pie plate.

● **Using an hors d'oeuvre** or cookie cutter, cut leaf shapes out of center of top crust; place crust over filling. Arrange leaf cutouts atop pastry. Seal and flute pastry edges in desired pattern. In a small bowl beat egg and stir in the 1 tablespoon water; brush onto crust.

● **To prevent overbrowning,** cover edge of pie with foil. Bake in a 375° oven for 25 minutes. Remove foil; bake about 25 minutes more or till golden. Cool on wire rack. If desired, serve with whipped cream. Makes 8 servings.

To freeze: Prepare pie as directed, *except* do not make cutouts in top crust; brush with egg mixture, or bake. Cover unbaked pie with an inverted 10-inch paper plate. Place in a freezer container. Seal, label, and freeze for up to 4 months.

To bake, uncover frozen pie. Prick or cut slits in top crust. Cover completely with foil. Bake in a 375° oven for 45 minutes. Uncover and brush with egg mixture. Bake about 40 minutes more

or till crust is golden brown. Cover edge of piecrust with foil the last 15 minutes to prevent overbrowning, if necessary.

Homemade Apple Pie Spice: In a storage container stir together 1 tablespoon *ground cinnamon,* 1½ teaspoons *ground nutmeg,* 1 teaspoon *ground allspice,* and ¼ teaspoon *ground cloves.* Store, tightly covered, in a cool, dry place.

Nutrition information per serving: 405 cal., 4 g pro., 64 g carbo., 16 g fat, 27 mg chol., 221 mg sodium, 261 mg potassium, and 4 g dietary fiber.

RIBBON-OF-CRANBERRY CHEESECAKE

The ribbon inside appears when you cut the first slice—

1½ cups finely crushed vanilla wafers (about 33)
6 tablespoons margarine *or* butter, melted
1 cup sugar
2 tablespoons cornstarch
1½ cups cranberries
2 teaspoons finely shredded orange peel (set aside)
1 cup orange juice
1 cup low-fat cottage cheese
2 8-ounce packages Neufchâtel cheese, softened
1 cup sugar
2 tablespoons all-purpose flour
2 teaspoons vanilla
3 eggs
1 8-ounce carton low-fat vanilla yogurt

● **For crust,** in a medium bowl combine vanilla wafers and margarine or butter. Press mixture onto the bottom and 1 inch up the sides of a 9-inch springform pan. Set aside.

● **For sauce,** in a medium saucepan stir together 1 cup sugar and cornstarch. Stir in cranberries and orange juice. Cook and stir over medium heat till bubbly. Cook and stir 2 minutes more. Remove ¾ *cup* of the sauce; cool slightly. Cover and chill remaining sauce till serving time.

● **Place the ¾ cup sauce** in a blender container or food processor bowl. Cover and blend or process till smooth. Set aside. Wash blender container or food processor bowl.

● **Place cottage cheese** in the blender container or food processor bowl. Cover

and blend or process till smooth. Transfer to a mixer bowl. Add Neufchâtel cheese, 1 cup sugar, flour, and vanilla. Beat with an electric mixer on medium speed till combined. Add eggs all at once; beat on low speed just till combined. Stir in orange peel. Pour *half* of the cheese mixture into crust-lined pan. Drizzle the blended sauce over cheese mixture in pan. Carefully top with remaining cheese mixture, covering the sauce as much as possible.

● **Place cheesecake** on a shallow baking pan in a 375° oven. Bake for 45 to 50 minutes or till center appears nearly set when shaken. Cool on a wire rack for 15 minutes; loosen the sides of the pan. Cool completely. Cover and chill till serving time.

● **To serve,** spread cheesecake with vanilla yogurt; top with some of the reserved chilled sauce. Pass remaining sauce. Makes 12 servings.

To freeze: Prepare, bake, and cool cheesecake as directed. Freeze on bottom of springform pan for 1 hour; remove bottom of pan. Transfer cake to a large freezer bag or container. Seal, label, and freeze for up to 3 months. Freeze reserved sauce separately. To serve, thaw the sauce and the cheesecake, loosely covered, in the refrigerator about 24 hours. Top as directed.

Nutrition information per serving: 407 cal., 10 g pro., 52 g carbo., 18 g fat, 92 mg chol., 362 mg sodium, 184 mg potassium, and 0 g dietary fiber. U.S. RDA: 26% vit. A, 21% vit. C, 21% riboflavin, 11% calcium.

To order *Better Homes and Gardens® Old-Fashioned Home Baking* cookbook, send check or money order for $27.95 to: Better Homes and Gardens® Reader Service, Department 8BB, Box 374, Des Moines, Iowa 50336. Specify Product Number 16327.

I bake extra stuffing with the turkey, because when seconds go around, it's the stuffing I reach for first.

—*Julia Malloy, Associate Food Editor*

THE HOLIDAY BIRD

When I think of turkey and stuffing, I picture the Iowa farm that's home to our Thanksgiving celebration every year. From the farm's sturdy apple trees (and Grandma's recipe box) comes a sweet apple stuffing that's a family legacy. I don't know which is older—Grandma's stuffing recipe or the farm, which has been in my husband's family for more than 100 years.

Grandma used to serve this stuffing in a farm-raised duck or goose. But when her children took over cooking the bird, they opted for turkey because it was easier to find. Knowing we are next in line to roast the Thanksgiving turkey, my husband and I now treasure the recipe and have fixed it several times already in our own kitchen.

Making this simple recipe proved to me that stuffing and roasting a turkey is surprisingly easy. The trickiest part is timing the bird and stuffing so they'll be ready at dinnertime. If they're done too early, the rest of dinner is underdone; if too late, dinner gets overcooked.

To make sure that you won't have a problem timing your bird to the appetites in your family, tear out and save the next few pages. On them, you'll find a turkey roasting time chart, complete with directions and photographs that'll help you get your bird on the table with a minimum of fuss. And for ideas to tuck inside your holiday bird, you'll find recipes for Grandma's apple stuffing and a rice stuffing that's a family favorite from my own recipe collection.

COOK-TO-COOK

ROAST TURKEY WITH SWEET APPLE STUFFING

Jonathan apples keep their shape and impart a tart-sweet apple flavor to the stuffing. Pictured on page 163—

- **5 cups dry bread cubes with crust (about 7 slices)**
- **½ cup milk**
- **2 eggs**
- **½ to ¾ cup sugar**
- **1 teaspoon ground cinnamon (optional)**
- **¼ teaspoon salt**
- **6 medium cooking apples (such as Jonathan *or* Newton Pippin), peeled, cored, and chopped (6 cups)**
- **1 cup raisins**
- **1 12- to 16-pound turkey**
- **Cooking oil *or* melted margarine *or* butter**

● **For stuffing,** in a large bowl combine bread and milk. In a small bowl beat eggs slightly with a fork. Stir in sugar, cinnamon (if desired), and salt. Stir egg mixture into bread mixture. Stir in apples and raisins; set aside.

● **Be sure frozen turkey** is thawed. Unwrap and remove excess fat. Remove giblets and neck; save for another use or cook as directed on *page 165*.

● **Under cold running water,** thoroughly rinse inside and outside of turkey. Pat dry with paper towels. Sprinkle inside with salt and pepper.

● **Set turkey in a large bowl,** with the neck cavity up. Spoon some of the stuffing loosely into neck cavity. Use skewers to hold neck skin to back. Turn the bird and spoon stuffing loosely into body cavity. Do not pack too tightly because stuffing expands during cooking and may not heat evenly if too densely packed. Spoon any remaining stuffing into a small casserole; cover and chill till the bird is almost done.

● **To keep stuffing** in the body cavity, tuck drumsticks under tail skin or use string to tie drumsticks securely to tail (see photo, *top right*). Twist wing tips under back so they won't overcook.

● **Place turkey,** breast side up, on a rack in a shallow roasting pan. Brush with oil, margarine, or butter to prevent drying. Insert a meat thermometer into the center of one of the inside

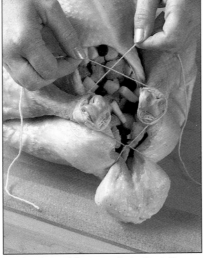

Tie the drumsticks securely to the tail or tuck them under the band of skin.

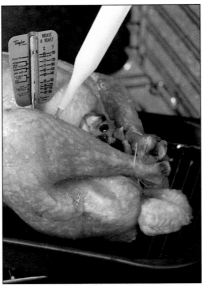

Baste or brush the bird occasionally with drippings during cooking.

Fresh fall vegetables season Golden Wild Rice Stuffing.

thigh muscles. For an accurate reading, the bulb should not touch bone.

● **Cover turkey loosely** with foil to prevent overbrowning and to keep the turkey moist. Roast in a 325° oven for 4 to 5 hours or till thermometer registers 180° to 185°. Baste occasionally with drippings during cooking, if desired (see photo, *center left*). After 3½ hours, cut skin or string between drumsticks, uncover turkey, and add stuffing in covered casserole to oven.

● **Remove bird** when it reaches 180° and stuffing when heated through. Cover turkey with foil and let stand 20 minutes for easier carving. Remove stuffing from bird and combine with stuffing in casserole. Serves 16 to 18.

Nutrition information per serving of stuffing: 127 cal., 3 g pro., 28 g carbo., 1 g fat, 27 mg chol., 171 mg sodium, 160 mg potassium, and 2 g dietary fiber.

Cooked Giblets: To cook, wash *giblets;* cover and chill *liver.* Combine remaining giblets, neck, ½ cup each chopped *celery* and *onion.* Add *water* to cover and a dash *salt.* Bring to boiling; reduce heat. Cover; simmer 1 hour or till tender. Add liver; cook 20 to 30 minutes more or till done.

GOLDEN WILD RICE STUFFING

For a savory stuffing, try this recipe in a 10- to 12-pound turkey—

- **½ cup wild rice**
- **2 cups chicken broth**
- **½ cup regular brown rice**
- **¼ teaspoon poultry seasoning *or* ground sage**
- **1 cup shredded parsnip**
- **1 cup shredded carrot**
- **1 cup chopped celery**
- **½ cup chopped onion**
- **2 tablespoons snipped fresh parsley**

● **Rinse wild rice** in a strainer under cold running water. In a 3-quart saucepan combine wild rice, broth, brown rice, and poultry seasoning or sage. Bring to boiling; reduce heat. Cover and simmer for 35 minutes.

● **Add parsnip, carrot,** celery, onion, and parsley. Simmer, covered, about 15 minutes or till tender, stirring often. Stuff turkey as directed at left and on *page 165.* Makes 10 to 12 servings.

Nutrition information per serving of stuffing: 87 cal., 3 g pro., 17 g carbo., 1 g fat, 0 mg chol., 173 mg sodium, 224 mg potassium, and 2 g dietary fiber. U.S. RDA: 39% vit. A, 13% niacin.

COOK-TO-COOK

TURKEY-ROASTING GUIDE

A tender, golden bird is easy enough with these helpful hints.

HOW MUCH TO BUY

For a 12-pound-or-less bird, buy 1 pound per serving. If the bird is over 12 pounds, buy ¾ pound per serving. For bone-in turkey breast, buy ½ pound per serving.

THAWING FROZEN TURKEY

Thawing in refrigerator: Place the wrapped bird on a tray in the refrigerator for 3 to 4 days (24 hours for every 5 pounds).

Thawing in cold water: Place the wrapped bird in a sink of cold water. Change the water every 30 minutes. (Allow 30 minutes per pound.)

Thawing at room-temperature: Do not thaw at room temperature, as the warm atmosphere promotes bacteria growth.

BEFORE ROASTING

Unwrap bird. Free legs and tail. Remove giblets and neck piece from the cavities. Thoroughly rinse bird; pat dry with paper towels. Don't stuff the bird till you're ready to roast it.

To stuff the bird, spoon some stuffing loosely into neck cavity. Pull the neck skin over the stuffing; fasten to the back of the bird with a skewer. Place the bird, neck side down, in a large bowl. Loosely spoon some stuffing into the body cavity; do not pack. (If packed too tightly, the stuffing will not reach a safe temperature soon enough.) Spoon any remaining stuffing into a casserole; cover and chill till the bird is almost done.

If a band of skin crosses the tail, tuck the drumsticks under the band. If the band is not present, tie the legs to the tail with some string or thread (see photo, *page 164*). Twist the wing tips under the back.

TURKEY-ROASTING TIMES

Because birds differ in size, shape, and tenderness, use these roasting times as a general guide.

Type of Turkey	Ready-to-Cook Weight	Oven Temp.	Guide to Roasting Time
Stuffed Whole Turkey* (open roasting)	6–8 lb.	325°	3–3½ hr.
	8–12 lb.	325°	3½–4½ hr.
	12–16 lb.	325°	4–5 hr.
	16–20 lb.	325°	4½–5½ hr.
	20–24 lb.	325°	5–6½ hr.
Unstuffed Foil-Wrapped Turkey	8–10 lb.	450°	1¼–1¾ hr.
	10–12 lb.	450°	1¾–2¼ hr.
	12–16 lb.	450°	2¼–3 hr.
	16–20 lb.	450°	3–3½ hr.
	20–24 lb.	450°	3½–4 hr.
Stuffed Oven Bag Turkey*	12–16 lb.	350°	2½–3 hr.
	16–20 lb.	350°	3–3½ hr.
	20–24 lb.	350°	3½–4 hr.
Turkey Breast and Portions (bone-in)	2–4 lb.	325°	1½–2 hr.
	3–5 lb.	325°	1½–2½ hr.
	5–7 lb.	325°	2–2½ hr.

Testing for doneness: Roast whole turkeys till the meat thermometer registers 180° (170° for turkey breast—*do not* overcook). The turkey meat should be fork tender, and the juices should not run pink when the turkey is pierced with a fork. (Pierce thigh meat on whole turkeys.) When done, remove the bird from the oven and cover it loosely with foil. Let the bird stand, covered, for 10 to 15 minutes before carving. The stuffing temperature should be at least 165°.
Unstuffed turkeys generally require 30 to 45 minutes less total roasting time than stuffed turkeys.

ROASTING DIRECTIONS

Open or covered roasting pan: Place the bird, breast side up, on a rack in a shallow pan; brush with cooking oil. Push a meat thermometer into the center of an inside thigh muscle so the bulb doesn't touch bone.

For open roasting, cover the bird loosely with foil, leaving space between the bird and foil. Press the foil in slightly at the end of drumsticks and neck. Roast in a 325° oven, basting occasionally. When the bird is two-thirds done, cut the skin or string between legs. Remove the foil the last 30 to 45 minutes to let the bird brown.

For covered roasting, do not add water. Roast, covered with the vent open, in a 325° oven for 20 to 25 minutes per pound. Uncover and drain, reserving juices. Turn the oven to 475°. Roast for 20 minutes more or till the bird is brown.

Foil-wrapped turkey: *Do not stuff bird* to roast this way. (Because the bird is roasted at a high temperature, the meat will cook before the stuffing reaches a safe temperature.) Wrap the *unstuffed* bird, breast side up, in greased, heavy-duty foil. Place in a shallow roasting pan. Insert a meat thermometer into the bird's thigh muscle through the foil, without touching fat or bone. Roast at 450° according to chart. Open foil the last 20 to 30 minutes.

Oven-bag turkey: Shake 1 tablespoon *all-purpose flour* in a turkey-size oven cooking bag. (This prevents the bag from bursting during roasting.) Add the bird to the bag. Place the bird, breast side up, in a large roasting pan at least 2 inches deep. Close the bag with a nylon tie. With a sharp knife, make six ½-inch slits in the top of the bag to allow steam to escape. Insert a meat thermometer into thigh muscle through a slit in bag. Roast in a 350° oven according to the chart.

Turkey breast and portions (bone-in): Thaw turkey, if frozen, as directed. Place turkey, skin side up, on a rack in a shallow roasting pan. Brush with cooking oil. Insert a meat thermometer into the center so the bulb does not touch fat or bone. Roast, uncovered, in a 325° oven, according to the chart, basting occasionally. Cover loosely with foil to prevent overbrowning, if necessary.

NEED EXTRA HELP? CALL

the U.S. Department of Agriculture's Meat and Poultry Hot Line. The toll-free number is 800/535-4555 or 447-3333 in Washington, D.C.

Home economists at the hot line take calls weekdays from 10 a.m. to 4 p.m. Eastern Standard Time (EST). The hours are usually extended around Thanksgiving.

MAKING

Christmas

Carols, candy, gatherings so jolly...Santa, gifts, and boughs of holly. These traditions of Christmas weave together a magical season. Whether you're baking cookies or trimming a tree with little ones at your knees, such times blend the warmth of the past with the glow of the present. To help you mold this Christmas into a memory, choose from more than 20 yuletide recipes created especially for your family gatherings. Several are quick to fix or can be made ahead, so you, too, can savor the season.

BY LISA HOLDERNESS

Sweeten your holidays with fabulous desserts. CRÈME BRÛLÉE TART layers custard and toasted sugar in a ginger crust. **CHERRY AND HAZELNUT SUNDAES** are a royal treat.

Memories

FESTIVE PARTY FOODS

The doorbell rings and the fun and feasting begin. After greetings of hugs and kisses, friends and family join in decorating the fragrant pine, singing carols, and sharing memories. Your gift in return for their company: a vivid buffet of delicious appetizers. To keep the cooking simple, pick out one or two special recipes and follow make-ahead directions where included. Round out your menu with purchased nibbles and beverages.

SPICED CRANBERRY TEA warms up holiday spirits. As the candy swizzle stick melts, it sweetens the hot tea.

WHOLE WHEAT PIZZA TART, cut into wedges, will disappear in a twinkling.

POTATO CAKES WITH SEAFOOD let you choose salmon, caviar, or shrimp for the toppings.

RED PEPPER DIP and fresh vegetables will brighten your holiday party table.

SPICY-SWEET CHICKEN "DRUMMIES" offer two glazes—mild cinnamon for kids, zesty red pepper for adults.

Christmas Memories

Christmas Memories

HOLIDAY BAKING   The buttery aroma of cookies in the oven draws all the family to the kitchen. It's time for that popular ritual—taste testing. Let everyone snitch a warm sample, then invite them to help with the baking. Prepare batches of cookies to freeze for serving throughout the season. When the baking's done, relax with all the bakers and a plateful of cookies.

Right: A TRIO OF COOKIES. Begin with one simple batch of dough and end up with three kinds of cookies, nine dozen in all:
● Lemon Almond Tea Cookies
● Choco-Mint Thumbprints
● Cherry Pistachio Rounds.

Below: BRANDIED FRUIT BARS offer a bite-size version of that old favorite, fruitcake, topped with a pecan-crumb mixture.
   EGGNOG KRINGLA is a variation of the traditional Scandinavian cakelike cookie.

170

Christmas Memories

CANDIES FOR GIFT-GIVING

Who doesn't love receiving the delicious gift of homemade sweets? This candy assortment offers recipes that both novice and seasoned candy makers can enjoy. For a quick candy, choose the bark or caramels—both use only three ingredients. For a big batch of candy that freezes well, try the classic fudge.

Stir nuts and dried apricots into white chocolate for big chunks of luscious APRICOT MACADAMIA NUT BARK.

For fudge-fancying friends, offer a tin of ROCKY ROAD FUDGE—rich with nuts, raisins, and marshmallows.

Let kids help with TOFFEE CARAMELS. Simply dip vanilla caramels into chocolate coating and roll in brickle pieces.

Christmas Memories

AN ELEGANT DINNER
Loved ones gather around the table—dressed in holiday finery—to share a splendid dinner and the special fellowship of the season.

Menu

SHIITAKE MUSHROOM AND SPINACH BROTH

•

BEEF TENDERLOIN WITH PORT SAUCE AND PASTRY LEAVES

•

GLAZED VEGETABLE TRIO

•

WHOLE WHEAT BRIOCHE

•

CRANBERRY-PEAR RELISH

•

DOUBLE-CHOCOLATE ORANGE TORTE

•

CRÈME DE MENTHE COFFEE

DESSERT—THE GRAND FINALE

Dessert? But of course! When dinner dishes are cleared, guests sit back and contemplate. Will it be a slice of the satin-glazed chocolate torte, a soothing after-dinner coffee, or both? As Christmas cook, give yourself the gift of time by assembling the cake earlier in the day. Brew the coffee just before serving.

DOUBLE CHOCOLATE ORANGE TORTE looks too pretty to cut, but the ultra-rich flavor gives you ample reason to do it anyway. This stunning dessert layers dense chocolate cake with a marmalade and orange liqueur filling.
  CRÈME DE MENTHE COFFEE is equally inviting. Top this chocolate-mint dinner coffee with a dollop of Minted Whipped Cream and mint candy shavings.

Christmas Memories

COOKIES ARE FOR KIDS

Share holiday rituals and fun with your children, too. Teach young chefs how to roll and pat balls of gingerbread dough into lovable cookies of all sizes. While the cookies bake, the kids can draw ponds for the bears to skate on before it's time to gobble them up.

Recipes begin on page 134.

Roll dough into little logs for the arms and legs. Attach to the body of the bear by pushing gently with fingers.

Use frosting to attach the candy cane runners and the bear bodies and legs to graham cracker sleds.

PHOTOGRAPHS: SCOTT LITTLE

CRÈME BRÛLÉE TART

Named after the elegant custard dessert that has a wonderful caramelized sugar topping—

1¼ cups all-purpose flour
 ½ teaspoon ground ginger
 ¼ teaspoon salt
 ¼ teaspoon ground cinnamon
 ⅛ teaspoon ground nutmeg
 ⅓ cup shortening
 3 to 4 tablespoons cold water
 3 eggs
1¼ cups light cream *or* milk
 ⅓ cup sugar
 1 teaspoon vanilla
 ¼ cup packed brown sugar

● **For crust,** in a medium mixing bowl stir together flour, ginger, salt, cinnamon, and nutmeg. Cut in shortening till pieces are the size of small peas. Sprinkle *1 tablespoon* of the water over *part* of the flour mixture; gently toss with a fork. Push to side of bowl. Repeat till all is moistened. Form dough into a ball.
● **On a lightly floured surface,** flatten dough with your hands. Roll dough from center to edges, forming a circle about 11 inches in diameter. Lightly wrap dough around rolling pin. Unroll into a 9-inch tart pan. Ease dough into tart pan, being careful not to stretch dough. Trim edges. *Do not* prick dough. Line dough with a double thickness of foil to prevent it from puffing. Bake in a 450° oven for 10 minutes.
● **Meanwhile, for filling,** in a bowl beat eggs and light cream slightly with a rotary beater or fork till combined. Stir in sugar and vanilla; mix well.
● **Remove foil from crust** and place tart pan on the oven rack. Pour filling into crust. Reduce oven temperature to 350°. Bake for 25 to 35 minutes or till a knife inserted near center comes out clean. Cool on a wire rack. Cover; chill at least 2 hours or up to 24 hours.
● **Before serving,** press brown sugar through a sieve, distributing it evenly over custard. Broil 4 to 5 inches from heat for 1 to 2 minutes or till brown sugar melts and forms a bubbly crust. Serve warm or chilled. Serves 8 to 12.
 Nutrition information per serving: 281 cal., 5 g pro., 32 g carbo., 15 g fat, 94 mg chol., 109 mg sodium, 118 mg potassium, and 1 g dietary fiber. U.S. RDA: 10% vit. A, 18% thiamine, and 21% riboflavin.

CHERRY AND HAZELNUT SUNDAES

These cookies are similar to brandy-snaps. They should be candy-crisp, yet tender enough to break easily with a fork or spoon. Our Test Kitchen found they could bake about three cookies at a time on a standard cookie sheet. This means you'll need three 6-ounce custard cups to drape the cookies over while the next batch is baking—

 ¼ cup packed brown sugar
 ¼ cup margarine *or* butter
 3 tablespoons light corn syrup
 1 cup ground hazelnuts (filberts) *or* almonds (4 ounces)
 ⅓ cup all-purpose flour
Vanilla ice cream
  Dried Cherry Sauce (see recipe *right*)

● **Line cookie sheets with foil.** Butter foil. Set aside.
● **In a small saucepan combine** brown sugar, margarine or butter, and corn syrup. Cook and stir over medium heat till margarine or butter is melted and mixture is smooth. Remove from heat. Stir in hazelnuts or almonds and flour.
● **For *each* cookie, drop** about *2 tablespoons* of the mixture onto the prepared cookie sheet, leaving about 5 inches between cookies. Flatten slightly, if necessary.
● **Bake in a 350° oven** for 8 to 9 minutes or till edges are golden. Let stand on cookie sheet for 1 to 2 minutes. Carefully loosen and immediately press the

To shape, press each cookie over a custard cup. If cookies harden before molding, pop the cookie sheet into the oven for 30 seconds to soften the cookies.

cookies over the ungreased bottoms of 6-ounce custard cups. Let stand while baking the next batch. Then, remove cookies from custard cups and cool on a wire rack. If desired, store in a moisture- and vapor-proof container at room temperature for up to 1 week or freeze for up to 6 months. For storage, use plastic wrap between cookies.
● **When ready to serve,** for each serving place *one* cookie cup on a dessert plate. Top each cookie with a scoop of vanilla ice cream and about ¼ *cup* of the Dried Cherry Sauce. Serves 8.
 Nutrition information per serving with 1/2 cup vanilla ice cream and sauce: 391 cal., 4 g pro., 53 g carbo., 19 g fat, 20 mg chol., 117 mg sodium, 218 mg potassium, 1 g dietary fiber. U.S. RDA: 14% vit. A, 39% vit. C, 14% thiamine, 14% riboflavin, 13% calcium.

DRIED CHERRY SAUCE

Look for dried cherries at your local gourmet food store. Or, you can order them through your favorite gourmet food mail-order catalog—

 ½ cup dried cherries *or* 1½ cups frozen pitted tart red cherries*
 ¼ cup packed brown sugar
 2 tablespoons cornstarch
 1 teaspoon finely shredded lemon peel
 ¼ teaspoon apple pie spice
 2 cups cranberry-cherry drink *or* unsweetened cherry juice*

● **In a small saucepan stir together** dried or frozen cherries, brown sugar, cornstarch, lemon peel, and apple pie spice. Stir in cranberry-cherry drink or cherry juice.
● **Cook and stir** till thickened and bubbly. Cook and stir for 2 minutes more. Serve warm. Makes about 2¼ cups.
 To make ahead: Prepare sauce as directed and pour into a storage container. Chill, covered, for up to 2 weeks. To serve, in a small saucepan heat sauce over low heat till warm, stirring occasionally.
 Note: If using frozen pitted tart red cherries, *decrease* cranberry-cherry drink or cherry juice to 1½ cups.
 Nutrition information per 1/4 cup: 76 cal., 0 g pro., 19 g carbo., 0 g fat, 0 mg chol., 4 mg sodium, 29 mg potassium, and 0 g dietary fiber. U.S. RDA: 30% vit. C.

SPICED CRANBERRY TEA

Rich and rosy red, this hot-tea punch is the perfect "warmer-upper"—

```
  6  inches stick cinnamon, broken
  2  teaspoons whole cloves
  1  cup water
 ¼  cup sugar
  1  quart apple juice or apple cider
  3  cups strong tea
  1  12-ounce can frozen cranberry-
     raspberry juice concentrate or
     cranberry juice cocktail
     concentrate
```
Lemon slices (optional)
Fruit-flavored striped candy sticks
     (optional)

● **For spice bag,** place cinnamon and cloves in the center of a 6-inch square of a double thickness of 100% cotton cheesecloth. Bring corners of cheesecloth together and tie with a clean string. Set spice bag aside.
● **In a 4-quart Dutch oven combine** water and sugar. Heat and stir till sugar dissolves. Add spice bag, apple juice or apple cider, tea, and juice concentrate. Heat through.
● **Remove and discard** spice bag. Pour into a heatproof punch bowl. If desired, add lemon slices. Ladle into mugs and, if desired, serve hot with candy sticks for stirrers. Makes 16 to 18 (4-ounce) servings.

To make ahead: Prepare Spiced Cranberry Tea as above, *except* after heating to dissolve sugar, add cider, tea, and juice concentrate, reserving spice bag to add at reheating time. Transfer mixture to a storage container; cover and chill for up to 1 week.

At serving time, in a 4-quart Dutch oven combine tea mixture and spice bag. Heat through. Remove and discard spice bag. Serve as directed.

Nutrition information per serving: 97 cal., 25 g carbo., 0 g fat., 0 mg chol., 3 mg sodium, 108 mg potassium, and 0 g dietary fiber. U.S. RDA: 24% vit. C.

POTATO CAKES WITH SEAFOOD

Look for bags of already-shredded hash-brown-style potatoes in the refrigerator case at your local supermarket—

```
1½  pounds potatoes (about 5
    medium), peeled, or one
    20-ounce package refrigerated
    shredded potatoes
  1  beaten egg
  1  tablespoon fine dry seasoned
    bread crumbs
  2  teaspoons chopped green onion
 ½  teaspoon pepper
 ¼  teaspoon salt
 ¼  teaspoon garlic powder
 ⅓  cup olive oil or cooking oil
 ½  cup dairy sour cream
```
Toppings such as thinly sliced
    smoked salmon, caviar, or tiny
    cooked shrimp, and snipped
    chives or green onions

● **If using whole potatoes,** in a food processor fitted with a medium shredding disc, coarsely shred potatoes. (Or, shred with a grater.) Place shredded potatoes in a large bowl of ice water. Let stand for 5 minutes; drain well. Thoroughly pat potatoes dry with paper towels.
● **Place shredded potatoes** or refrigerated shredded potatoes in a large mixing bowl. Stir in beaten egg, bread crumbs, green onion, pepper, salt, and garlic powder; mix well. (The mixture will be dry).

● **In a large skillet heat** *2 tablespoons* of the oil. For *each* cake, drop a *heaping tablespoonful* of the potato mixture into the skillet; spread the mixture to 2½ to 3 inches in diameter. Fry potato mixture, a few cakes at a time, over medium-high heat about 2 minutes or till bottoms are brown. Carefully turn cakes over. Fry about 2 minutes more or till brown and crispy. Add more oil as needed. If cakes begin to burn, reduce heat. Transfer cakes to a baking sheet. Repeat frying with the remaining potato mixture.*
● **Bake in a 400° oven** for 15 minutes or till potato cakes are tender inside. Drain on paper towels. Transfer to a serving platter.
● **To serve,** place a slice of smoked salmon atop each cake, dollop with sour cream, and sprinkle with chives or green onion. *Or,* dollop each cake with sour cream and top with caviar or shrimp and sprinkle with chives or green onion. Makes 25 appetizers.

*****To make ahead:** Fry the potato cakes as directed; do not bake. Freeze the cakes on a baking sheet about 45 minutes or till firm.

Transfer cakes to a freezer container. Seal, label, and freeze for up to 3 months. To serve, transfer frozen cakes to a baking sheet. Bake in a 400° oven for 15 to 18 minutes or till potato cakes are tender inside. Drain on paper towels; serve as directed.

Nutrition information per appetizer with 1/2 ounce salmon and 1 tablespoon sour cream: 62 cal., 1 g pro., 6 g carbo., 4 g fat, 11 mg chol., 37 mg sodium, 95 mg potassium, and 0 g dietary fiber.

WHOLE WHEAT PIZZA TART

Use frozen whole wheat bread dough for a quick-to-fix crust—

- 1 16-ounce loaf frozen whole wheat bread dough, thawed
- 1 green onion *or* leek
- ¼ of a small sweet yellow *or* green pepper
- ¼ cup pizza sauce
- ¼ cup purchased pesto
- 1½ cups shredded provolone *or* mozzarella cheese (6 ounces)
  Toppings such as sliced pepperoni, sliced eggplant, sliced tomatoes, sliced fresh mushrooms, and sliced pitted ripe olives

● **On a lightly floured surface, roll** bread dough into a 9-inch circle. Place in an 11-inch tart pan with a removable bottom, pressing to fit into pan. Prick crust with a fork.
● **Bake in a 400° oven** for 12 to 15 minutes or till brown.* Transfer to a cooling rack, leaving oven on.
● **Meanwhile, cut** the green onion or leek into long, thin strips. Reserve all but 2 or 3 strips for another use. Cut sweet pepper into long, thin strips.
● **In a medium saucepan cook** the green onion or leek and sweet pepper, covered, in a small amount of boiling water for 2 to 3 minutes or till tender; drain completely.
● **Spread pizza sauce** over *half* of the crust; spread pesto over the remaining half. Sprinkle with cheese. Arrange green onion or leek, sweet pepper, and other desired toppings atop cheese.
● **Bake for 10 to 15 minutes** or till heated through and cheese is melted. Remove from pan and place on a serving platter. Cut into wedges to serve. Makes 10 to 12 appetizer servings.
  To make ahead: If desired, prepare, bake, and cool crust up to several hours ahead. Let stand, covered, at room temperature till you're ready to finish preparing the recipe.
  Nutrition information per serving: 244 cal., 11 g pro., 23 g carbo., 12 g fat, 16 mg chol., 600 mg sodium, 343 mg potassium, and 7 g dietary fiber. U.S. RDA: 23% thiamine, 18% riboflavin, 15% niacin, 19% calcium.

RED PEPPER DIP

For an even creamier dip, stir in an extra ¼ cup yogurt or sour cream—

- 1 7¼-ounce jar roasted red sweet peppers, drained, *or* 1 or 2 red sweet peppers, roasted, peeled, and cut up*
- ½ cup blanched whole almonds *or* walnut halves, toasted
- ¼ cup plain low-fat yogurt *or* dairy sour cream
- 2 teaspoons anchovy paste
- 2 cloves garlic, quartered
- ¼ teaspoon ground cumin
  Sweet red pepper strips
  Assorted vegetables such as fresh *or* frozen sugar snap peas *or* fresh pea pods**, peeled whole small carrots, baby yellow patty pan squash, broccoli flowerets**, jicama strips, *and/or* zucchini slices

● **For dip,** in a blender container or food processor bowl combine roasted red sweet peppers, almonds or walnuts, yogurt or sour cream, anchovy paste, garlic, and cumin. Cover and blend or process till smooth. Chill the dip till serving time.
● **Place dip in a small dish;** top with red pepper strips. Serve on a platter with assorted vegetables. Serves 8.
  To roast sweet peppers: Place peppers on a broiler pan 4 inches from the heat. Broil, turning often, till the peppers are charred on all sides. Place the broiled peppers in a paper bag. Close the bag tightly and let stand for 10 minutes. This steams the peppers so the skin peels away easily.
  Cut the stems off the peppers. Peel skin off peppers. To remove seeds and ribs, slit the peppers open and place them seed side up on a flat surface. Use a knife to scrape seeds and ribs from the flesh. Cut up peppers as directed in the recipe.
  Note: If using fresh or frozen sugar snap peas, fresh pea pods, or broccoli flowerets, blanch for 30 seconds and chill before serving with dip.
  Nutrition information per serving: 76 cal., 3 g pro., 6 g carbo., 5 g fat, 2 mg chol., 81 mg sodium, 149 mg potassium, and 2 g dietary fiber. U.S. RDA: 10% vit. A, 63% vit. C.

SPICY-SWEET CHICKEN "DRUMMIES"

If you like, save the two-part wing-tip section of each chicken wing to use in making stock or soup—

- 32 chicken wings
- 1 10-ounce jar apple jelly
- 1 teaspoon ground cinnamon
- 1 teaspoon finely shredded lime peel
- ½ teaspoon ground red pepper

● **Preheat broiler.** Rinse chicken; pat dry. To make the mini drumsticks, cut off and discard the 2-part wing-tip section of *each* chicken wing, reserving the largest portion of the wing. Use a small knife to cut the cartilage loose from the cut end of each bone. Push meat and skin to top of bone, shaping it into a compact ball.
● **Place mini drumsticks** on a rack in an unheated broiler pan. Broil 4 to 5 inches from the heat for 10 to 12 minutes or till light brown.
● **Meanwhile,** in a small saucepan heat jelly over medium heat till melted, stirring constantly. Divide jelly in half. To *one half,* stir in cinnamon; to the remaining jelly, stir in lime peel and ground red pepper.
● **Brush** *some* of the cinnamon jelly on *half* of the drumsticks. Brush *some* of the pepper jelly on the remaining drumsticks. Broil for 2 to 4 minutes or till drumsticks are brown.
● **Turn drumsticks** and brush with remaining jellies. Broil for 2 to 4 minutes more or till drumsticks are no longer pink. Transfer to a serving platter. Makes 16 appetizer servings.
  Nutrition information per serving (2 mini drumsticks): 105 cal., 6 g pro., 13 g carbo., 4 g fat, 21 mg chol., 23 mg sodium, 68 mg potassium, and 0 g dietary fiber. U.S. RDA: 11% niacin.

EGGNOG KRINGLA

Two Christmas traditions (eggnog and kringla) rolled into one soft, cakelike cookie. Be sure to use butter to make the soft dough manageable—

     4 **cups all-purpose flour**
     1 **teaspoon baking powder**
    ½ **teaspoon baking soda**
    ½ **teaspoon ground nutmeg**
    ¾ **cup butter**
    1½ **cups sugar**
     1 **egg**
     1 **cup dairy eggnog**
Sifted powdered sugar (optional)
Ground nutmeg (optional)

● **In a large bowl stir together** flour, baking powder, baking soda, and the ½ teaspoon nutmeg. Set aside.
● **In a large mixer bowl beat** butter with an electric mixer on medium speed for 30 seconds or till softened. Add the 1½ cups sugar and beat till fluffy. Add egg and beat well. Add flour mixture and eggnog alternately, beating till well mixed. (If the dough gets too stiff for your mixer, stir in the last part of the flour by hand.) Cover and chill for at least 4 hours or overnight.
● **Working with *half* of the dough** at a time, on a lightly floured surface, roll *rounded tablespoonfuls* of the dough into pencillike strips about 8 inches long and ½ inch thick. (Keep the remaining dough chilled.) On an ungreased cookie sheet overlap one end of the strip over the other end to form an oval (see photo, *below*).

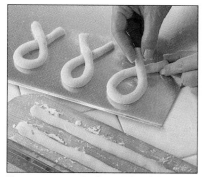

Loop one end of an 8-inch strip over the other end, forming an oval with the two ends overlapping.

● **Bake in a 350° oven** for 6 to 8 minutes or till edges just turn light brown. Transfer to a wire rack; cool. If desired, sprinkle with the powdered sugar and nutmeg. Makes about 60 cookies.

Note: These instructions are for a simplified kringla shape. The traditional kringla looks like a pretzel. For this shape, roll dough into 10-inch ropes. Shape each into a loop, crossing 1½ inches from ends. Twist rope at crossing point. Lift loop over to touch ends and seal, forming a pretzel shape.

Nutrition information per cookie: 77 cal., 1 g pro., 12 g carbo., 3 g fat, 12 mg chol., 35 mg sodium, 18 mg potassium, and 0 g dietary fiber.

BRANDIED FRUIT BARS

Two tips for easy cutting: First, line the pan with foil, extending the foil over the edges. After the bars cool, lift the foil out—bars and all. Peel off the foil and discard. Second, use a sharp knife to help avoid crumbling—

     1 **cup mixed dried fruit bits**
    ¼ **cup brandy *or* apple juice**
     1 **cup whole wheat flour**
    ¾ **cup all-purpose flour**
    ½ **cup finely chopped pecans**
    ¾ **cup margarine *or* butter**
    ½ **cup packed brown sugar**
    ⅓ **cup apricot preserves *or* orange marmalade**

● **In a small saucepan combine** fruit bits and brandy or apple juice. Carefully bring to boiling. Reduce heat; simmer, covered, for 3 to 5 minutes or till liquid is absorbed.
● **In a medium bowl stir together** whole wheat flour, all-purpose flour, and pecans.

● **In a large mixer bowl beat** the margarine or butter with an electric mixer on medium speed for 30 seconds or till softened. Add brown sugar and beat till fluffy. Add flour mixture and continue to beat till crumbly. Reserve *1 cup* of the crumb mixture. Press remaining crumb mixture onto the bottom of an ungreased 9x9x2-inch baking pan. Stir preserves or marmalade into fruit bits. Spread mixture atop crumb mixture in pan. Sprinkle with reserved crumbs; lightly press crumbs into fruit layer.
● **Bake in a 375° oven** for 20 to 25 minutes or till top crumbs are golden. Cool. Cut into bars. To store, place in a moisture- and vapor-proof container. Store bars at room temperature for up to several days. *Or*, store in the freezer for up to 12 months. To thaw, let bars stand, covered, at room temperature. Makes 24 bars.

Nutrition information per bar: 150 cal., 2 g pro., 20 g carbo., 8 g fat, 74 mg sodium, 103 mg potassium, and 1 g dietary fiber. U.S. RDA: 11% vit. A.

A TRIO OF COOKIES

Attention busy bakers. Here's a time-saving dream come true—

    ¾ **cup shortening**
    ¾ **cup margarine *or* butter**
    4½ **cups all-purpose flour**
    1½ **cups sugar**
     1 **egg**
     3 **tablespoons milk**
     1 **egg yolk**
    1½ **teaspoons vanilla**
    ¼ **teaspoon baking soda**
    ¼ **teaspoon salt**

● **In a large mixer bowl beat** shortening and margarine or butter with an electric mixer on medium to high speed about 30 seconds or till softened.
● **Add about *half* of the flour,** all of the sugar, egg, milk, egg yolk, vanilla, baking soda, and salt. Beat till thoroughly combined, scraping sides of bowl occasionally. Beat or stir in the remaining flour.
● **Divide dough into thirds.** Use it to make Choco-Mint Thumbprints, Cherry-Pistachio Rounds, and Lemon Almond Tea Cookies (see recipes, *page 182*).

CHOCO-MINT THUMBPRINTS

Christmas wouldn't be complete without a "grasshopper" treat—

⅓ recipe A Trio of Cookies dough
(see recipe, *page 181*)
2 squares (2 ounces) semisweet
chocolate, melted and cooled
2 teaspoons milk
½ recipe Basic Frosting (see recipe,
right)
1 teaspoon milk
¼ teaspoon peppermint extract
Few drops green food coloring
(optional)
¼ cup chopped candy canes *or*
peppermint candies

● **In a medium mixing bowl combine**
the ⅓ recipe cookie dough, the chocolate, and the 2 teaspoons milk. Mix till
thoroughly combined.
● **Shape dough** into an 8-inch-long
roll. Wrap in waxed paper or clear plastic wrap. Chill for at least 1 hour. (Or,
freeze for same amount of time if dough
was made with corn oil margarine.)
● **Cut dough** into ¾-inch slices. Cut
each slice into *quarters*. Shape each
quarter into a ball. Place balls 2 inches
apart on an ungreased cookie sheet.
Press down in the center of each ball
with your thumb.
● **Bake cookies in a 375° oven** for 8 to
10 minutes or till tops look dry. Transfer cookies to a wire rack. Cool cookies
completely.
● **For filling,** in a small mixing bowl
combine the ½ recipe Basic Frosting,
the 1 teaspoon milk, the peppermint
extract, and, if desired, food coloring.
Mix thoroughly. Spoon a *scant teaspoon*
of the filling into the center of each
cookie. Sprinkle *each* cookie with *some*
of the chopped candy. Makes about 48
cookies.
Nutrition information per cookie:
75 cal., 1 g pro., 11 g carbo., 4 g fat, 3 mg
chol., 29 mg sodium, 12 mg potassium.

BASIC FROSTING

Smooth and creamy—

½ cup margarine *or* butter
4 cups sifted powdered sugar
3 tablespoons milk
½ teaspoon vanilla

● **In a small mixer bowl beat** margarine or butter with an electric mixer on
medium to high speed about 30 seconds
or till softened. Gradually add *2 cups* of
the powdered sugar, beating till combined. Beat in milk and vanilla. Gradually beat in remaining powdered sugar
till smooth. Divide frosting in half. Use
to frost Choco-Mint Thumbprints and
Lemon Almond Tea Cookies.

CHERRY PISTACHIO ROUNDS

A takeoff on Santa's Whiskers, a BH&G
all-time favorite recipe that first was
published in the late '60s—

⅓ recipe A Trio of Cookies dough
(see recipe, *page 181*)
¾ cup maraschino cherries,
drained and finely chopped
Few drops red food coloring
(optional)
½ cup finely chopped pistachio
nuts, pecans, *or* walnuts

● **In a medium mixing bowl combine**
the ⅓ recipe cookie dough, the maraschino cherries, and, if desired, food coloring. Using a wooden spoon, mix till
thoroughly combined.
● **Shape dough** into a 10-inch-long
roll. Roll dough in nuts till covered.
Wrap in waxed paper or clear plastic
wrap. Chill for at least 4 hours. (Or,
freeze for same amount of time if dough
was made with corn oil margarine.)
● **Cut dough** into ¼-inch-thick slices.
Place slices 2 inches apart on an ungreased cookie sheet.
● **Bake in a 375° oven** for 8 to 10 minutes or till edges are firm and bottoms
are light brown. Transfer cookies to a
wire rack; cool. Makes about 36 cookies.
Nutrition information per cookie:
68 cal., 1 g pro., 8 g carbo., 4 g fat, 4 mg
chol., 23 mg sodium, 27 mg potassium,
and 0 g dietary fiber.

LEMON ALMOND TEA COOKIES

Pucker up for a sweet-tart taste—

⅓ recipe A Trio of Cookies dough
(see recipe, *page 181*)
2 teaspoons finely shredded
lemon peel
1 teaspoon almond extract
½ recipe Basic Frosting (see recipe,
left)
1 teaspoon lemon juice
Few drops almond extract
½ cup toasted, sliced almonds

● **In a medium mixing bowl combine**
the ⅓ recipe cookie dough, the lemon
peel, and the 1 teaspoon almond extract. Using a wooden spoon, mix till
thoroughly combined.
● **Shape dough** into an 8-inch-long
roll. Wrap in waxed paper or clear plastic wrap. Chill for at least 4 hours. (Or,
freeze for same amount of time if dough
was made with corn oil margarine.)
● **Cut dough** into ¼-inch slices. Place
slices 2 inches apart on an ungreased
cookie sheet.
● **Bake in a 375° oven** for 8 to 10 minutes or till edges are firm and bottoms
are light brown. Transfer cookies to a
wire rack; cool.
● **For the frosting,** in a small mixing
bowl combine the ½ recipe Basic Frosting, lemon juice, and the few drops almond extract. Mix thoroughly. Spread
about *1 teaspoon* of the frosting atop
each cookie. Sprinkle with sliced almonds. Makes 32 cookies.
Nutrition information per cookie:
108 cal., 1 g pro., 14 g carbo., 5 g fat, 5 mg
chol., 43 mg sodium, 22 mg potassium,
and 0 g dietary fiber.

APRICOT MACADAMIA NUT BARK

Tart apricots create a delightful contrast to the sweet bark—

- ½ cup coarsely chopped macadamia nuts, hazelnuts (filberts), *or* almonds
- 1 pound white baking pieces with cocoa butter, cut up, *or* 1 pound vanilla-flavored confectioner's coating, cut up (3 cups)
- ⅓ cup finely snipped dried apricots
- 2 tablespoons finely snipped dried apricots

● **Spread nuts** in a single layer in a shallow baking pan. Bake in a 350° oven for 7 to 9 minutes or till toasted, stirring occasionally. Cool.

● **Meanwhile, line** a baking sheet with foil; set aside.

● **In a heavy 2-quart saucepan heat** baking pieces or confectioner's coating over low heat, stirring constantly till melted and smooth. Remove from the heat. Stir in the toasted macadamia nuts, hazelnuts, or almonds and the ⅓ cup dried apricots.

● **Pour mixture** onto the prepared baking sheet, spreading to about a 10-inch circle. Sprinkle with the 2 tablespoons apricots, lightly pressing into mixture. Chill about 30 minutes or till firm. (Or, if using confectioner's coating, let stand at room temperature for several hours or till firm.)

● **When firm,** use the foil to lift candy from the baking sheet; break candy into pieces. Store candy, tightly covered, in the refrigerator. (Or, if using confectioner's coating, you can store, tightly covered, at room temperature.) Makes about 1¼ pounds nut bark.

Nutrition information per ounce: 159 cal., 2 g pro., 14 g carbo., 11 g fat, 0 mg chol., 21 mg sodium, 117 mg potassium, and 0 g dietary fiber.

ROCKY ROAD FUDGE

Is it worth the time it takes to make this holiday treat? Our taste panel voted an enthusiastic "yes!" You just can't buy a fudge that's this creamy and uniquely flavored—

- 2 cups packed brown sugar
- 1 cup sugar
- 1 8-ounce carton dairy sour cream
- ½ cup margarine *or* butter
- ½ teaspoon ground cinnamon
- ½ teaspoon finely shredded orange peel
- ⅛ teaspoon ground nutmeg
- 3 cups semisweet chocolate pieces (18 ounces)
- 1 7-ounce jar marshmallow creme
- 1 teaspoon vanilla
- 1¾ cups tiny marshmallows
- 1 cup chopped walnuts *or* almonds
- ⅔ cup raisins

● **Line a 13x9x2-inch baking pan** with foil, extending foil over edges of pan. Butter the foil; set pan aside.

● **For fudge,** butter the sides of a heavy 3-quart saucepan. In the pan combine brown sugar, sugar, sour cream, margarine or butter, cinnamon, orange peel, and nutmeg. Cook over medium-high heat to boiling, stirring constantly with a wooden spoon to dissolve sugar.

● **Carefully clip a candy thermometer** to side of pan. Cook over medium heat, stirring frequently, till thermometer registers 232°*. Remove pan from heat; remove candy thermometer from pan.

● **Add the chocolate pieces,** marshmallow creme, and vanilla. Stir till well blended and chocolate is melted. Quickly spread about *half* of the fudge mixture in the prepared pan. Sprinkle with

marshmallows, *half* of the walnuts or almonds, and all of the raisins. Quickly top with the remaining fudge mixture (see photo, *below*). Sprinkle with the remaining walnuts or almonds, pressing lightly into the fudge.

While fudge is warm, score it into small squares. When firm, lift out of pan and cut into squares. Store, tightly covered, in the refrigerator. Makes about 4 pounds (70 servings).

*Note: Use a candy thermometer to cook this creamy fudge to perfection. Test your thermometer for accuracy by placing it in boiling water. If the thermometer registers above or below 212°, add or subtract the same number of degrees from the recipe temperature and cook candy to that temperature.

Nutrition information per serving: 119 cal., 1 g pro., 18 g carbo., 6 g fat, 1 mg chol., 24 mg sodium, 74 mg potassium, and 0 g dietary fiber.

TOFFEE CARAMELS

- 1 14-ounce package vanilla caramels (approximately 48 to 50 caramels)
- 12 ounces chocolate-flavored confectioner's coating, coarsely cut up
- 2 6-ounce packages almond brickle pieces (about 2 cups)

● **Unwrap caramels.** Set aside.

● **In a small heavy saucepan** heat confectioner's coating over low heat, stirring occasionally, just till melted. Remove from heat.

● **Meanwhile, place** brickle pieces in a small bowl.

● **Drop caramels,** one at a time, into melted coating; turn to coat. With a fork, lift caramel out, drawing fork across rim of pan to remove excess coating. Drop into brickle pieces, turning to coat entire caramel. Transfer caramel to a waxed-paper-lined baking sheet. Repeat with remaining caramels. Let stand 30 minutes or till firm. Or, chill 10 minutes or till firm. Store in a tightly covered container for up to 7 days. Makes 48 to 50 caramels.

Nutrition information per caramel: 108 cal., 0 g pro., 16 g carbo., 5 g fat, 0 mg chol., 58 mg sodium, 21 mg potassium, and 0 g dietary fiber.

Pour remaining fudge quickly over marshmallows, nuts, and raisins before it starts to set up and harden.

SHIITAKE MUSHROOM AND SPINACH BROTH

Look for shiitake mushrooms, a Japanese variety also called black mushrooms or winter mushrooms, in gourmet markets or near other Oriental products in your grocery store—

- **7 or 8 dried shiitake mushrooms *or* other dried mushrooms**
- **1 large carrot**
- **4 14½-ounce cans chicken broth**
- **2 tablespoons minced dried onion**
- **1 tablespoon lemon juice**
- **½ teaspoon dried basil, crushed**
- **⅛ teaspoon garlic powder**
- **1½ cups chopped fresh spinach *or* watercress**

● **In a small bowl soak** mushrooms for 30 minutes in enough *hot water* to cover. Rinse well and squeeze to drain thoroughly. Thinly slice mushrooms, discarding the stems.

● **For carrot flowers,** use the sharp tip of a clean bottle opener to make 5 grooves lengthwise down the side of the carrot (see photo, *right*). Slice carrot. (Or, slice carrot and use hors d'oeuvre cutters to cut flowers or other designs from each slice.)

● **In a large saucepan** or Dutch oven combine mushrooms, carrot flowers, broth, onion, lemon juice, basil, and garlic powder. Bring to boiling; reduce heat. Cover and simmer for 8 to 10 minutes or till carrot is nearly tender, stirring occasionally.*

● **Stir in spinach** or watercress. Cover; simmer about 2 minutes more or till spinach is tender. Ladle into 8 soup bowls. Makes 8 appetizer servings.

*To make ahead: Prepare broth as directed, *except* do not add the spinach. Cool. Transfer to a storage container and chill for up to several days. To serve, transfer to a large saucepan and heat through. Stir in spinach or watercress and continue as directed.

Nutrition information per serving: 53 cal., 5 g pro., 6 g carbo., 1 g fat, 1 mg chol., 666 mg sodium, 341 mg potassium, 2 g dietary fiber. U.S. RDA: 49% vit. A, 11% riboflavin, 26% niacin.

To carve carrot flowers, run the sharp tip of a bottle opener down the carrot, making five lengthwise grooves; slice carrot.

BEEF TENDERLOIN WITH PORT SAUCE AND PASTRY LEAVES

A spectacular entrée for your annual holiday dinner—

- **½ of a 17¼-ounce package (1 sheet) frozen puff pastry, thawed**
- **1 egg white**
- **1 3-pound beef tenderloin**
- **1½ cups beef broth**
- **¾ cup tawny port *or* dry red wine**
- **2 tablespoons finely chopped shallot *or* onion**
- **½ teaspoon dried rosemary, crushed**
- **1 bay leaf**
- **3 tablespoons margarine *or* butter, softened**
- **2 tablespoons all-purpose flour**
- **Fresh rosemary sprigs (optional)**

● **Unfold pastry.** On a lightly floured surface roll puff pastry to eliminate crease. With a small knife or leaf-shaped cookie cutter, cut 16 leaf shapes out of puff pastry (see photo, *right*).

● **Transfer pastry leaves** to an ungreased baking sheet. To make the leaf veins, score each pastry leaf with the tip of a sharp knife. Brush *each* leaf with *some* of the egg white. Bake in a 400° oven about 10 minutes or till golden and flaky. Cool. If desired, store, tightly covered, at room temperature for up to 12 hours.

● **If tenderloin is long and thin,** fold narrow ends under and tie. If tenderloin is flat and wide, tie crosswise in two or three places to form a rounder shape. (The tenderloin should be about 8x4½ inches after tying.) Place tenderloin on a rack in a shallow roasting pan.

● **Roast tenderloin, uncovered,** in a 425° oven for 45 to 60 minutes or to desired doneness (140° for rare or 145° for medium rare). With a sharp knife, slice into 8 portions.

● **Meanwhile, for port sauce,** in a medium saucepan combine broth, port or wine, shallot or onion, dried rosemary, and bay leaf. Bring to boiling; reduce heat. Simmer, uncovered, for 15 to 20 minutes. (You should have about 1⅓ cups sauce after simmering.) Remove the bay leaf.

● **Stir together** margarine or butter and flour. Add to wine mixture. Cook and stir till thickened and bubbly. Cook and stir for 1 minute more.

● **To serve,** place a portion of tenderloin on *each* dinner plate. Spoon about *3 tablespoons* of the port sauce over *each* portion. Top *each* with *two* pastry leaves and some fresh rosemary sprigs. Makes 8 servings.

To make sauce ahead: Prepare and simmer but don't thicken. Cool. Transfer to a storage container and chill for up to 2 days. Before serving, return to a medium saucepan and heat through. Continue by stirring together margarine or butter and flour and thickening sauce as directed.

Nutrition information per serving: 460 cal., 39 g pro., 13 g carbo., 25 g fat, 108 mg chol., 431 mg sodium, 603 mg potassium, and 0 g dietary fiber. U.S. RDA: 20% thiamine, 37% riboflavin, 43% niacin, 29% iron.

With a small knife, cut out pastry leaves. The leaves should be the same size, in order to cook evenly.

WHOLE WHEAT BRIOCHE

*For variety, omit the almonds on top
and instead sprinkle with poppy seed or
caraway seed after brushing with the
egg white mixture—*

   1 package active dry yeast
   1 cup warm water (105° to 115°)
   ½ cup margarine *or* butter
   ⅓ cup packed brown sugar
   ½ teaspoon salt
   3 cups all-purpose flour
   3 eggs
   1¼ cups whole wheat flour
  24 whole almonds
   1 egg white
   1 tablespoon water

● **In a small mixing bowl soften** yeast
in ¼ cup of the *warm* water.
● **In a large mixer bowl beat** margarine or butter, brown sugar, and salt
with an electric mixer till fluffy. Add
the remaining warm water, *1 cup* of the
all-purpose flour, and the whole eggs.
Beat well. Add softened yeast and beat
well. Using a spoon, stir in the remaining all-purpose flour and whole wheat
flour till dough is smooth.
● **Place in a greased bowl.** Cover; let
rise in a warm place till double (about 2
hours). Punch down. Cover with plastic
wrap. Chill for 2 to 24 hours.
● **Punch dough down.** Turn out onto a
lightly floured surface. Cut dough into
6 portions; cut each portion into 5
pieces. With floured hands, shape each
piece into a ball. (You will have 30 balls
of dough.)
● **Place rolls** into greased muffin pans
or individual brioche pans. Using a
sharp knife, cut a little slit in the top of
each roll. Place *one* almond sideways
into *each* slit. Cover; let rise in a warm
place for 30 minutes.

● **In a small mixing bowl combine** the
egg white and the 1 tablespoon water.
Brush over tops of rolls and almonds.
● **Bake in a 425° oven** for 12 to 15 minutes or till rolls sound hollow when
tapped. Remove from pans; cool on a
wire rack. Makes 30 rolls.

   *Nutrition information per roll: 113
cal., 3 g pro., 16 g carbo., 4 g fat, 21 mg
chol., 81 mg sodium, 63 mg potassium,
and 1 g dietary fiber. U.S. RDA: 13%
thiamine, 10% riboflavin.*

GLAZED VEGETABLE TRIO

*If it's easier for you, cook the brussels
sprouts and corn on the stove top according to package directions—*

   1 8-ounce package frozen brussels
      sprouts
   1 8-ounce package frozen baby
      corn on the cob
   2 tablespoons water
   3 tablespoons brown sugar
   3 tablespoons margarine *or* butter
   1 teaspoon vinegar
   1 large onion, thinly sliced and
      separated into rings

● **In a 2-quart microwave-safe** casserole combine brussels sprouts, baby
corn, and water. Micro-cook, covered,
on 100% power (high) for 8 to 10 minutes or till vegetables are just crisp-
tender, stirring once. Drain.
● **Meanwhile,** in a large saucepan combine brown sugar, margarine or butter,
and vinegar. Cook and stir over medium heat for 1 to 2 minutes or till blended. Add onions. Cook, uncovered, over
low heat for 10 to 12 minutes or till
onions are glazed and tender, stirring
occasionally.
● **Add corn mixture** and stir to coat.
Cook for 1 to 2 minutes more to heat
through. Makes 8 side-dish servings.

   *Nutrition information per serving:
84 cal., 2 g pro., 10 g carbo., 4 g fat, 0 mg
chol., 63 mg sodium, 135 mg potassium,
and 2 g dietary fiber. U.S. RDA: 25%
vit. C.*

Planning an Elegant Dinner Menu

DAYS AHEAD:
● Make and chill Cranberry-Pear
Relish.
● Prepare and freeze cake layers for
the Double-Chocolate Orange Torte.
● Whip Minted Whipped Cream; freeze
the dollops.
● Shave and freeze candy curls for the
Crème de Menthe Coffee and chocolate
curls for the torte.

UP TO 2 DAYS AHEAD:
● Make and chill the Port Sauce.

UP TO 1 DAY AHEAD:
● Prepare and chill dough for Whole
Wheat Brioche.
● Make and chill Bittersweet Choco-
late Icing for the torte.

THE MORNING OF:
● Cut out and bake pastry leaves. Store
leaves, tightly covered, at room temperature.
● Cut carrot flowers and chop spinach
for Shiitake Mushroom and Spinach
Broth.

TWO HOURS BEFORE DINNER:
● Let chocolate icing come to room
temperature.
● Assemble torte.
● Shape brioche; let rise.

ONE HOUR BEFORE DINNER:
● Bake brioche.
● Roast tenderloin.
● Soak mushrooms for Shiitake Mush-
room and Spinach Broth.

BEFORE DINNER:
● Prepare Glazed Vegetable Trio.
● Finish cooking (or reheat) the Shii-
take Mushroom and Spinach Broth.
● Heat and thicken the Port Sauce.
● Brew coffee for Crème de Menthe
Coffee.

CRANBERRY-PEAR RELISH

Make this vivid red relish ahead, transfer to a storage container, and chill for up to one week—

- 1½ cups sugar
- ½ cup water
- 1 12-ounce package (3 cups) cranberries
- 2 medium pears, cored and cubed (2 cups)
- ½ teaspoon ground nutmeg
- ½ teaspoon ground allspice
- 4 inches stick cinnamon

● **In a 2-quart saucepan bring** sugar and water to boiling, stirring to dissolve sugar. Boil rapidly, uncovered, for 5 minutes.

● **Add** cranberries, pears, nutmeg, allspice, and cinnamon. Return to boiling. Cook for 3 to 4 minutes or till cranberry skins pop, stirring occasionally. Remove from heat. Cover and chill. Remove cinnamon before serving. Makes about 3¼ cups.

Nutrition information per 1/4 cup: 117 cal., 0 g pro., 30 g carbo., 0 g fat, 0 mg chol., 1 mg sodium, 52 mg potassium, and 2 g dietary fiber.

BITTERSWEET CHOCOLATE ICING

Only three ingredients, but oh so wonderfully decadent—

- ¼ cup whipping cream
- 1 tablespoon light corn syrup
- 4 ounces semisweet chocolate, finely chopped *or* ⅔ cup semisweet chocolate pieces

● **In a small heavy saucepan combine** whipping cream and corn syrup. Bring just to boiling, stirring constantly. Remove from heat; stir in chocolate till chocolate is melted and mixture is smooth. Cool to room temperature. Stir before icing the Double-Chocolate Orange Torte. Makes ¾ cup.

DOUBLE-CHOCOLATE ORANGE TORTE

Moist, fudgy, and incredibly rich—a perfect last course for a grand celebration dinner. For a nonalcoholic version, simply replace the orange liqueur with orange juice. Or, if you're making the raspberry version, just leave out the raspberry liqueur—

- 3 squares (3 ounces) unsweetened chocolate, coarsely chopped
- 1 cup sugar
- ¾ cup all-purpose flour
- 1½ teaspoons baking powder
- ½ teaspoon baking soda
- ½ teaspoon salt
- ½ cup margarine *or* butter
- ½ cup water
- 2 tablespoons orange liqueur
- 1 tablespoon finely shredded orange peel
- 4 eggs
- 1 tablespoon orange liqueur
- 1 tablespoon orange juice
- ½ cup orange marmalade

Bittersweet Chocolate Icing (see recipe, *left*)
Chocolate curls (optional)

● **Grease** an 8x8x2-inch baking pan. Line the bottom with waxed paper; grease the paper. Dust the paper and pan with flour; tap out excess flour.

● **In a heavy saucepan place** chopped unsweetened chocolate over low heat, stirring constantly, till chocolate just starts to melt. Remove from heat; stir till smooth. Cool.

● **In a large mixer bowl stir** together the sugar, flour, baking powder, baking soda, and salt. Add the margarine or butter, water, the 2 tablespoons orange liqueur, and the finely shredded orange peel.

● **Beat with an electric mixer** on medium speed till mixture is combined. Beat on high speed for 2 minutes. Add melted chocolate and eggs; beat with electric mixer for 2 minutes more. Pour the batter into the prepared pan.

● **Bake in a 350° oven** for 30 to 40 minutes or till a wooden toothpick inserted near the center comes out clean. Cool cake on a wire rack for 10 minutes. Loosen edges of cake with a spatula. Invert. Remove the pan and peel off the waxed paper. Cool cake completely.

● **Combine** the 1 tablespoon liqueur and orange juice. Split cake in half horizontally. Sprinkle *each* cut side with *half* of the liqueur mixture. Place bottom half of cake on a platter; spread marmalade evenly atop. Top with remaining cake layer.

● **Frost the cake** with the Bittersweet Chocolate Icing. (The frosted cake will hold up to several hours.) If desired, decorate the sides of the frosted cake with chocolate curls pressed into icing. Makes 10 to 12 servings.

Double-Chocolate Raspberry Torte: Prepare Double-Chocolate Orange Torte as directed, *except* omit the orange peel and orange juice. Substitute *raspberry liqueur* for the orange liqueur. Use *2 tablespoons* raspberry liqueur to sprinkle on the cake. Substitute *seedless red raspberry preserves* for orange marmalade.

Nutrition information per serving: 412 cal., 5 g pro., 51 g carbo., 22 g fat, 93 mg chol., 329 mg sodium, 159 mg potassium, and 2 g dietary fiber. U.S. RDA: 22% vit. A, 10% thiamine, 16% riboflavin, 10% iron.

CRÈME DE MENTHE COFFEE

To make the chocolate-mint candy curls, use a vegetable peeler to shave the long, narrow edge of chocolate-mint candy—

- 1 **cup water**
- ⅓ **cup sugar**
- 6 **layered chocolate-mint candies**
- ¾ **cup milk**
- ¾ **cup light cream**
- 2 **cups freshly made, hot, double-strength coffee**
- **Minted Whipped Cream**
- 4 **to 6 layered chocolate-mint candies, shaved into curls**

● **In a small saucepan stir together** the water, sugar, and the 6 whole chocolate-mint candies. Heat and stir till the sugar dissolves and the chocolate-mint candies melt.

● **Add** milk and cream; heat through. Stir in coffee.

● **Pour** into eight 6- to 8-ounce heat-proof mugs, cups, or glasses. Top *each* serving with a dollop of the Minted Whipped Cream, then sprinkle with some of the chocolate-mint candy curls. Makes 8 (5-ounce) servings.

Minted Whipped Cream: In a chilled small mixer bowl stir together ¾ cup *whipping cream,* 3 tablespoons *crème de menthe* or *crème de menthe flavoring,* and 2 tablespoons *sugar.* Using chilled beaters, beat with an electric mixer on medium speed till soft peaks form when beaters are lifted. Makes 4½ cups.

Nutrition information per serving: *210 cal., 2 g pro., 22 g carbo., 12 g fat, 41 mg chol., 42 mg sodium, 120 mg potassium. U.S. RDA: 16% vit. A.*

SKATING BEARS AND SLEDDING TEDDYS

Ginger cookies were never so fun—

- 1 **cup margarine *or* butter**
- ⅔ **cup packed brown sugar**
- ⅔ **cup corn syrup *or* molasses**
- 4 **cups all-purpose flour**
- 2 **teaspoons ground cinnamon**
- 1 **teaspoon ground ginger**
- ¾ **teaspoon baking soda**
- ¾ **teaspoon ground cloves**
- 1 **beaten egg**
- 1½ **teaspoons vanilla**
- **Decorating Frosting (optional), (see recipe, *right*)**
- **Miniature semisweet chocolate pieces**
- **Medium candy canes (about 6 inches long) (optional)**
- **Graham crackers (optional)**

● **In a medium saucepan combine** margarine or butter, brown sugar, and corn syrup or molasses. Heat and stir over medium heat till margarine melts and sugar dissolves. Pour into a large mixing bowl; cool for 5 minutes.

● **Meanwhile,** in a bowl combine flour, cinnamon, ginger, soda, and cloves.

● **Add** egg and vanilla to margarine mixture; mix well. Add the flour mixture and beat till combined. Cover and chill dough for 2 hours or overnight.

● **To make *each* adult bear,** shape dough into one 1½-inch ball (for body), one 1-inch ball (for head), three ¼-inch balls (for nose and ears), two 1¾-inch-long by ½-inch-wide logs (for arms), and two 1½-inch-long by ¾-inch-wide logs (for legs). If desired, taper arms and legs so they are slightly wider at hand and feet ends.

● **On an ungreased cookie sheet** flatten the 1½-inch ball for body to a 2-inch round. Attach the 1-inch ball for head, and flatten to a 1½-inch round. Attach the ¼-inch balls to the head for nose and ears. Attach the 1¾-inch-long logs for arms and the 1½-inch-long logs for legs. (*Do not* attach legs if making sledding bears). (See photo, *page 177.*)

● **To make youth bears,** make balls and logs a little smaller than those for adult bears. To make baby bears, make pieces a little smaller than those for the youth bears. On an ungreased cookie sheet assemble as for adult bear, flattening the body and head. Attach nose, ears, arms, and legs. (*Do not* attach legs if making sledding bears.)

● **For bears holding hands, assemble** side by side on baking sheet. Press ends of inside arms together.

● **To decorate all bears** before baking, press in miniature chocolate pieces, point side up, for eyes. For paws, press miniature chocolate pieces, point side down, into ends of arms and legs. (Press chocolate pieces into arms only if making skating bears.)

● **Bake in a 325° oven** 15 minutes for adults, 12 minutes for youths, or 8 minutes for babies or till edges are light brown. Transfer to a rack; cool.

● **For skating bears,** cut small rectangles of heavy foil; diagonally trim ends to resemble skate blades. Attach under end of bears' legs with some of the Decorating Frosting, leaving the longer side of each foil "blade" showing.

● **For sledding teddys,** make a sled by attaching 2 candy canes (for runners) to a whole graham cracker with Decorating Frosting. Attach bodies upright to the sled with Decorating Frosting. (You may find it helpful to cut off the rounded end of the body, making it easier to attach to the sled.) Then, use Decorating Frosting to attach legs to body and sled as if the bear were sitting with legs out front on the sled (see photo, *page 177*). To have a baby bear sitting on the larger bear's lap, attach the baby bear's body to larger bear with Decorating Frosting. Attach legs with frosting to larger bear's legs. Makes 12 adult or 21 youth or 36 baby bear cookies.

Nutrition information per youth cookie: *227 cal., 3 g pro., 34 g carbo., 9 g fat, 10 mg chol., 143 mg sodium, 64 mg potassium. U.S. RDA: 14% vit. A, 19% thiamine, 11% riboflavin, 11% niacin.*

DECORATING FROSTING

Use this frosting as glue when making the skating and sledding bears—

- ¼ **cup shortening**
- ¼ **teaspoon vanilla**
- 1¼ **cups sifted powdered sugar**
- **Milk**

● **In a small mixer bowl beat** the shortening and vanilla with an electric mixer 30 seconds or till softened. Gradually beat in powdered sugar. Beat in enough milk (about *1 tablespoon*) to make a frosting of spreading consistency.

INDEX

D-F

Index

Index

T-Z

Microwave Wattage

All microwave recipes were tested in high-wattage (600 to 700 watts) and low-wattage (400 to 550 watts) microwave ovens. If the low-wattage cooking times differ from the high-wattage times, they appear in parentheses in the recipe methods. The cooking times are approximate because microwave ovens vary by manufacturer.

Nutrition Analysis

Some nutrient information is given by gram weight per serving. The United States Recommended Daily Allowances (U.S. RDAs) for selected vitamins and minerals are given in the recipes when the value exceeds 10 percent. The U.S. RDAs tell the amounts of certain nutrients necessary to meet the dietary needs of most healthy people.

To obtain the nutrition analysis of each recipe, the following guidelines were used:
● When ingredient options appear in a recipe, the analysis was calculated using the first ingredient choice.
● Optional ingredients were omitted in the analyses.
● The nutrition analyses for recipes calling for fresh ingredients were calculated using the measurements for raw fruits, vegetables, and meats.
● If a recipe gives optional serving sizes (such as "Makes 6 to 8 servings"), the nutrition analysis was calculated using the first choice.

Have BETTER HOMES AND
GARDENS® magazine delivered to
your door. For information, write to:
MR. ROBERT AUSTIN
P.O. BOX 4536
DES MOINES, IA 50336